"Miriam Adeney takes us on a richly illustrated journey in order to teach us how to (re)think globally while loving and acting locally. Moving with creative ease between narrative and dialogue, she tells fascinating stories with a sensitive cross-cultural touch, crossing all given and imposed borders and barriers with passion that inspires."

DR. PETER KUZMIČ, Eva B. and Paul E. Toms Distinguished Professor of World Missions and European Studies, Gordon-Conwell Theological Seminary

"Kingdom Without Borders is a fresh look at the question, What is God doing in the world? In this book, Miriam Adeney again combines the work of a scholar with the skill of a writer. She draws us into the story of the global Christian family while introducing us to the trends and theological conversations so vital to our understanding. Between Adeney's mastery of storytelling and the profound insights she reports, the reader gains a greater appreciation for God's greatness. This creative combination of voices from many sources is an important contribution to the growing conversation surrounding globalization."

DOUG MCCONNELL, dean, School of Intercultural Studies,
Fuller Theological Seminary

"A delightful and accessible introduction to global missions—God's foreign policy among the nations. A masterful storyteller, Miriam introduces us to her multicultural family, from Cesar in the Philippines to Ruth in Rwanda, in this flyover perspective on the move of the Spirit through the peoples of our world. Bible teaching, economic theory, comparative religions or insights on intercultural communication provide lively connecting tissue you will not find in dry missions texts. It is a bold call to serve vulnerably, sharing in suffering until Christ's resurrection power is released among *all* peoples!"

STEVE HOKE, vice president of people development,
Church Resource Ministries, and coauthor of *Global Mission Handbook*

"Miriam Adeney has once again written a powerful and accessible book on a topic of profound importance. Readers will be humbled and inspired by what they find in these pages—testimonies that show how the gospel is changing lives all over the world."

DANA L. ROBERT, Truman Collins Professor of World Christianity and History of Mission, Boston University School of Theology

"The fact of the vibrancy and growth of the church around the world is one many of us have come to learn in the past few decades. Like no other account I've read, Miriam Adeney compellingly weaves individual stories from every nook and cranny of the globe into a tapestry that reflects God's burden and passion for every person and community. She takes what others report as data and brings it to us through the lives of the people who have been transformed by encountering the living Christ, and ultimately paints a masterpiece of God at work across our planet. Reading the journeys of brokenness, trauma, pain, hope, sacrifice, joy and redemption will change your perspective on how God is at work—and just maybe your life."

SCOTT MOREAU, professor of intercultural studies,
Wheaton College, and editor of *Evangelical Missions Quarterly*

"*Kingdom Without Borders* invites us into a magnificent tapestry of the glory of God alive in the peoples and nations of our world. Miriam Adeney weaves the dominant designs of God's global mission with and through countless stories of people and friends. We meet sisters and brothers in Christ in contexts of joy and profound sadness; in China, Latin America, the Islamic and the Buddhist worlds; in the arts and persecution, in the Word and the Spirit. I cannot recommend any book higher than *Kingdom Without Borders* as *the* introduction to worship the God of mission."

WILLIAM D. TAYLOR, global ambassador, World Evangelical Alliance,
and coauthor of *Global Mission Handbook*

KINGDOM

WITHOUT

BORDERS

THE UNTOLD STORY OF

GLOBAL CHRISTIANITY

MIRIAM ADENEY

An imprint of InterVarsity Press
Downers Grove, Illinois

InterVarsity Press
P.O. Box 1400, Downers Grove, IL 60515-1426
World Wide Web: www.ivpress.com
E-mail: email@ivpress.com

InterVarsity Press® is the book-publishing division of InterVarsity Christian Fellowship/USA®, a movement of students and faculty active on campus at hundreds of universities, colleges and schools of nursing in the United States of America, and a member movement of the International Fellowship of Evangelical Students. For information about local and regional activities, write Public Relations Dept., InterVarsity Christian Fellowship/USA, 6400 Schroeder Rd., P.O. Box 7895, Madison, WI 53707-7895, or visit the IVCF website at <www.intervarsity.org>.

All Scripture quotations, unless otherwise indicated, are taken from the Holy Bible, New International Version®. NIV®. Copyright 1973, 1978, 1984 by International Bible Society. Used by permission of Zondervan Publishing House. All rights reserved.

Excerpts from Sadhu Sundar Singh: Essential Writings, ed. Charles E. Moore (Maryknoll, N.Y.: Orbis Books, 2005). Used by permission.
Excerpts and material adapted from the DVD The Cross—Jesus in China (China Soul for Christ Foundation, P.O. Box 1600, Rohnert Park, CA 94927. Tel 707.585.9588. www.chinasoul.org). Used by permission.
Excerpts from After the Tsunami, by Ajith Fernando (Colombo, Sri Lanka: RBC Ministries: 2005). Used by permission.
Lyrics from "This Kingdom," by Geoff Bullock. Used by permission.
Excerpts from After the Locusts, by Meg Guillebaud (Oxford U.K.: Monarch Books, 2005). Used by permission.
Excerpts from Following Jesus in the Hindu Context, by H. L. Richard (William Carey Library, 1605 E. Elizabeth St., Pasadena, CA 91104, www.missionbooks.org). Used by permission.
Excerpts from The Lord of Bellavista, by David Miller (London: Triangle Publishers, 1999). Used by permission.

All excerpts of conversations, narratives or poetry by individuals are used by permission. Every effort has been made to trace and contact copyright holders for all material quoted in this book. The author will be pleased to rectify any omissions for future editions if notified by copyright holders.

Design: Cindy Kiple
Images: For cover image credit, please see p. 295.

ISBN 978-0-8308-3849-3

Printed in the United States of America ∞

Library of Congress Cataloging-in-Publication Data

Adeney, Miriam, 1945-
    Kingdom without borders: the untold story of global Christianity/
Miriam Adeney.
        p. cm.
    Includes bibliographical references.
    ISBN 978-0-8308-3849-3 (pbk.: alk. paper)
    1. Christianity—21st century. 2. Church history—21st century. I.
Title.
    BR121.3.A34 2009
    270.8'3—dc22
                                                                          2009031644

P   22   21   20   19   18   17   16   15   14   13   12   11   10   9   8   7   6   5   4   3   2   1

Y   27   26   25   24   23   22   21   20   19   18   17   16   15   14   13   12   11   10   09

CONTENTS

Then Jesus asked, "What is the kingdom of God like?
What shall I compare it to? It is like a mustard seed,
which a man took and planted in his garden.
It grew and became a tree and the birds
of the air perched in its branches."

LUKE 13:18

Again, the kingdom of heaven is like a merchant looking
for fine pearls. When he found one of great value, he went
away and sold everything he had and bought it.

MATTHEW 13:45

INTRODUCTION

WHAT I LEARNED
FROM FILIPINOS

"Why are you in the Navy, Cesar?"

"To make money."

When I was four years old, a Filipino taught me about culture.

My dad was a medical doctor who was going to direct the leprosarium that served the entire northern Pacific, the region called Microne-
sia. Following World War II, the United Nations had commissioned the
United States to administer the area. A call had gone out for a doctor to
run the leprosarium. My father and mother decided to respond.

On the way to the island of Tinian, where the leprosarium was located, we stopped in Hawaii so my dad could study leprosy on the island
of Molokai. Meanwhile, my mother and my baby sister and I were
housed in the Navy's Bachelor Officer Quarters on Oahu.

I was popular with all the bachelor officers, but my best friend was a
Filipino steward named Cesar. During his afternoon coffee breaks, we
would sit on a bench overlooking the Pacific and talk about life.

"What are you going to do with all the money you make?" I
asked him.

"Go back to the Philippines, start a business, and marry Lily," he smiled.

"You want to go back? But Cesar, you've arrived! You're in America! Why would you want to live anywhere else?" Even at age four, American ethnocentrism popped out.

"Hawaii's fine," he answered calmly. "But it's not home."

America is not the center of the universe. Cesar helped me see that. I thank God for that man. Of all the Navy stewards I could have met, God sent Cesar. He taught me a lesson that I have passed on to generations of students. America is precious, but so are other places. Home can be anywhere in the world.

Cesar went back to work. I looked around. The Pacific stretched as far as I could see. Powder-blue billows darkened to pewter gray where the sea met the sky. Maybe it was raining there. Greens shimmered from jade to lime near the shore. Azure spots sparkled so bright that they hurt my eyes. The sun's heat poured down, but it was comfortable under the palm and banana trees, and the sea breeze tickled my hairline. I swung my feet, peeked at my toenails and thought about homelands.

Since then it has been the joy of my life to walk alongside Christian brothers and sisters on five continents. In this book I introduce some who have influenced me. Think of this as a continuation of Hebrews 11, that great list of people down through the ages who lived and died by faith. Some stories come from my own encounters, and others are from books. Check the titles and read the originals to get the full drama. Sometimes I've changed narrative to dialogue. Sometimes I've used aliases for my interview subjects.

The chapters in this book alternate between great regions and key topics, such as the Word (chap. 3), the Spirit (chap. 5), catastrophes and Christian responses (chap. 7), and media for witness and discipling (chap. 9). Other broad themes are woven through certain chapters, including suffering (chaps. 2, 4, 6, 8, 10, 11), poverty (intro., chaps. 4, 7, 11), ecology (chaps. 5, 7), world religions (chaps. 6, 8, 10, 12), contextual theology (chaps. 1, 3, 4, 5, 6, 8), training leaders (chaps. 1, 4, 5, 6,

9, 10), mission history (chaps. 3, 6, 10, 11), and best practices in mission (chaps. 1, 4, 8, 11).

This book is not primarily statistics or strategies or critique, though those are present. Here and there you will find a little Bible teaching or economic theory or comparative religion. Some memorable speeches and writings will be quoted. But your favorite organization or leader may be missing. This book is illustrative, not exhaustive. As the apostle John wrote at the end of his Gospel, if all the relevant data were included, the whole world would not be able to contain the books.

Mostly you will find stories. Are these the most important ones? Who knows? I have tried to select stories that represent central themes. But there are thousands more waiting to be told.

People Power

Years after Cesar and I both left Hawaii, I joined the staff of the Philippine InterVarsity Christian Fellowship. There I met Melba Maggay, who was a freshman in journalism at the University of the Philippines. Short, bright, passionate for justice but quick to smile, Melba had moved from following Marx to following Jesus.

One afternoon at camp we walked down a path together.

"I wouldn't have walked with you like this last year," she remarked.

"Why not?" I blurted.

She shrugged. "I would have been afraid of benevolent assimilation."

Right away I knew what she meant. At the end of the Spanish-American War in 1898, President McKinley decided that God had guided the United States to absorb the Philippines. Filipinos disagreed. They fought for their freedom for two more years. McKinley called his policy "benevolent assimilation." When Melba looked at me, she thought in those terms. Yet God enabled her to love me anyway.

Three decades later this friend of my heart is CEO of the Institute for the Study of Asian Church and Culture. She writes for national newspapers as well as for the stage at the Philippine Cultural Center. Her Ph.D. dissertation has pioneered the use of Tagalog, the most widely spoken of Philippine languages, as an academic language. She mentors many.

Facing the artillery in the People's Power Revolution in 1986 was one of the great moments of her life. Massive intimidation of voters and fraud in ballot counting had stained the presidential election, but Ferdinand Marcos had claimed another victory. Two weeks after the election, two of the highest ranking government officials defected, Fidel Ramos, Deputy Chief of Staff, and Juan Ponce Enrile, Minister of Defense. Barricading themselves and their followers in key military installations, they recognized Marcos's opponent, Cory Aquino, as the legitimate president.

Immediately the archbishop of Manila urged Filipinos to take to the streets to surround the two rebel officials' bases. Rich and poor responded.

"Bring your sleeping mats," they hollered to each other. "We'll settle in for a long vigil. Twenty years of corruption is enough."

Then Marcos ordered out the artillery.

"Link arms!" the masses called out, standing at attention. Melba and her evangelical friends prayed. Beside them on the left, Roman Catholics fingered their rosaries. On their right, Muslim separatist soldiers down from their hideout in the hills breathed the name of Allah. Together, ranging as far as the eye could see, hundreds of thousands of Filipinos faced the tanks.

As the behemoths crunched closer, the people walked forward to meet them. Many began singing the Lord's Prayer in Tagalog.

> Our Father in heaven,
> Hallowed be your name,
> Your kingdom come,
> Your will be done, on earth as it is in heaven,
> Give us this day our daily bread,
> And forgive us our debts, as we also have forgiven our debtors.

"Pray with us," they pleaded with the soldiers on the tanks. "If you can't pray aloud, pray in your hearts."

Some poked flowers into the cannons' barrels.

Three times the tanks revved up their motors and advanced. But each time more soldiers defected, and the tanks stopped.

The following day, Marcos resigned and left the country.

In the Philippines it is known as the People's Revolution. In the annals of world history it is a remarkable example of nonviolent political change with strong Christian input. Five days after the revolution, I myself landed in the Philippines for a short teaching stint. On every bus I rode I overheard strangers exclaiming to one another about how God had delivered them.

Tragically, the Philippines' social, economic and political problems remain dire. Recently Melba wrote, "There is a hardness to evil, a mystery to its persistence, that cannot be fathomed nor remedied by mere politics. . . . We continue the fight. Yet we need to mine more deeply the resources of our faith if we are to make even a small dent in the monolith of injustice that fazes us."

Applying it more personally, she continues,

> *I* need a deeper rootedness in God, a closer walk with him so that I am able to hear the thud of his footfall in our history. Amid the gore, and grime, and grinding poverty, among people who serve quietly in the armpits of cities, making a space for grace in the squalor and violent hate, life springs forth from the Word, bringing a fresh blast of wind, carrying the weary and the wounded on its wings. . . .
>
> While all my professional expertise is useful, it cannot hold a candle to the clean white flame that descends upon us when the Spirit speaks. I had not noticed that through the years I had become technically proficient, like a highly trained monkey performing tricks. Confronted once again with the wonder of his Word, I feel shame at how I had allowed myself to coast along, just sailing with my usual stock in trade.[1]

Melba's words speak profoundly to leaders everywhere. So often we are tempted to "sail along with our usual stock in trade . . . like trained monkeys performing tricks." So often we expect that the next social reform will solve the problems. Melba reminds us that while we work for justice and order and beauty in small and large arenas, our hope is not in the systems of this world, nor in ourselves, but in Christ and his kingdom.

I HAVE A DREAM

Yet Christ calls us to be his hands and feet. When I was with the Philippine InterVarsity, our director, Isabelo Magalit, gave a speech titled "I Have a Dream," inspired by Martin Luther King Jr.

"I dream," Magalit said,

> that from the student world of this nation will come a steady stream of men and women who love nothing more than they love Jesus and hate nothing more than they hate sin. . . .
>
> People who know their God, who are alive to their times, and who are therefore able to serve the living God in their generation. . . .
>
> They must know first that God is alive, and that he is the God who acts. He is not a dumb idol or the vain product of wishful thinking.
>
> They cannot be hermits up in a monastery forever contemplating the divine mysteries. They must live in the middle of injustice. . . .
>
> They must recognize the spirit of the times, they must have insight into the peculiar opportunities of the day. . . .
>
> Some will be pastors, occupying the great evangelical pulpits of the cities. The vigor of the Church is determined by the power of the preached Word. Can we overemphasize the ministry of the Word?
>
> But the pastors will not only be in the big pulpits. They will also be in the villages and urban neighborhoods. People are not so sophisticated there. Neither are they able to pay a big salary. But they need the ministry of the Word, and they form the great bulk of our population. How can able men and women be motivated to live and work in the backwoods? This is part of the dream: that people who love Jesus and his word will count themselves as of no reputation. The communists are willing to spend a lifetime in the mountains. Why should less be expected of the servants of God?

Next Magalit mentioned seminary and university professors, and doctors and engineers, lawyers, businessmen, and mass media people. "Consider"—he said—"consider what it would mean to have a few committed Christians in the Philippine Medical Association. Perhaps adequate medical service for the 60% of our people who today do not get to see a physician even at their deathbed?"

Next he mentioned politicians and social reformers who would meet around the Word of God, discussing the nation's needs and planning to meet those needs through political and social action.

Finally he urged,

> My dream is to see Christian homes where love and justice are dressed in the flesh and blood of daily existence. Where future citizens are educated, where young Christians are nurtured to maturity in the faith, where neighbors are evangelized by Christians who really care about them.

"Share my dream!" Magalit concluded.[2]

Hundreds of young Filipinos did. On their fiftieth anniversary the Philippine InterVarsity Christian Fellowship published a book, *Broad Strokes of a Dream Fulfilled,* containing stories of more than fifty Filipino graduates who followed God's call and blessed their communities. The foreword is by Isabelo Magalit.

CREATE WEALTH

The sun goes down in the blink of an eye in the tropics, but the evenings stretch out wonderfully. People amble, gratefully inhaling the night breeze. Friends laugh, families meander companionably, couples nuzzle. Vendors, alert and awake, cater to everyone's desires. In upscale places like The Fort or the Mall of Asia or the Podium, stylish people flock to coffee shops and bars.

Yet not far away, cardboard shacks hover on the banks of fetid canals thick with unspeakable garbage. The night breeze and the family and friends and vendors are here too, but the options are limited and the milieu squalid.

Ruth Callanta decided to do something about this divide. On a broad scale she determined to narrow the gap between the mall and the canal. On a personal scale she wanted to bless men and women and children who deserved more.

Today the Center for Community Transformation that Ruth directs has 150 branches in 19 provinces, 47 cities and 35 municipalities, and 130,000 "community partners"—micro-entrepreneurs and street dwellers and urban youth who are involved in the Centers' programs. Jesus' name is mentioned constantly, and a discipleship program runs through all the activities, because CCT has come to believe this is essential to development.

When Ruth attended the Lausanne Conference in 1989, she already had experience as a community-development consultant in several countries. At this conference she was challenged to step out in faith and launch something for her own nation.

CCT's first project served employees who were being fired from their jobs. San Miguel, one of the biggest corporations in the country, was retrenching. It hired CCT to help its employees cope psychologically and economically when they were laid off. While enabling these people to develop small businesses to carry them through the next stage of their lives, CCT also made sure they knew that their intrinsic value did not depend on their jobs.

Other big corporations like Shell and Meralco followed suit and hired CCT to "humanize the retrenchment process."

From this beginning CCT has grown. Recent annual statistics show these figures:

- community partners: 130,000

- Bible study groups: 5,713

- persons committing to Christ as Lord: 45,221

- Muslim partners (borrowers): 2,654

- total loans: 1.8 billion pesos

- repayment rate: 99%

- savings mobilized: 170 million pesos

- outstanding loans: 430 million pesos

- community partners with health insurance: 69,032[3]

The quality of CCT's work was evident when in 1999 the United Nations' Development Program chose just twenty Philippine microfinance organizations to mentor. CCT was one.

No matter what the context, CCT's Christian witness shines. When CCT switched from the Grameen bank model to the Association for Social Advance—switching from group to individual liability for loans—the ASA asked Ruth to tone down their spiritual emphasis. But CCT held firm. To ASA's surprise, CCT's repayment rate continued to improve significantly.

Such prominent witness was not always the case. There were periods when the Christian thread was thin. Today, however, CCT's vision statement aims for "Christ-centered faith communities where Christ is honored and worshipped and where people live in dignity and sufficiency in accord with God's plan for a just, humane, and caring society."[4]

That vision is being fulfilled. "We've begun to read God's Word, and it's shaping the way we live," say a group of women entrepreneurs whose businesses include manicure, dry goods, food stalls and selling rags from discarded cloth remnants.

In December 2008 CCT opened a site for street dwellers, complete with showers, a cafeteria and a crafts center. An empty lot formerly used by drug dealers in Manila has been transformed into an oasis of hope. It is named *Kaibigan* (Friend) Ministry.

As the sun goes down along the canals, 130,000 people are moving up into a wholesome future because people like Ruth have taken action.

TRANSFER WEALTH

Lina Padilla was tooling around on the Internet. She and Carmena Cruz manage MEANS (Mission: East Asia National Support). This organization began in 1971 to serve as a conduit through which Filipinos in the

United States could donate to the InterVarsity in the Philippines and get U.S. tax receipts. Lina and Carmena live in Chicago. They are two of the many Filipinos outside the Philippines.

With time, MEANS's vision has grown. Today donors' contributions are forwarded to two hundred organizations or individuals, called "ministry partners." In the future, as the Philippines increasingly becomes a missionary-sending country, MEANS envisions "One country, One missionary, One Filipino"—at least one Filipino missionary for every country.

That vision sent Lina to the Internet to troll for Filipino witnesses across the nations.

Sarita. Up popped Sarita's blog from Ukraine.

"Carmena, look at this!" Lina sputtered.

"Interesting. I'll follow it up," Carmena decided as she glanced through Sarita's post.

So she wrote to Sarita.

"Are you a Filipina?" she asked.

"Yes," Sarita answered.

"How did you get to Ukraine?" Carmena wondered.

God had put Ukraine on Sarita's heart back in the Philippines, she explained. She earned a certificate from the Asia Center for Mission, procured funds from her church and friends, and bought a ticket to the Ukraine. Even while learning the Ukrainian language, she began to approach people on trains and invite them to English classes. She talked to people about the meaning of life, about spiritual power and about Jesus. Some believed. She formed Bible study groups and worship fellowships. She began training young Ukrainian believers in Christian leadership skills. Now she is learning about gardening and small-scale agriculture in order to help people put more food on their tables.

After Carmena and Sarita had chatted for some days, Carmena explained MEANS's purpose. "MEANS doesn't support missionaries directly, but we connect missionaries with donors. Would you like us to send our donors information about you? We would be honored to help a Filipina who is serving in that part of the world."

So Sarita's story appeared in MEANS's newsletter.

Edith. Enter Edith, a Filipina nurse in Texas. In her sister's apartment Edith saw the MEANS newsletter in which Sarita's story was featured.

"Oh, that is what I want!" Edith exclaimed. "I would love to give to a Filipina woman who is serving so far away from home. Send me some more information," she e-mailed Lina and Carmena—"and I will mobilize all my friends to contribute to Sarita's work."

Jay. The final character in this story is Jay, graduate of the Ateneo University, a first-class Catholic institution. He became a vibrant follower of Jesus in New York. Today he sings in the Brooklyn Tabernacle Choir.

Like Edith, Jay "accidentally" picked up a copy of the MEANS newsletter and read Sarita's story. He began to contribute money. Yet he wanted to do more.

"I'm an English teacher," he told Carmena and Lina. "I'd like to take a trip to Ukraine to help Sarita run a short-term English institute." And he did.

Much later Sarita confided to Carmena, "When you responded to my blog, I was desperate." Her only funds came from her Philippine church, and difficult economic conditions had reduced those. She didn't know where to turn. Then, truly out of the blue, MEANS showed up, and shortly after that Edith and Jay became Sarita's partners.

Business basics. Donations to MEANS totaled about $20,000 during its first year. Today the organization receives about $350,000 annually. By day, Lina works as the serials manager of the Northwestern University Law School library. Carmena has been the accounts payable manager for U.S. Robotics. Although MEANS has no paid staff—not even a secretary—it has thirty-four committed volunteers.

"Here are your donors," the founder had told Lina and Carmena when in 1986 he handed them a box of file cards with donors' names and addresses, transferring the leadership to them. "God will send you money. And God will send you volunteers."

God did. People with remarkable expertise—accountants, IT specialists, engineers, nurses, doctors—show up for the monthly work days. They bring specialized computers and video cameras, and create media packages beyond Carmena's and Lina's dreams. Starting with a box of file cards, today the MEANS office features computers with flat screens all networked to their own server.

Not long ago, MEANS's excellent board treasurer was transferred to Singapore. He didn't want to quit the ministry, so now their board meetings are conducted through teleconferencing.

Children's tutorial centers. MEANS continues to pioneer. Take the area of books. Filipino Christians in the United States discovered bilingual children's books created by OMF Publishers in the Philippines. "*Our* children need these!" they exclaimed. "These books would help them remember their Tagalog language."

OMF Publishers asked MEANS to serve as U.S. distributor.

Meanwhile, Carmena and Lina and others were sending Christian books to the Philippines. When they visited their home country, however, they were disappointed. The book boxes they had sent moldered in the corners of churches. People liked the pictures, but didn't know how to read very well.

From these experiences the "Read to Grow" program was born, a joint project between OMF Publishers and MEANS. One hundred children's libraries and reading-tutorial centers have been established throughout the Philippines. OMF has supplied the books. MEANS has supplied the funds, about $5,000. Churches often supply the space and personnel. Communities enjoy the benefits of tutorial help and Christian children's books.

MEANS is also funding libraries in the communal InterVarsity staff homes located in various Philippine cities. They aim for two hundred books in each home. These will attract not only Christian students but also non-Christians. Buying two hundred books from OMF costs about $500, compared to $5,000 if they had been bought in the United States, not to mention shipping cost and time.

A terrorist organization? Since September 11, 2001, MEANS's paperwork has become much more complicated. The Philippines is classed as a terrorist site by the U.S. government, so donors have to comply carefully with legal regulations.

Recently the government made a routine request for the names of all recipients. Lina wrote a letter of protest. "Some of our missionaries serve in countries where publishing their names might endanger them," she explained. Others wrote similar letters. As a result, the IRS changed Form 990. Because of security concerns, nonprofit agencies now are allowed to report workers by region rather than by country or by name.

Through MEANS, missionaries are blessed, donors are blessed and volunteers are blessed as MEANS ushers them into a larger world. "If we weren't volunteers with MEANS, we'd buy a big house and a big car, and spend all our time going to parties," one couple told Lina and Carmena. "Our values have totally changed though our work with MEANS."

PRAY AND PARTY

"*Tumatakbo.* He is running," Lisa spoke in my ear. "Practice now. Let's take advantage of this opportunity."

"*Tumatakbo,*" I mumbled.

"*Tumakbo, tumatakbo, tatakbo.* He ran, he runs, he will run. Repeat," she ordered.

"Tuh . . . tuh . . . Sorry." Failed again. Would I ever remember? If not, how would I communicate?

In a jeepney crawling through Manila, my large pasty body was crammed on a bench beside five trim, tan ones. The air was a soup. I felt almost asphyxiated. On the opposite bench swayed six more people. We grabbed metal rods overhead as the vehicle zoomed around obstacles and lurched through potholes.

"*Tumakbo, tumatakbo, tatakbo,*" Lisa chanted on. Today Lisa Espineli Chinn is the beloved director of International Student Ministry for InterVarsity in the United States, but on that afternoon we were single women who lived and worked together for the Philippine InterVarsity.

"*Tumatakbo ako.* I am running. *Tumatakbo tayo.* We are running. *Tumatakbo sila.* They are running," Lisa persisted. "Come on, try it."

"Will this woman never stop? Give me a break," I grumbled to myself as we bounced through another crater and my head cracked into the metal roof. I felt short of breath from the weight of the heat. My body seemed almost ready to explode. Would I have a stroke?

Yet what a blessing it was to live and work with Lisa and the other staff workers. Reading the English Bible did not come naturally to them, but they immersed themselves in it because it was precious. They struggled to grasp each nuance of God's nature. As a result, their prayers resonated richly with biblical symbols:

> Thank you, Jesus, for being our rock. Especially with the riots at the university this week—
>
> Today is so hot, and our bus ride is so long. Please be our green vine—
>
> Thank you for being our door . . . our bread . . . our water . . . our light.

Through friends like these I learned new dimensions of worship. I also learned about community and hospitality and courtesy and respect and gracefulness and poverty and justice. I learned that women can do anything. I learned that parties are essential to life!

Not that Filipino Christians are flawless. I saw Christian leaders who betrayed financial trust and led others to join them in networks of massive dishonesty. I saw Christian leaders who not only patronized promiscuous homosexual clubs but also led others to do the same. I saw jealousy. And gossip. And simple stupidity, setting projects back for years. Filipinos can sin as much as any of the rest of us.

We all are imperfect. The Bible refers to us as crude clay lanterns, "jars of clay" (2 Cor 4:6-7). Yet when God's light shines through us, we can be beautiful.

My life in the Philippines was not all work. There were idyllic days when I went snorkeling. It was another world altogether the minute I dipped my mask into the Pacific. Bold brown-and-gold-striped clownfish swam safely among big white stinging sea anemones. Blue starfish. Lionfish. Eels. Sea slugs. Schools of tiny dili. Black sea urchins. They neither "toil nor spin" (Mt 6:28 NKJV), but their feeding cycles progressed with stately rhythm. Coral polyps undulated. Seaweed forests waved and bent in the current. Everything felt cool, even in the noon heat. No wonder the Filipinos of old spent so much time on and in the water.

Like the fish, Filipinos interact gracefully, colorfully, unhurriedly. They make hospitality an art. Filipinos also interact symbiotically. When kin or friends have needs, no one thinks, *My apartment. My car. My salary.* Filipinos do not sleep in a room alone, nor work or relax alone. Often I watched my landlord's grandchildren play together, five children in one family ranging in age from one to ten. For hours they had fun without squabbles, the older ones adjusting the games so the little ones could join at varying levels of skill. Filipino children are trained that way. Certainly there are tensions in Philippine society, and they are exacerbated by globalization. But no Filipino is an island.

When I was four years old I learned some theology of culture from a Filipino. Throughout my life Filipinos have continued to bless me. This chapter could have been about God's people in the Congo or Guatemala or Malaysia because God is just as much at work there. His people are thinking as deeply and acting as wisely in those places. But I learned first from Filipinos. In gratitude I have begun this book with a glimpse of how they make a difference.

THESE ARE MY PEOPLE

WHAT IS THE FUTURE? "BACK IN THE DAY . . . " WE SAY. BUT WHAT IS "FORWARD IN THE DAY"? WHAT'S COMING TOWARD US?

- Is a clash of civilizations inevitable—or should we eventually expect the triumph of the golden arches everywhere?

- Will we see the "end of history," the flattening of ideologies so we can all do business more efficiently—or will we see a rise of passionate fundamentalisms?

- Will hunger, disease, illiteracy and injustice be reduced—or will disasters and wars devastate large regions and destabilize economies?

- Will we work hard to resolve conflicts and build relationships—or will broken families, depression and loneliness be widespread?

- Will the next generation die for a cause—or for an iPod?

- Will Jesus' followers flourish—or will persecution increase?

- Will the number of churches grow—or will they splinter into factions?

- Will more Christians get training and lead with maturity—or will prideful competition preoccupy us?

- Will carefully defined "best practices" structure our ministry and
  mission—or will the Spirit blow where it wishes, pole-jumping all
  our boxes?

Yes. All of the above.

So what will hold us together in this vortex?

Pawns in a Global Game

In 605 B.C., the Babylonian army rolled over Judah and marched a lot of
the people to Babylon in chains. One captive was a young man named
Daniel. Although he was slotted into the "gifted" group and got extra
privileges, he was a slave, subject to the whim of his captors.

At one swoop Daniel lost his family. His country and culture. His
girlfriend, if he had one. His career plans. His freedom and his rights—he
could be thrown into a lions' den at any moment. He even lost his name
and was renamed for a pagan god. He spent the rest of his life working
for megalomaniacs like Nebuchadnezzar.

Following Daniel in history were Esther and Nehemiah. All three
believers lived in exile at the mercy of global forces beyond their control. All three model strategies important for us as we cope with globalization in our time, when jobs are outsourced, terrorism erupts and we
sometimes feel like pawns in a giant game.

Nehemiah was called to build the wall around Jerusalem. Esther
served in a larger arena. When genocide threatened her people, she was
called to confront the powers and engage in advocacy with international repercussions. Nehemiah worked at the microlevel, Esther at the
macrolevel.

What about Daniel? He worked at the missional level, giving words
to a vision of God in an upside-down world. Up to now, God had been
in the temple but now the temple was smashed. God had been in the
land, but now the boundaries of the land were erased. God had been
with the people, but now the people were scattered throughout the
alien empire from North Africa to India. Where was God? Esther and
Nehemiah needed to know before they could do their work.

God gave Daniel a vision (Dan 7). This provided the foundation on which people like Esther and Nehemiah could build. Previously Daniel had interpreted visions for rulers. Now he received his own. In his vision the snow-white "Ancient of Days" presided from a throne blazing like fire. A hundred thousand people vibrated around him. Court books were opened, a cruel, powerful beast was judged and executed, and its body was thrown into fire.

Then the "Son of Man" entered. Clouds surrounded him as he approached the Ancient of Days. Everyone turned, and he became the focus of worship. "He was given authority, glory, and sovereign power; all peoples, nations and men of every language worshiped him. His dominion is an everlasting dominion that will not pass away, and his kingdom is one that will never be destroyed" (Dan 7:14).

Snagging Nebuchadnezzar. "Everlasting dominion." A kingdom "that will never be destroyed." These words captured the imagination of Nebuchadnezzar, that great Babylonian emperor. Although he was a brilliant military strategist, architect, philosopher and civic planner, Nebuchadnezzar had weaknesses. For example, he built a statue of himself and threw people in a red hot furnace when they wouldn't bow to it (Dan 3). Yet during the decades that Daniel served Nebuchadnezzar they must have talked about God, because Nebuchadnezzar progressively expressed a more complete understanding of who God is. The last time we see him, Nebuchadnezzar has issued a proclamation:

> To the peoples, nations, and men of every language, who live in all the world: May you prosper greatly!
>
> It is my pleasure to tell you about the miraculous signs and wonders that the Most High God has performed for me.
>
> How great are his signs,
>> how mighty his wonders!
> His kingdom is an eternal kingdom;
>> his dominion endures from generation to
>> generation. (Dan 4:1-3)

At the end of his proclamation, Nebuchadnezzar repeated what so impressed him: *"His dominion is an eternal dominion; his kingdom endures from generation to generation"* (Dan 4:34, emphasis added).

What poignant longing these words convey. Every great person wants to create something that will last. I live in the same city as Bill Gates. He hopes that Microsoft will last. Meanwhile he has taken early retirement to create a legacy through philanthropy. Nebuchadnezzar hoped that his empire would endure. But in fact it lasted only a few years after his death. Then it was overthrown by the Medes and Persians

After the lions. Yet the Medo-Persian ruler Darius commented on the very same characteristic of Daniel's God. Darius ordered Daniel thrown to the lions, then retrieved him from the den and issued a proclamation about "the God of Daniel . . . *his kingdom will not be destroyed, his dominion will never end"* (Dan 6:26, emphasis added). Darius too longed for a rule that would last.

However, the Medo-Persians were overthrown by the Greeks. Not long afterward, Alexander the Great's empire blew up and fragmented into four parts, as pictured in Daniel 11.

Only one person in this story lived in the everlasting kingdom: Daniel the slave. Because he did, because he was not totally captured by the systems of this world, he could make important contributions *to* this world. This he did in a long life of service under several emperors.

Daniel was called to put words to a vision, to articulate who God is, a God of love and power, a God who cares and who rules even when the foundations are shaking, even when the lights are going out. Microlevel work like Nehemiah's is essential. Macrolevel work like Esther's is too. Yet we can burn out in microlevel projects. We can burn out in macrolevel advocacy. To keep going, we will need missional vision, kingdom vision continually renewed. "Where there is no vision, the people perish" (Prov 29:18 KJV).

That's why there is no work more important than telling the story of Jesus. He brings the vision to life. In our time it is in Jesus that we see who God is.

BODIES FOR HIRE

A few years ago I spent time in the Arabian Gulf. Hundreds of gleaming skyscrapers thrust out of the sand, row after row. Men in spotless white robes and white head cloths and women in elegant silky black designer robes and scarves swished from air-conditioned offices to air-conditioned cars.

Out in the heat were Filipinos. In the richer Gulf countries the grunt work is done by foreigners. Sometimes 80 percent of the labor force comes from outside. The Philippine economy is set up to facilitate overseas employment. Without enough jobs at home, there is a push to work in richer countries and send back foreign exchange.

Many Filipino university graduates take jobs as maids or nannies if they are women, or as construction workers if they are men. In the homes where they work they risk sexual abuse. On job sites they risk injuries. Legal protection is rare, and medical help for foreign labor is unreliable.

Meanwhile, back in the Philippines they have left their parents and brothers and sisters, and often wives and husbands and children too.

Witness to local Muslims is illegal, and in countries like Saudi Arabia even Christian worship is banned.

Yet many Filipinos have grown in their faith in this hard setting. For some nominal Christians it has been a wake-up call. They are stressed. They are spiritually starving. To help them, multilevel discipleship-training programs have been developed on the spot.

Others came prepared to witness in spite of the risk. Back home there are at least ten Philippine agencies that provide mission training for workers going abroad. On the field such laborers share their faith with office mates or house mates who show interest. And they sing. Whenever there is a lull, a Filipino sings. If he or she is a believer, Christian lyrics bubble up.

Some have done time in jail, and others have given their lives for this witness. Nevertheless, fruit grows.

Where I traveled, it was legal to worship inside a church. I sought out a Filipino service where about 150 people gathered. The worshipers glowed. When they began to sing, the place rocked. One song focused on Jesus the king. Clerks and nannies, maids and managers belted out—

And this Kingdom's reign
And this Kingdom's rule
And this Kingdom's power and authority
Jesus, God's righteousness revealed.

As the decibels rose, I squirmed and muttered under my breath, "This is a little loud, don't you think? Let's keep it down. Don't you all remember where you are? Don't you know who's in charge?"

Then I realized they *did* know. That's why they were so radiant and so uninhibited. They were singing to the same power and authority that Christians have honored a hundred thousand times in a hundred thousand hard places. Like Daniel they were living and loving in the kingdom of everlasting dominion that will never be destroyed. It was this cosmic reality that empowered them to be salt and light wherever their labor was needed around the world.

Someday the Arab world may be different because Christian Filipinos—and Koreans and Pakistanis and others—took lowly jobs and let the love of Christ flow through them.

Faithful and Alive

Different kinds of people call themselves Christians. Centuries ago some groups converted for political reasons. Today many of their members have little personal interest in Christ, though they still wear the label "Christian." By contrast, "evangelicals" emphasize Jesus' death and resurrection, Bible study, personal conversion, and outreach.[1] They are not necessarily members of certain churches nor bound to certain geographical regions as "Christian cultures" or "Christian nations." Some even reject the word *Christian* and call themselves "Jesus Muslims" or "Jesus Hindus," yet share evangelical commitments. Whatever else they call themselves, evangelicals want to be Jesus' disciples, faithful and alive.

To be evangelical is "not just a doctrinal position with a pietistic lifestyle attached (which is how most non-evangelicals seem to see it)," according to J. I. Packer,

> but rather is an organic reinvigorating of life in Christ . . . a particular divine operation: namely, an animating and revitalizing activity whereby . . . the Holy Spirit impacts individuals and groups to reconfigure and direct their lives towards the mature fullness of Christ . . . life maintained in intensity . . . [as] vigor and enterprise overflow. . . . The end product of the Spirit's action is lively godliness . . . radical personal convertedness . . . [and] a vivid sense of new identity in the body of Christ linked with . . . concern for . . . Christians everywhere.[2]

At least eighty million Chinese in China name Jesus as Lord. So do millions more Chinese outside the country. In Africa four hundred million Africans praise Jesus. There are fifteen times more Anglicans worshiping in Nigeria every Sunday than there are in Britain. There are more Free Methodists in the small countries of Rwanda and Burundi than there are in the United States. There are forty-five million evangelicals in Brazil supporting 4,700 Brazilian missionaries.

In Latin America there are more Christians than in all of the United States and Europe. The same is true in Africa, and again in Asia. By 2025 there will be as many Pentecostals as there are Hindus, and twice as many Pentecostals as Buddhists, according to Philip Jenkins in his award-winning book *The Next Christendom: The Coming of Global Christianity.* "We are currently living through one of the transforming moments in the history of religion worldwide," Jenkins says. "The center of gravity in the Christian world has shifted inexorably southward to Africa, Asia, and Latin America. Already today the largest Christian communities on the planet are to be found there." He adds, "By 2050 only about one fifth of the world's three billion Christians will be non-Hispanic Whites."[3]

Not only is Christianity the wave of the future. It is also the wave of the past. As Jenkins says, "Christianity never has been synonymous with Europe or the West."[4] Early Christian art was shaped in places like Syria and Iraq and even Africa. Early New Testament manuscripts were developed in Africa. So was monasticism. In his book *How Africa Shaped the Christian Mind*, Thomas Oden discusses seven ways that Africa helped to form the European Christian mind.

A written Gospel and written book of psalms were in the African Coptic language by A.D. 300. Today there are ten million Coptic Christians. The Syrian Orthodox church still uses Aramaic language, which is close to what Jesus spoke.

There is strong tradition that the apostle Thomas took the good news of Jesus to India, and there are documented Christian communities in that land before A.D. 200. There is tradition that Mark took the good news to Africa, as did the Ethiopian eunuch who was baptized by Philip. Visiting Jews came to faith in Jesus when Peter preached in Jerusalem at Pentecost (Acts 2), and they carried the good news home to communities across North Africa and Asia, laying foundations for the first churches in those regions.

China's early records of the gospel stretch to 600. Missionaries who belonged to the Nestorian church traveled east along the Silk Road. They translated parts of the Bible and planted monasteries in many Chinese cities.

God was in all these countries before our records, of course. God created every individual person in his image. Through nature (Ps 19), conscience (Rom 2), dreams and visions (Acts 10), human witnesses, and Scripture—and today through the Internet—God speaks to those who look for him.

This revelation culminates in Jesus, the Word made flesh. "No one comes to the Father except through me," Jesus said (Jn 14:6). "There is no other name under heaven . . . by which we must be saved," according to the apostle Peter (Acts 4:12). God has ways to make Jesus known to those who want to meet him.

SAVING CULTURES

Sometimes the gospel saves a whole people from annihilation. In Borneo I have worshiped with Kelabit and Lun Bawang tribespeople. Their grandfathers hunted rhinoceros. They picked fruit by swinging from vines eighty feet above the jungle floor and rafted through class-six whitewater rapids as a routine means of transportation.

In the middle of the nineteenth century an Indian-born Britisher named James Brooke arrived. For the next hundred years, he and his successors constituted the government throughout the region. Head-hunting was prohibited. Agricultural methods were improved.

Unfortunately, more rice and more freedom to live without fear meant more fermented beverages, more partying and more heavy drinking.

Alcoholism became a major scourge. Violence erupted frequently. Families were broken. Community social structures were in tatters.

Then on the continent of Australia, several Christians felt called to serve the Lun Bawang and Kelabit people.

When they arrived, officials tried to discourage them. "Your ideals are commendable. But, frankly, it's not worthwhile going up those mountains because in another generation those people will be gone. It's not worthwhile to learn those languages, because they are going to disappear."

Nevertheless, the missionaries did go up the mountains. They shared God's good news. The people responded. Lives changed. They quit drinking. Families healed. They asked the government for schools. Today they are literate, contributing citizens. Including believers in nearby tribes, there are 150,000 followers of Jesus, and more than one thousand churches.

"If not for the gospel, you would be dead," I blurted out one Sunday after worshiping with them.

"That's absolutely right," they agreed. "The gospel saved us, not only as individuals but as a people."

Daniel, Esther and Nehemiah. Filipino and Australian and Borneo Christians. All who worship King Jesus. These are my people. I belong with them.

FLEAS ON THE DOG

But Christians can break your heart.

One Sunday evening in a tropical country Peter and Rebecca ushered me into a lovely eating place. My work introduces me to some of the finest human beings on earth, intelligent evangelical leaders who are contextualized in a dizzying spectrum of cultures. That Sunday was no exception. I had been bathed in rich worship. Now, as the three of us sat down and opened our menus, I was thanking God for the beauty of his church in their land.

Peter threw cold water on my bliss.

"For twenty years I've poured my life into students," he said. "I've discipled them, cried with them, celebrated with them. Then they graduate and take good jobs. Ten years later all they can talk about is the house and the car and the promotion and the vacation and the big church remodel. The poor are still all around, but they no longer see them. It happens student generation after generation." He sat with eyes downcast and shoulders slumped, this gifted, highly placed leader.

It was a helpful corrective to my rosy picture.

"The church is made up of sinners. The fleas come with the dog," says Eugene Peterson.

> We expect a disciplined army of committed men and women who courageously lay siege to the worldly powers. Instead we find some people who are more concerned with getting rid of the crabgrass in their lawns. We expect a community of saints who are mature in the virtues of love and mercy, and find ourselves working on a church supper where there is more gossip than there are casseroles. We expect to meet minds that are informed and shaped by the great truths and rhythms of Scripture, and find persons whose intellectual energy is barely sufficient to get them from the comics to the sports page. . . . Faith in Christ does not in itself make a person an interesting conversationalist or stimulating companion. [Sometimes you just have to] endure tedious relationships with unimaginative pilgrims.[5]

Then we realize it is not the kingdom that holds us together, but the King.

> Our little systems have their day,
> They have their day and cease to be.

They are but broken lights of thee
And thou, O Lord, art more than they.[6]

A PURE PILGRIMAGE CHURCH

We are in process. We are not finished. Sometimes others' sins, or our own, make us cry. Yet the thrill of the journey always returns.

When the cornerstone for a major ecumenical church was laid in Qatar in 2007, Paul Hinder, Catholic Bishop of Arabia, spoke of this journey. "We have to accept that we are expatriates in every sense of the word. We are a pure pilgrimage church. A multicultural, multilingual, multiracial church composed of the faithful more or less from all over the world."[7]

Simultaneous with the inauguration of that church in Qatar in 2008, the Evangelical Community Church of Abu Dhabi—the church where I worshiped with Filipinos—dedicated a new building extension. There were two morning services for the dedication, standing-room only. These were followed by the Filipino service, which was packed. That was followed by the Ethiopian service. That was followed by a special Chinese New Year service, for which the uncompleted building was booked in faith months in advance. About 450 Chinese workers crowded into that event, 90 percent of whom never had entered a church before. It took working in the Gulf to draw them to the gospel.

The church is on a journey, not in a box. Global flows are taking us in new directions. Not only "extreme" Gulf congregations are multicultural. The nations are in *our* neighborhoods. Wherever we live, we hardly can go to the mall without passing people from half a dozen countries.

Reaching across these cultural boundaries should feel natural. It always has been our call. Abraham was commissioned to bless *all* the families of the earth (Gen 12:3). Moses charged God's people to love the aliens as they loved themselves (Deut 10:19). David sang, "May *all* the peoples praise you" (Ps 67:5). Isaiah envisioned God's followers being light to the nations (Is 51:4). Habakkuk pictured the day when "the earth will be filled with the knowledge of the glory of the LORD, as the waters cover the sea" (Hab 2:14). Paul was propelled by a passion for the unreached peoples (Rom 15:20). John vibrated with a vision of peoples and tribes and kindreds and nations gathered together around the throne of God at the end of time (Rev 7:9-10).

Our loyalties cannot stop at the edge of our culture. While culture is a treasured gift of God, outsiders are God's gifts too. So even though the overall emphasis of this book is indigenous believers, now and then foreign missionaries will appear. These are sojourners who have stepped out into the margins to demonstrate with their bodies God's "pure pilgrimage church."

IT TAKES A KINGDOM FAMILY

"I'm so hungry I could devour a rock," Peter growled as he somersaulted into the soft sand.[8]

"Don't think about it," counseled Joel. "Look at that sunset." Hunkering down, he drummed a soft beat on a piece of driftwood.

Peter got out his guitar and began to strum. He licked his lips and eyed the lapping waves of the Mediterranean. Although their homes were south of the Sahara, they had come to North Africa to further their education. The richer nations in the north had granted them scholarships. Yet the people in these nations thought of Jesus merely as a prophet. They had no idea that he was savior and king and God and friend. Peter and Joel longed for their classmates to hear this good news.

Along with other Christian students from the south, they had formed a student group. When there were ten fellowships linked across the band of solidly Muslim nations, they decided to hold a leadership-training camp.

By faith, even though they hardly had the funds to survive month by month, they had reserved a site at the beach. Twenty-seven students arrived at the camp. Then they discovered that nobody had any money for food.

So they went down to the shore and stared at the waves. As the sun crept toward the crests, they began to sing songs of praise.

A fishing boat drifted past, then pulled up on the sand nearby. The fishermen approached. "What are you doing?" they asked.

"Singing," Peter smiled.

"Songs to God," Joel added.

"Songs to Jesus," Peter clarified. *Might as well let our witness shine.*

The fishermen looked at each other. "You believe in Jesus?"

"Yes."

"Are you students?"

"Yes."

"So you're just sitting here singing?"

"Well, to be honest, we'd also like to be eating. But it took all our money to get here. We have no food." Joel shrugged and forced a smile. "At least we can sing."

The fishermen looked at each other. "We have plenty of fish. Take some. Take lots. We're from Korea, and we're Christians too."

God had brought African students from the south to the universities in Muslim lands. Over the years they would have a significant quiet witness. But they were not self-sufficient. At this camp, at least, God used members of the global church to keep them alive. Every night that week the fishing boats pulled up with fish for all the campers.

"Take as much as you like," the fishermen said. "We pray God's blessing on you. This is not an easy place to be a Christian."

Encouraged, the campers returned to their universities ready to pray with those in need and to point them to Jesus.

Today one of the Africans who studied and witnessed in that region, Daniel Bourdanne, is global director of the International Fellowship of Evangelical Students (IFES), the movement that networks InterVarsity movements globally.

Grow Up

Disciples are more than converts. Knowing the King is more than cheerleading. If we truly love God and our neighbors, we have to apply our brains. We have to immerse ourselves in "the whole counsel of God."[9]

Where do we find that? In Scripture stories, doctrinal themes, spiritual presence, obedient practice (because we learn by doing) and community application (because faith is not just private).

Growing up to spiritual maturity is a challenge that faces Christians everywhere. Some turn to formal institutions like Asian Graduate School of Theology, a consortium of eight seminaries that offer M.A. and Ph.D. degrees, with a home base in the Philippines. AGST models cooperative sharing of finance, personnel, library and facilities. In another partnership the South American Theological Seminary reaches from Brazil to Africa, to help the Mozambique Graduate School of Theology offer an M.A.

At the other end of the training spectrum are oral Scripture programs, as we will see in chapter nine. Mentored nonformal apprenticeships play a big part too.

Training requires financial investment. Overseas Council, based in Indianapolis, is one group that has stepped up to the plate. Over the past thirty years, OC has helped one hundred schools in sixty countries with computers, libraries, buildings, scholarships, administrative skills training and faculty development.

Maintaining academic standards is another unglamorous requirement. Various bodies like the Asian Theological Alliance sacrificially conduct accreditation visits to hold schools accountable.

God gives us brains and he expects us to develop them, whether through seminaries or private study or radio teaching or training camps or other programs. How else can we help with the issues of our day— oil, water, violence, hunger, disease, joblessness, lovelessness—unless we can think Christianly? This must be done in the context of our own culture, with its categories of community and time and justice and everyday values, if we are to create "ethnotheology" that is appropriate for our people.

Thoughtful Christians are found at all levels. Esme Bowers of the Africa Evangelical Alliance trains women. Her books are manuals stored on her laptop. Whenever she deplanes, she considers the situation of the local women. Has war swept through? She downloads the manual on soldiers and prostitutes. Is the region agricultural? She downloads the manual on earthkeeping.

Recently Esme conducted a workshop in Zimbabwe. There a local woman approached her. "I had twelve children," she told Esme. "They were all married. But they all died of AIDS. All their spouses died too. Now I'm left with thirty-two grandchildren to support on a little plot of ground."

Yet in spite of horrendous burdens, this woman had come to Esme's workshop to be trained as a thoughtful Christian leader. She knew that every Christian needs to learn to think.

In today's chaotic world, people are hungry for meaning. They wonder if there is any big picture. They long for explanatory paradigms. Great biblical themes like creation, stewardship of the earth, incarnation, sacrificial life-giving, resurrection, new birth, spiritual empowering, heaven and a God both powerful and personal can speak volumes. It is our privilege to present these ideas winsomely in the marketplace of ideas.

LATIN AMERICANS AND THE BEAUTY OF JESUS

One afternoon in Guatemala I listened to a courtyard fountain spill, trickle, gurgle and sing. It restored my soul. I was aware that Guatemala had problems. As we had been driving to my first meeting, my friend Armindo had received a call telling him that his partner had been shot in the leg during a car hijacking. Wrenching the steering wheel around and zooming to the hospital, Armindo took the news calmly. No big deal. He had had *two* cars stolen himself. But I was shaken. It took the soothing sound of the water later to remind me that there is also beauty in this "country of eternal spring."

I was there to teach Guatemalans who were heading to places like Mauritania, Kurdistan and Sudan. My topic was Muslim women. Many Spanish-speaking missionaries serve in such countries. Like Jesus' people elsewhere, Latin Americans not only worship and witness and network and grow to maturity, but also reach across borders in well-planned mission.

There is a large ethnic group in the Middle East where several hundred former Muslims follow Jesus because of the witness of a team of Latin American professionals.

When they first arrived, these Latin Americans immersed themselves in local life. "We learned what their profiles were for an ideal man and woman, and we tried to fulfill those standards," says the leader, Abraham Duran. "We tried to walk, behave, eat, drink, talk, share, keep silence, sleep, and relate in ways that our people group considered right, proper, and ideal. . . . We tried to dispel their prejudices. . . . We never initiated apologetic discussions, but we responded. . . . People cannot see the beauty of Jesus if they see only our ugliness."

> We presented the beauty of Christ's teachings about God, human beings, society, religious leaders, and God's kingdom before we talked to them about who Jesus is. . . . His teaching "rings true."
> . . . We think we are good, and discover that we are unable to keep "the law" or noble "New Year" or "new life" resolutions consistently. We are sure we can fix society with more education, and our best projects end in chaos. We insist that the revolution will solve the problems, and it multiplies them. We affirm that we can manage wealth and power, and they become our masters. We know we can change the world if religion is in power, and religion in power turns people into rebels and saints into monsters.

People discovered that Jesus was the hero they were looking for. They saw Jesus' compassion demonstrated by missionaries who "took the side of justice, served the poor, healed the sick, educated the ignorant, and provided for the needy." Most of all the missionaries prayed. Miraculous healings occurred. Dreams and visions happened. The team also was willing to suffer, and people saw their joy. During times of turmoil, people saw their peace. They practiced community, and welcomed new believers, even as they encouraged them to stay close to their families and friends.

"Jesus did not arrive from heaven as an adult and say to the monotheistic, legalistic Jews: 'I am God Almighty fresh from heaven, and if you, right now, will repent and put your trust in my atoning sacrifice, you will be saved,' " says Duran. "If we want to share the good news of the gospel with our monotheistic, legalistic Muslim friends, we must follow his example—a gradual approach that will lead people to discern the truth and beauty of Jesus' personality, teachings, and life, motivating them to be his followers."[10]

These Latin Americans deliberately traded the beauties of countries like Guatemala—the colorful flowers and textiles, the familiar spices and fruits, the greenery and flowing water, the language of Cervantes—to share the beauty of Jesus.

It's Not about Us

"Tell me, Doctor. If you were in the uterus, would you want to come out into a world like this?"

The speaker was a pregnant woman. A nuclear bomb had just exploded, and radiation sickness was spreading. The scene is from the movie *The Day After.*

The doctor shook his head. "I can't argue with you," he said.

She jumped up and grabbed his lapels and begged, "Argue with me! Tell me about hope!"

Hope. That woman's cry echoes in our hearts. We do not know the future. There may be tidal waves. Terrorism. Germs that do not respond to antibiotics. Water shortages.

Five hundred years from now our universities could be ashes. Our churches, even our denominations, might have disappeared. The United States of America could be gone.

But Jesus' church will be alive, blossoming in a million places in several thousand languages, "salting" the earth, lighting neighborhoods, blessing broken people and connecting them with the God who made them and loves them and can empower them to live with meaning and joy in this terrifying and beautiful world.

These are my people. They tell me about hope.

I love America. When I fly home from Asia and first see land, whether the beaches of Los Angeles or the Strait of Juan de Fuca—that blue furrow that arrows between green firs toward SeaTac airport—a lump forms in my throat. I treasure the words, "We hold these truths to be self-evident, that all men are created equal, that they are endowed by their Creator with certain inalienable rights." I sing "God Bless America" with feeling.

Yet the future global church may not be Western-led, and that's OK. Let the mantle pass. We in the West can learn to follow, can't we? True, most of the money, power, training institutions, publishing houses and international organizations still are based here. But God is doing something new in our time. People of every nation are joining in. We can too, wherever we are. This book is not primarily about us or what we should do. It is a humble celebration of the kingdom that glows from generation to generation and will never be destroyed.

"I will build my church," Jesus said, "and the gates of hell shall not prevail against it" (Mt 16:18 KJV). Today we have the great privilege of being part of that together, linked as never before.

THE ELEPHANT
IN THE ROOM

Jesus' People in China

"TAKE ME WITH YOU."

Heads swiveled and eyebrows rose. The men shook their heads and turned back to their plans.

The young woman edged forward. "Take me along."

"Shhh, let them plan," an older woman murmured as she patted Liang's shoulder. "You've paid such a price already. Come over here." She tugged on the young woman's arm.

But Liang stood her ground. "I want to go. Haven't I earned the right?"

Heads swiveled back. Faces scrunched up, perplexed. "Your husband was martyred in that Li village just a week ago," the group leader said kindly, "and yet you want to join us on this very risky return trip?"

"Yes."

The men looked at each other. First of all, Liang was a woman. Second, she already had suffered severely with the loss of her hus-

band. Third, she was young. Fourth, she had no special Bible knowledge. Wouldn't she be an impediment to their mission team rather
than a help?

Still, when the team left, Liang traveled with them. The air steamed
as they tromped past pineapple fields, alongside rubber plantations,
through the jungle and finally down the path to the very village where
Wang had been smashed into the ground.[1]

An island province facing Vietnam across the sea, Hainan is the
most southerly part of China. While most of Hainan's population is
Chinese, there are also a number of indigenous peoples. The largest
group is the Li.

Wang's and Liang's church in Hainan wanted to share the good news
about Jesus with the Li. So they sent a mission team. But when the tribal
people saw the Chinese-speaking missionaries, they remembered centuries of domination and got very angry.

"The spirits of the mountains rule our land. You Chinese dogs have
been here only 500 years. You know nothing. You have stolen our land
and now you wish to steal our gods as well? You will pay for this!"

Brandishing hoes and rakes and other farm implements, a mob rushed
at the missionaries. Wang was beaten to death.

For three weeks the whole church grieved. For three days they
prayed and fasted. Then they sent the mission team back to the site of
the murder.

What would they encounter?

Surly looks greeted them. But before anyone on either side could
open their mouths, Liang took a few paces forward and raised her voice
so she would be heard clearly. "I am the widow of the man you killed
three weeks ago," she said.

Shock covered the villagers' faces.

"My husband is not dead, however," she continued, "God has given
him eternal life. Now he is living in paradise with God. When he came
here to your village, he wanted to tell you how you could have that life
too. If he were here now, he would forgive you for what you did. In his
place I forgive you. I can do this because God has forgiven me. If you

want to hear more about God, meet us under the big tree outside of town this evening."

People listened quietly. Nobody raised a hand against the missionaries. So the team members put their heads together. It was clear that God had given Liang an opening. Maybe she should continue to be the spokesperson.

"What do I know? I am not a teacher. I simply gave a witness," she exclaimed.

"We'll teach you," Wang's father counseled her. "Every day we'll prepare you for what to say."

So when villagers gathered under the tree at the end of the day, Liang passed on what she had been taught that afternoon. After a week and a half, many tribal people had believed. When the mission-team departed, Wang's father stayed to instruct the new Christians and baptize them.

Two months later he showed up at the home church with three men from the new Li church. During the service, these young believers gave greetings.

"I am the man who murdered Wang," one began.

There was a hiss of indrawn breath, but the congregation listened as the Li man told how God had forgiven him. He asked forgiveness from God's people, expressed an eternal debt of gratitude and brought a money gift from the new church to show thanks to the church that had sent them the good news.

In a kaleidoscope of ways this experience is being repeated across China—across all the provinces, across all educational and social levels, and across a wide variety of ethnic groups. Liang and Wang are part of a massive movement. People are thinking and talking about Jesus throughout the land, and many are owning Jesus as Lord. There are at least eighty million Christians inside China, and millions more Chinese believers outside. The Church is now larger than the Communist Party.

SUPERPOWER ON THE WORLD STAGE

On the world scene at the beginning of the twenty-first century, China is the "elephant in the room." What does that mean? If you are in a room with an elephant, you move carefully. Every country planning to take new steps today must consider China. Whether you lunch with businessmen in Costa Rica or Angola, Vietnam or Kazakhstan, eventually the conversation turns to China.

For over twenty years China's annual economic growth has been at least 8 percent, and sometimes as high as 14 percent. Five thousand years of literacy have laid a foundation for progress. Habits of networking, hard work, taking the long-term view and approaching life actively are bricks laid on this foundation. Chinese emphasize community in their social structure and cooperation in their set of values. Their population looks unstoppable. At 1.3 billion, China is largest nation in the world.

Of course there are blips. Milk products tainted with melamine have sickened thousands of children, and some will have serious kidney problems. Air pollution can be severe. A disastrous water shortage is a possibility. Deforestation threatens floods. People in some rural regions lack necessities, so 150 million of them have migrated to cities. Since they lack proper documentation in their new locations, they may not get health care, schooling for their children or other basic services. They become a shadow society.

Advertisements display Chinese wearing stylish clothes, buying cars and using new technology. For some businessmen, politicians and media people this picture is accurate, especially in the southeast. Yet emotional bankruptcy is widespread among the population at large. The suicide rate is so high that the government has stopped publishing it.

A person can be jailed or sent to labor camp without trial— "reeducated through labor"— if he or she spouts ideas that the government considers inappropriate. This includes Christians. Whole regions, like Tibet, see their language and culture eroded with government approval.

Nevertheless, China has made amazing progress on many fronts. It is no easy feat to whoosh a billion people out of superstitious and hierarchical mindsets into prosperity. It is even harder when the physical resource base is so barren in some large regions, when the area and population are so vast, and when there is so much diversity within the nation.

Yet by the 1990s, fifty-eight million fewer people experienced chronic hunger than in the preceding decades.[2] This is major success.

Nor does China ignore potential problems. Ambitious new schemes to empower farmers and distribute water are under way. In the past some ambitious schemes have failed drastically. The costs have been tragic for ordinary people. To its credit, however, China faces up to disasters in the making. It takes practical steps to avert them. After the 2008 earthquake in Sichuan where ten thousand children died, the government swiftly provided shelters, medical care, trauma counseling and other services for the hordes who were displaced.

LIGHTS IN THE POWERHOUSE

If China is a powerhouse, Jesus' people are its lights. Some fellowships register with the government. Others do not. Among the unregistered are at least twenty large house church networks with millions of members. Some unregistered churches may have two thousand people meeting for Sunday worship, even though the maximum gathering allowed by law without official permission is twenty-five.

There is a growing "Third Church" movement as well. Though unregistered, these churches don't hide. They make their presence known, pointing to the official constitution of China, which guarantees freedom of religion. They want to make China live up to its claims, to be all that it should be. Lawyers from such churches advocate for human rights, for rights of conscience and speech and assembly. They defend the cases of people who are unjustly accused, both Christian and non-Christian. Members of these churches create programs to help disadvantaged groups like migrants to the cities or victims of earthquakes or floods. They contribute visibly to the welfare of the nation.

In the secular arena some Chinese Christians run factories or other businesses that employ thousands. In their factory complexes they bless the community by offering clinics, computer classes, libraries, gyms and even karaoke rooms.

China is not a monolith. The government is not one giant mind. There are layers and layers, and winds that blow from many directions.

In most cities there are vibrant open churches. The sermons are excellent. The study of the Bible is balanced and rich. It is possible to order Christian materials through the mail or buy them at bookstores.

In some regions church members witness by performing as street entertainers or by showing videos or inviting people to faith-based events.

Technically, this public witness is not legal. That is one of the restrictions the government religion bureau has placed on churches. Another restriction prohibits youth ministry. Children and youth are not to be taught in church programs. And certain Bible themes cannot be taught, such as Jesus' kingdom at the end of time. That is banned because it contradicts Marxist theory.

Whether these restrictions are enforced depends on local officials' interpretations. They in turn respond to political currents. Before the 2008 Olympics, for example, many local evangelists were arrested and foreign missionaries were deported because the government did not want to risk any disruptions during the international sports events.

Two reasons. In some regions police have been brutal, charging into unregistered worship services, flailing bamboo rods, kicking people who fall down, fining the participants and sentencing them to hard labor. This happens more in the countryside than in the cities because urban persecution may be flashed around the world immediately. Rural persecution can be hidden away.

Why does the government restrict and even persecute Christians? For two reasons, one religious and the other social. At the beginning of the communist movement, Karl Marx called religion "the opiate of the people." Religious people have their eyes on heaven; "so heavenly minded they are no earthly good," in a common phrase. When Christians do think about life here and now, they tend to focus on individual morality. Given massive injustices in so many places, such a focus is trivial, Marx believed. It distracts people from the struggle for equal rights, yet that is the struggle that will usher in a healthier, happier society for everyone. So, as an opiate, as a distraction, religion is harmful and must be opposed.

Atheism remains a pillar of Marxism in China. However, in the 1980s Deng Xiaoping turned the economy in a more efficient direction, including greater participation in the global economy. Instead of focusing on ideology, the government emphasized effectiveness. "It doesn't matter whether a cat is black or white as long as it catches a mouse," Deng is reported to have said. Pragmatic business successes were praised while religious issues became less important as long as social order was not disrupted.

"Disrupting social order" is the second reason why officials may crack down on unregistered meetings. Respect for elders and authorities is a bedrock value in Chinese culture. Confucius taught it. Respect contributes to social harmony, which is vital for a successful society. Individuals should defer to the common good, subordinating personal whims to their leaders' plans. This will result in the best situation for everybody in the long run. Resources are limited. Economic and social challenges are huge. Collaboration is essential. A country with such a large population cannot afford the luxury of too much diversity.

Unregistered groups seem to challenge all this. Their existence is an affront, implying that government structures do not serve the people adequately, so the people find it necessary to create their own. Furthermore, many churches *do* teach children and youth, and *do* preach about the kingdom of God at the end of time with Jesus on the throne. These teachings sow seeds of chaos, some officials believe.

What a sad irony. "The party line is stability and prosperity. Why does it act as if truth will destabilize?" asks one local Christian.

One neighbor helping another. Meanwhile, Jesus' people shine as lights, one workmate sharing with another, one neighbor helping another.

"I have had eight abortions already," says Mei. "What am I going to do about this new pregnancy?"

"My husband wants me to have a second child," says Wan, "If I do, we'll lose our benefits. We'll break the law on the "one child policy." But if I don't give him a child, he says he'll find another woman to do it. What shall I do?"

"My water pump only goes down 30 feet," says the sweaty farmer, "and the water table has receded to 70 feet, and in some places 120 feet.

What shall *I* do?"

These are real questions that ordinary people are asking. Christians don't have all the answers, but they can come alongside and love, listen, *encourage*, pray and testify to the God whose grace has helped them through one crisis after another.

There are no parallels in history to the Chinese church's huge growth since 1960. It is unprecedented. Will it continue indefinitely? Some fear there is a ten-year window before materialism saps vitality. Yet the global Chinese church exhibits breadth (variety), depth (organizational infrastructures, leader-training institutions, publishing, missions), social networking among Chinese worldwide, literacy, technological sophistication and confident activism. Both as thinkers and as actors, Chinese Christians demonstrate dynamic vitality.

Fifty years from now Chinese may lead the world church. In that case, like all peoples who lead the church for a period of time, they would do well to remember Constantine. Before the emperor Constantine (d. A.D. 337), Christianity was a minority faith. He installed it as the preeminent religion throughout the empire. Thereafter the church bogged down in bureaucracy. Faithful Christians continued, but there was unrelenting pressure to wed faith to power. This remains a perennial temptation for leaders. Humility is good policy and a Chinese virtue as well.

Jesus Is Lord of Art, Science, Sociology

"Do you think human beings are basically good?" Chou asked. He and En were taking a tea break before they tackled their textbooks. They were two of the privileged intellectuals who had received scholarships for advanced studies.

"I used to," En answered. "Like Confucius, I believed men just needed education in order to do what is right."

"You changed your mind?"

"Well, look at our history. Even in our own lifetime," En shrugged. "In the 1980s, the economy opened up. We pursued the Four Modernizations. We traveled abroad, we read widely, we raised questions. Then in 1989 it all crashed down, with the bloody massacre of students in Tiananmen Square, right in front of our central government buildings and ancient monuments."

"Yes, a lot of illusions were destroyed there. Many of us lost hope. What could we believe? Why put out effort? Why sacrifice?"

"And that isn't the first time reform efforts have crashed. Think of our parents' time."

"Very true. The Cultural Revolution." Chou sighed. "Chairman Mao wanted to recapture the fire of the revolution and reinvigorate the country. So he challenged the youth to purge traditional institutions."

"And it ended in tragedy," En murmured. "Priceless books burned. Paintings slashed. Worse, teachers and religious leaders paraded naked through the streets with dunce caps on their heads, then beaten or even killed. Worst of all, parents denounced by their own children for innocent remarks."

"And when the young leaders realized what they had done, when they woke up to the disaster and saw the part they had played, how traumatized they were. Now they're numb. They no longer trust any cause."

"No wonder we call them the 'Lost Generation.' "

"They had good intentions," Chou reflected. "In the 1980s, *we* had good intentions. The original revolutionaries had good intentions too. Where did we all go so wrong?"

"Well, in answer to your original question, I'm no longer sure that human nature is good," En replied. "Evil just seems to keep cropping up."

A Chinese Christian mind. Following the Tiananmen Square massacre in 1989, many students turned to Christ. At least six of the top thirty protest leaders became Christians. Today in the universities, the media, the arts and the professions, thoughtful people like Chou and En are exploring new ways to think about the world. Many are investigating the Christian faith.

Christianity is associated not with tradition and ritual but with modernity, business and science. "We are first-generation Christians and first-generation businessmen," says one house-church pastor. "Christianity is the basis for good citizenship in China," says another, a former party official. "The market economy discourages idleness. [But] it cannot discourage people from lying or causing harm. A strong faith discourages dishonesty."[3]

Many thousands of Chinese study overseas. By the hundreds they are meeting Jesus. After training in discipleship, they return to China and salt universities and professions.

In 2008 the Chinese student association at a major American university teamed up with several Christian groups to sponsor a benefit concert for victims of the recent earthquake. The concert venue was a large local church. Here gifted Chinese musicians performed on heritage instruments. Then the eighty-member choir of the Chinese student association filed in, all dressed neatly in matching colors. They lifted up their voices in rousing and triumphant songs of China. On the last piece they invited Chinese in the audience to sing along. As I slipped out, I encountered the Chinese janitor sitting alone in the narthex, listening to the piped music, eyes closed, singing softly, smiling. Through such friendships with scholars inside and outside of China, the gospel spreads.

Some who are known as "cultural Christians" ask, "What can Jesus do for China?" For them Christianity is a lode to mine for ethics. Their interest is intellectual, not personal.

But others have come to see that Christianity is not merely academic. It requires commitment of mind, heart and action. It means obeying Jesus as Lord. A decade of discrete conferences run by Chinese scholars inside China have clarified the matter.

Christian intellectuals have a passion to relate their faith to all of life. Often grassroots believers have not been allowed to take leading roles in society. Shunted to the margins, they have loved God, loved each other, loved their neighbors and looked forward to heaven. They have not spent energy struggling with broader social issues. Many have received little education. But scholars care about science and arts and social organization. They believe that any ideology worth following must relate coherently to all these areas, and must do so in a Chinese way.

Leadership training. The Bible can be downloaded in China. So can discipleship and leadership-training materials. But Christians in poor rural areas may have limited Internet access.

During times of persecution like the Cultural Revolution, Bibles were few and were kept well-hidden. In secure settings they would be brought out. It was a privilege to be able to borrow one. Some believers copied the Bible by hand, or at least as much as they could manage before they had to pass it on to the next person. Some memorized whatever portions they could.

Today Bibles are printed in China exclusively by Amity Press in Nanjing. Between two to three million Bibles are produced each year for sale inside the country. Because the Bible does not have an ISBN number, however, it is not sold in Chinese bookstores. Amity Press also publishes Bibles in eight Chinese minority languages, in Braille for Chinese and in non-Chinese languages for sale globally.

Yet believers multiply so fast that the demand for Bibles exceeds the supply. Getting mature pastors is another challenge. "In China the two-year-old Christian teaches the one-year-old."[4]

Without grounded teaching, heresies can develop. Some strange and terrible cults have swept across China. One is described in chapter five. These cults not only seduce sincere seekers but also give Christians a bad reputation with the government and the larger community.

ORDINARY TWENTY-FIRST-CENTURY CHRISTIANS

As the people of China move to the cities, new material desires grip them. They want to own things they never thought about before. New lifestyles become possible once they are freed from the eyes of gossips back in the village. New tensions strain families. Divorce rates rise. Generation gaps widen. As they access the Internet, new ideas percolate.

When rural Christianity goes to the city, it has to adapt. Putting it very bluntly, one dedicated fifty-year-old leader comments, "The youth of today cannot be Wang Ming Dao."

Who is Wang Ming Dao? A hero of the Chinese church who spent two decades in prison. While there, he was tortured badly. For all time he will be respected and revered. The way he lived brings honor to all Chinese Christians. His teachings have enriched millions. But youth can identify with Wang Ming Dao only to a limited degree. Their circumstances are diametrically different. They need new patterns and models if they are going to cope with new stresses.

Grassroots Christians come in many sizes and shapes, and so do the models they offer. Here are three.

The playboy. Zhu Yi was a media producer and, in his own words, a "big sinner." He tells his story in *The Cross,* a riveting four-part documentary on Jesus' people in China today.[5]

"There are two kinds of men," Zhu Yi says. "One kind finds the virtues of all women in *one* woman. The other finds the virtues of one woman in *all* women. I chose to be the latter."

Zhu Yi had numerous love affairs, many simultaneous. But eventually this deceit felt like a trap closing around him. It was exhausting to balance the women. He knew he was hurting his wife. In time he saw that he was destroying himself, numbing his own conscience.

What about a divorce? Wouldn't that simplify things? he wondered. But "I didn't have the guts to do it," he admits.

Then his wife became a Christian. "After I converted, I found peace," she says. "There was nothing worth getting angry over. . . . I had to endure all kinds of abuse from Zhu Yi. But God gave me strength and patience. When my husband attacked me, I just found a quite corner and prayed."

Zhu Yi was confused. "Sometimes I tried to provoke a fight, but to my surprise instead of fighting with me she would go into the kitchen or the bathroom to pray. I said to myself, 'This is impossible! This girl doesn't have strength like that!' "

Before her conversion, Zhu Yi's wife had been very suspicious whenever he went out. Now she just smiled and said, "All right."

"Gradually I stopped lying to her because I didn't want to be unworthy of her trust," he says.

One evening he volunteered to drive her to church. Beijing is not safe at night, he reasoned. He would wait outside in the car until the meeting finished. Yet somehow he found himself inside, seated in the front row.

On the way home he said to his wife, "I want to pray, but I don't know how."

Because she was used to praying in the bathroom, she took him there. They knelt down. "Repent," she advised him.

"So I did," he says. Soon he was sobbing. "I felt the sky had turned into a huge book in front of my eyes. After I repented for a sin recorded on a particular page, that page would be turned to the next one. I remembered things I'd long forgotten. It was miraculous. If I hadn't decided to follow Jesus Christ at the time, I might have ended up dead."

Today the couple are in love again. "I didn't realize what a new life we'd receive until we both accepted God. We're so grateful to the Lord," she says.

"Now we have good communication," he says.

She understands me and I understand her. We have become one as God says. It feels so good to come close to God together as husband and wife. I feel she's not hard to talk to, and she needs my love so much. And I feel that with her as the only woman to love in my life, I am complete. One time I told her I felt like we were falling in love all over again. God is full of wonder. He brought love into our home and saved us from the hands of Satan. Our life has gone back to the state of Eden. There is no deception. In the past I hid my cell phone and beeper because I did not want her to find out about all my love affairs. But now I can leave her my cell phone and beeper if I'm not available. I ask her to help answer the calls and take care of my stuff. She has become my personal secretary, and I've become hers, too. There are no secrets between us. We have become one, physically and spiritually.

The Cross, in which Zhu Yi's story appears, is made by a gifted Chinese documentary filmmaker. It features artists, dancers, orphans, gangsters, professors, casino bosses, farmers and factory workers who have come to Jesus. It also introduces evangelists who have spent long years in prison. Taken together, these provide a mosaic of role models for urban youth and adults.

The martyr. "I wish I could give you better news," the doctor said, "but unfortunately your disease is incurable."[6]

"Isn't there something more you can try?" Steven sputtered.

"No. I'm very sorry. I advise you to go home and put your affairs in order. You don't have very long."

In his anxiety, Steven listened to a gospel witness and responded. To everybody's surprise, Steven's disease disappeared. He was healed completely. Overflowing with gratitude, he told people his story. He was a poor farmer, but in the winter season when the ground lay fallow he had free time. He began to travel and preach. Although he was illiterate, he had an oral command of biblical teaching and spoke with authority. He established four small house churches.

It wasn't long before he was arrested and sentenced. The prison was in the Muslim region of China. In the jail was a Muslim who had been sick for a long time. Steven prayed for him, and he was healed. Shortly after that, ten Muslim prisoners put their faith in Jesus as their Lord.

To keep this movement from spreading throughout the prison population, the officials released Steven early. However they escorted him out of the prison at midnight into bitter cold, four degrees below zero. Steven was wearing thin clothes. Without transport he started walking, crunching one foot in front of another through snow and ice. Nine miles later he arrived at the home of a Christian. He discovered that it was full of people who had gathered there to pray for him that very night.

Steven planted two more churches before he was rearrested. This time he was beaten so badly that he died. But in five years—five extra years of life that he had never expected to see—Steven planted six churches, won 150 Chinese to Jesus and encouraged many more.

The husband who brews tea. Yin's administrative job gave her a feeling of importance. She lost that feeling when she went home at the end of the day. There she was ignored while she cleaned and picked up after her husband.[7]

They had been married twenty years when she was offered a promotion in a different city. She accepted, leaving Lai behind. They didn't divorce, but they were on the verge.

Then Lai became a Christian.

"Come home," he urged, "and see the changes in my life because of my new beliefs."

"What new beliefs?" she responded. "You smoke and drink. You don't know how to love anyone. You're a lazy slob and you never help around the house."

But when she did come home, Yin was stunned. "He never treated me so well. Not since the day we got married. When I was young, I wasn't ugly. Actually I was quite a pretty girl," she says straightforwardly. "But even back then I wasn't able to change him. Now I'm old, yet he's so nice to me. . . . I was always the one who made the tea for my husband, but now when I wake up from my afternoon nap, a cup of oolong tea is always there. It's my favorite tea and my husband makes it specially for me. If it weren't for God's power, this never would have happened."

Their adult daughter adds, "Five years ago we had three cars. Now we have three bicycles instead. But I have no desire to go back to the life we had before. Although we only have bicycles, our life has completely changed."

BACK TO JERUSALEM AND THE ENDS OF THE EARTH

Who knows when the gospel first came to China? Not everybody writes things down. We do know that by A.D. 578, Nestorian Christians had arrived. They traveled overland along the Silk Road from the area that is now Iran and Iraq. During the next several centuries many thousands of Chinese believed in Jesus through their witness.

Today believers want to carry the gospel back along the Silk Road in the opposite direction. They want to plant churches in Muslim and Buddhist and Hindu communities all the way between China and Jerusalem. In many of these places there is no established church.

This is a long-term vision. A group known as the Jesus Family pioneered it in the 1920s. They moved to the region in west China where Muslims are the majority, got jobs, built houses, raised children and shared their faith.

In the 1940s, Mark Ma, who was vice principle of Northwest Bible Institute in Shaanxi province, testified that he received a direct revelation from God. So did several others. They formed the "Preach Everywhere Gospel Band," but agreed to refer to it in English as the "Back to Jerusalem Evangelistic Band." Seven men and women were commissioned to go. They reached the western edge of China by 1950. The Northwest Spiritual Movement was another group that sent missionaries.[8]

But World War II and the national struggles culminating in the communist revolution caused disruptions all along the way. Internal tensions and splits among the missionaries hampered outreach too.

In the 1980s and 1990s the dream revived. Millions of Chinese now followed Jesus. Churches were growing. In some places Christians were experiencing more freedom than they had in earlier decades. Leaders began to talk again about mission to the west. They tried to recover the history of the Back to Jerusalem movement.

Brother Yun was the leader of a large house-church association. He located some of the original songs from that movement. One night in 1995 he challenged believers to expand their vision, to imagine witnessing to unreached nations. Then he began to sing one of the songs.

In the audience an old man sobbed. After the song ended, he shuffled to the front. "My name is Simon Zhao," he said. "I went to Muslim China in the 1940s as a missionary in this movement. But I was arrested. For 31 years I have been in prison. I have been tortured brutally. My wife was kept apart from me, and eventually she died. So did all my friends. But I used the years to pray that God would raise up a new generation of Chinese believers to fulfill the vision." He looked at Pastor Yun. "Thank you for that song. I am the composer. I created those lyrics 48 years ago."[9]

Simon Zhou helped many young people in the churches across China recover the vision of their forefathers, the dream that had been all but forgotten.

In 1996 a ground-breaking event took place. Leaders from large networks of churches met. They pledged to ignore their divisions and instead work together to spread the gospel to the unreached peoples west of China. Eight adjacent countries were chosen for pioneer work. The missionaries would evangelize. They would revive existing churches. They would share some resources but divide some geographical areas so as not to conflict. They expected God to guide them through dreams as well as through planning. They expected him to provide financially. And they determined to send some of their top church leaders as missionaries. They wanted to give their best, even though they expected that some of them would be martyred.

"The Back to Jerusalem missionary movement is not an army with guns or human weapons. It is not a group of well-dressed, slick professionals. It is an army of broken-hearted Chinese men and women whom God has cleansed with a mighty fire," says church historian Paul Hattaway.[10]

This is not the only Chinese mission thrust. Because Africa has minerals and oil, the Chinese government is investing heavily there. In Congo alone China is pouring in twelve billion dollars. But before the government's African economic push began, diaspora Chinese missionaries were on the ground. In 1998 Chinese formed a mission society to reach out to that continent. In April 2008 they celebrated their tenth anniversary.

In the Middle East thousands of Chinese labor as temporary workers, both in Israel and in the Arab countries. Diaspora Chinese missionaries have brought the good news here too. As a result, five hundred Chinese workers committed their lives to Jesus as Lord at one recent Moon Festival in Dubai.

ETERNITY IN THE ALPHABET
AND CONFUCIUS AS THE OLD TESTAMENT?

Chinese culture contains great gifts. Yet sometimes good cultural elements can be turned into idols. Take the alphabet.

Many Chinese Christians believe that God revealed himself to their forefathers even before the time of Abraham. Their argument runs like this. The written language of the Chinese is five thousand years old. Various ideographs combine a strange assortment of symbols which make more sense if they are part of a biblical story. For example, the word for "boat" combines the symbols for "eight" and "mouths." Could this point to the eight members of Noah's family who were saved in a boat?

Proponents of this view argue that because the earliest biblical patriarchs lived such long lives, only a few generations separated Adam from the tower of Babel. From Babel, people dispersed to new regions with new languages. As the Chinese' ancestors moved east from the tower, might they have brought with them hints of God's original revelation embedded in roots of their language?[11]

Other Chinese disagree. Theologian How Chuang Chua is one. He contends that the dates assigned to Adam, the tower of Babel and so forth are unsubstantiated. He faults the description of the language, as well as the exegetical method.[12]

Either way, that history is lost to us. We do know that God "has planted eternity in the human heart" (Eccles 3:11 NLT), and communicates in a variety of ways. Confucianism, for example, might be seen as a kind of Old Testament preparation for the gospel. The apostle Paul once said that "the law [of God] was our schoolmaster to bring us unto Christ" (Gal 3:24 KJV). By this he meant that the law reveals our inadequacy to keep it. The law makes well-intentioned people hunger for the power to live righteously. They become aware of their need for something more. The law causes them to long for grace. Confucianism is like that. It holds up an ethical standard that we cannot keep. Some Chinese theologians emphasize this.

One Good Friday I spoke about Jesus' death to a gathering of international students. A Chinese woman talked with me afterward, discussing great thinkers like Darwin and Freud. Then she turned to the subject of Christianity.

"Back in China, I knew some Christians," she said. "They were admirable people. But I never saw any need for Christianity until I came to the

U.S. Here I realized that if you Americans didn't have Christianity, you would be a very immoral people." Then she added something surprising. "But we Chinese are naturally moral. So we don't need Christianity."

She was wrong. Confucianism encourages virtue, but thoughtful Chinese know they fall short as individuals and as a society.

In any case, Confucianism does not parallel the Old Testament completely. Jesus saw himself fulfilling the Old Testament specifically, not any other religion's ideals. Abraham, Moses, David, Isaiah, Jeremiah, Daniel, Esther and Nehemiah described key dimensions of the God whose love led him to the cross and whose power burst the bounds of death. No other religion foreshadows this so comprehensively.

Still, the ethics Confucius taught, as well as the questions Lao Tse raised, can be seen as gifts of God's creational, common grace.

All this has implications for Chinese missionaries. Because Chinese culture is so rich, it may subtly become an idol even for Christian workers. The Back to Jerusalem movement was birthed amid awesome testimonies of steadfastness and martyrdom. Yet "although house church Christians have served in northwest China for thirty years, scarcely any have learned the local language. To the indigenous people, these Chinese missionaries appear to be one more arm of the imperialistic Han (majority Chinese)," according to a missionary with much experience in west China. He adds, "Chinese missionaries desperately need missiological underpinnings." Not only Chinese need this. We all do, especially if we come from large and powerful cultures.

Chinese Everywhere

When I did consulting work in Mali, I could not switch on a fan. No electricity was available in this West African country until the rainy season began. The Niger river had been overused, we were told. So our team returned home in the evenings with acrid liquid pouring down our bodies, and just sweated it out.

Then, out of the swirls of dust, a miracle appeared: the Hong Kong Café. This humble establishment had a generator, and, wonder of wonders, air conditioning. It became our home away from home.

Just as Chinese restaurants like the Hong Kong Café refresh tired people in the most surprising spots, so do Chinese churches. From Tahiti to Paris they flourish. At least seventy million Chinese are scattered across the globe outside China. Amid this diaspora, Jesus' people bless many societies.

Wherever they live, Chinese continue to identify with their heritage. Emigrants from other countries may merge into the populations of their new nations and forget their roots. Chinese remain Chinese. Even though they may lose the ability to speak their language and may never set foot on their ancestral soil, still they maintain ties to China in their hearts. Like the American Chinese janitor singing softly in my church, they feel honored to be part of this great people

Particularly in East and Southeast Asia—in countries like Thailand, Singapore, Malaysia, Indonesia, Philippines and Taiwan—Chinese have been influential in business and society, and also in big churches, theological seminaries, publishing houses and missions. The renowned China Graduate School of Theology is in Hong Kong, part of China but also part of Southeast Asia.

In Singapore some churches focus on specific minority peoples inside China. A church will send a short-term team. They try to understand the culture and some of the language. They share the gospel in various ways. They pray. The next year they send another team. Over time relationships are built and fellowships are planted. Other Singaporean churches focus on one *city* in China. They send a family to set up a business as a base for the church's long-term ministry. Singapore's mission research centers also are state of the art.

Electrifying evangelist. A lot of the spiritual vitality in Southeast Asia can be traced to an evangelist named John Sung. Born in China in 1901, graduating with high honors from Ohio Wesleyan University, he was offered prestigious professorial posts in Germany, the United States and China. One night, gazing at the moon, he tried to choose between the offers. But a silent voice spoke to him. "What good is it for a man to gain the whole world, and yet lose or forfeit his very self?" (Lk 9:25).

Sung returned to China. It is said that during the ship journey he deliberately dropped all his medals and honors into the Pacific except for his final diploma. For the next thirteen years, preaching across Asia, Sung "moved Chinese hearts as no Christian preacher has ever moved them, before or since."[13]

In Surabaya, Indonesia, for example, Sung conducted twenty-one meetings, morning, afternoon and evening, every day for a week in 1939. People said the program would not succeed because merchants had to be in the stores in the mornings. But the storekeepers shuttered their businesses and came. Some people kept their seats all day long and bought their meals from vendors, who went up and down the aisles. Many lives changed that week.

Seven months later Sung returned for a ten-day training school. Two thousand people participated in daily studies on the Gospel of Mark. Five thousand people came to the evangelistic meetings every night. He had to preach on his knees because he was not well.

Afterward, churches had to be expanded to make space for all the new believers.

Historian David Bentley-Taylor critiques Christian Chinese in Indonesia for "certain deficiencies," such as unwittingly flaunting wealth among the poor through their "splendid homes, luxurious cars, sumptuous wedding feasts, and lavishly furnished clubs." Yet, he continues,

> they are also marked by an emphasis upon personal repentance and the forgiveness of sins, by an ardent love for the Bible expressed in diligent reading of it, and by a strong urge to witness to others and lead them to the feet of Christ. . . . There are many prosperous Chinese homes in which the truths of the New Testament and Christian standards of morality and family life are treasured above all treasures, and in which business is driven forward with the special motive of devoting ten per cent of all profits to Christian work . . . for well-equipped buildings and for the support of students and pastors."[14]

A lot of this is the legacy of John Sung.

CHINA'S CHRISTIAN MARTYRS

"You have some nerve!" shouted the judge as he struck the bench. "You are so young and yet you dare to deceive the People's government. . . . Little child, I promise you there is no heaven for you here. If you continue to be stubborn and resist, I will sentence you to eight or ten years in prison. Your future will be finished! Don't think this is some game."

"Since I have fallen into your hands I have no plans to return home," sixteen-year-old Shi Xiaoxiu answered sweetly. "My family is prepared to finish the course our Lord Jesus has determined for us."[15]

The year was 1983 and the place was the province of Henan. This story has been recorded in *China's Book of Martyrs* by Paul Hattaway. Drawing on Catholic archives, records of Protestant massacres like those during the Boxer Rebellion, and contemporary house church historians' reports, Hattaway has amassed a spine-tingling account of faithfulness across time and space. While it is true that many Christians in China move freely, others have suffered. The history of their faithfulness is part of the noble heritage of Jesus' people in that land.

Seven years before the judge shouted at Xiaoxiu in the court room, her mother had fallen sick. Xiaoxiu's ancient great-grandmother urged the woman to trust in Jesus. Lishi did and recovered. Over time other family members believed, and a house church began.

Then a young woman named Meichun was diagnosed with a terminal illness. Meichun's sister was married to Xiaoxiu's brother, Wuting. Meichun came to the Shi household for prayer. But she died.

When someone dies in a house other than his or her own, the householders may be held responsible legally. Grieving, Meichun's family filed a complaint. So police arrived at the Shi home and arrested all but the youngest children.

In the courtroom the next day Lishi, the mother, was the first person to stand trial. When she described how the family had prayed, the judge got so mad that he told the guards to kick her to the ground. They beat her until she fainted. Then they poured a bucket of water over her to revive her and sent her to her cell.

Although her face was bloody and her arms were bruised, she whispered to her children, "Remain strong! We are considered worthy to suffer reproach for the Lord."

Her two sons, Wuting and Wuming, were unrecognizable when they were returned to their cells because they had been beaten so badly.

Their twenty-four-year-old sister, Meizhen, was a school teacher. She was beaten so severely during several "confession" sessions that witnesses said there was not a square inch of her body where her skin had not been broken or scarred.

Finally the three minor children were called to give testimony. Xiaoxiu was one of those. Each child claimed responsibility for praying for Meichun. Each one wanted to take the blame and shift it away from their mother and older brothers. The court never had seen anything like it.

When the court convened for its final session, seven members of the family were sentenced to prison, one for life. Lishi and her son Wuting were sentenced to death.

With a fatal sentence hanging over his head, Wuting paused as he walked past his wife. "Meiying, my beloved wife, why are you crying?" he said softly. "How can I not drink the cup that the Lord has given me? . . . Beloved Meiying, it is only that I will be one step ahead of you. . . . Don't be sad. Be strong and courageous. Whatever happens, you must live fully for the Lord. Don't waste any time."[16]

Meiying and her mother-in-law, Lishi, shared a cell. One night they both dreamed that they were flying, dressed in white. As they rose, they saw "The Beloved." His arms stretched out to welcome them and his scarred hands wiped their tears.

Two weeks later Lishi and Wuting were executed on the side of a hill known as Frog Mountain. They showed no fear, according to a house church historian named Danyun.

"May we pray?" Lishi asked. A soldier nodded. They knelt, and prayed to the Creator, "Forgive our country and our people. . . . Save our country and our people. . . . Lord, we ask you to receive our spirits."

They were shot.

When relatives retrieved the bodies, they found a note in Wuting's clothes. "It is now finished. Do not be sorrowful for me. I am only going to that place before you. . . . For my funeral, make it very simple. Take care of my two children and let them know that I died for the Lord."[17]

REX JESUS

From martyrs to missionaries, from intellectuals to farmers to businessmen, Chinese Christians are blazing trails. To me this story is personal. My father-in-law, David Adeney, went to China in 1934. There he met and married Ruth. The happiest years of David's life, I suspect, were 1946 to 1950, when they worked with students. In 1946 the Chinese InterVarsity Christian Fellowship was born. When the global network of university movements was formed in 1947, the Chinese group was the largest.

By 1950, it was outlawed and David and Ruth had to flee.

But he never left China in his heart. Right before he died, he gave me a book that he had taken into China and brought out again. Published in 1903—before communism existed—the book is entitled *Rex Christus: An Outline Study of China.*

When David hurriedly packed his books to leave China in 1950, the title may have mocked him. In the decades that followed, Jesus' kingship over China increasingly looked doubtful.

Who could have predicted the millions and millions of Chinese praising Jesus today?

Rex Jesus.

3

WORD

ELEPHANTS STOMPED THE PRISONER TO DEATH WHILE THE KING LOUNGED ON HIS CUSHIONS AND WATCHED.

Ann cuddled her baby and trembled. What next? Her husband had been rotting in prison for almost two years. With stars in their eyes the new couple had sailed from Boston in 1812, heading for Burma, known today as Myanmar. They were among America's first foreign missionaries. They would translate the Bible into Burmese, and Ann would translate part of it into Thai. They would face hardships they could not imagine. But that was all in the future when they waltzed on the deck by the light of the moon on their honeymoon voyage.

Now, cowering, Ann realized they were deep in the thick of trouble. She had seen her first two babies die. One was wrenched from her by a miscarriage when the couple hid from officials during their first eighteen months in Asia. Slipping from ship to shore and back again in various ports, they had evaded British, Burmese and Indian governments. But it had cost Ann her baby.

Their second child, Roger, lived six months before he started to cough and run a fever. When he died, Anne wrote, "Nothing but experience can teach us what feelings agonize the soul of a parent when he puts his face to that of his dear, his only child, to find out whether there may not be one breath more; and when sure of the truth, when hope goes out with life, he tries to raise the bursting desire: 'O Lord, receive the spirit!'"[1]

Dangling until the blood drains out. Watching the king watch the elephants, Ann stroked Maria, who had been born seven months after her daddy was put in jail. Maria would die at the age of two. None of Ann's children would grow to maturity. But Ann had no way of knowing that. At present, her thoughts were on her husband. He had three sets of shackles on his feet. In the evening, guards passed a bamboo pole through the foot shackles of a half dozen prisoners and lifted the pole until the men were dangling upside down, their weight resting on their shoulders. The blood drained out of their legs, leaving them numb, and that is how they slept, their upper bodies lying in filth. At times, one hundred prisoners were crowded into a windowless room. Every day some were summoned for execution. Ann had to hold her nose as she walked past executed prisoners hanging on a wall, their bodies hacked open and their organs dangling out. Among those who stayed alive, tropical diseases flourished.

As soon as Adoniram was arrested, Ann began visiting government officials and their wives. Nearly every day she showed up, bringing a petition or simply speaking by her presence. Sometimes she was allowed to take food to her husband. Sometimes she brought medicine. She built a hut in the prison courtyard, and got permission for Adoniram to sleep there where there was more fresh air and fewer germs.

Then one day the prisoners disappeared. Where had they gone? When Ann learned of the region they might have been taken to, she bundled up her baby, two orphans and her cook, and set out in pursuit. Adoniram nearly died on the forced march to the new prison. Yet when he arrived, the first thing he heard was the wail of a baby coming from a cart right behind the prisoners. And there was Ann.

"What are you doing?" he groaned. "You can't stay here."

But she did. The very next day one of her orphans came down with smallpox, so she took a needle and informally inoculated the rest of her party. Again she made friends with local officials, got permission to take Adoniram food and medicine, and eventually got him healthier housing—in the cage of a lion.

Better housing in the lion's cage. A huge lioness had been brought to the prison. Her roars were terrifying. What was her purpose there? No one knew. Since the guards had no instructions to feed her, they didn't. After three weeks of neglect, she died. Her cage was light and airy, and because of Ann's request it became Adoniram's cell.

Then Ann fell sick with dysentery and could no longer nurse baby Maria. Before she collapsed, she panted a request. Could Adoniram under guard take Maria every day to a nearby village? Nursing mothers there might share a little milk with her. That is what happened. Shackles clanking, Adoniram shuffled from door to door and women took pity on Maria and nursed her from their own breasts.

Finally Adoniram was freed. As the family sailed toward Rangoon, he wrote, "What do you think of floating down the Irrawaddy on a cool, moonlit evening with your wife by your side, and your baby in your arms, free—all free? I can never regret my twenty-one months of misery when I recall that one delicious thrill. I think I have had a better appreciation of what heaven may be."[2]

Ann lived only thirty-seven years, but she made them count. During peaceful interludes she cared for her husband, children, seekers and disciples, learned languages, ran a girls' school, did regular evangelistic itineration over a large area, wrote a catechism, and translated several books of the Bible into both Burmese and Thai.

Adoniram at the University of Washington. Before she left the United States, Ann had prepared well. After her conversion experience, she wanted to learn theology. Seminary was not open to women, so she developed her own course. She read extensively in the works of five leading theologians, especially Jonathan Edwards. She studied Scripture daily, using commentaries and keeping notes on what she did not understand. Whenever a visiting preacher came along, she would consult with him on obscure points.

After the couple arrived in Burma, they hired a local scholar to teach them the Burmese language. It took some persuading before he was willing to tutor a woman. At first the three sat and stared at each other. The teacher had no training, and they had no common tongue. Finally Adoniram pointed at something. The scholar gave the word for it. Then learning took off.

Twelve hours a day they studied. Paper was unavailable, so they used palm leaves. Burmese looks like a long line of circles and part circles, with no punctuation. They persevered, learned to read and write it, and became fluent. Years later, when the Burmese and British made a truce, they brought the treaty documents to prison for Adoniram to check because there was no British person who read Burmese and no Burmese who read English. Eventually Adoniram would author a definitive Burmese-English dictionary—six hundred pages. As I prepared to travel to Burma this year, I ran my fingers over Adoniram's dictionary, still in use in the library at the University of Washington.

It was not all work and no play. There is much in Burmese culture that is lovely. For example, when baby Roger died, the Burmese governor's wife wanted to console Ann and cheer her up. She sent an elephant to take the Judsons on an outing. They joined a royal procession of elephants pushing through the jungle for ten miles until they came to a wild fruit grove surrounded by flowers and pools. Here they had a magical jungle picnic.

War? Cholera? Keep studying! In 1817 Adoniram set off on a trip, expecting to return home in three weeks. Three months later Ann learned that his ship had never arrived at its destination. Then Burma's first reported cholera epidemic exploded. To frighten the death devils, the people set up an earsplitting clamor of gongs.

Meanwhile, war loomed on the horizon. In the nineteenth century British colonial power ruled India. As the British looked at the teak forests across the Burmese border, they wanted access. Burma's rulers resisted. While not particularly interested in the welfare of the common person nor in due process of law, they did treasure their historic heritage. They did not want it obliterated or submerged by Western culture.

Tensions grew, war threatened and persecution of foreigners increased. Friends told Ann that Adoniram probably was dead. She should not stick around in such a dangerous place. Eventually all the other foreigners pulled out.

Ann stayed. And she kept on studying. "I know I am surrounded by dangers on every side, and expect to see much anxiety and distress; but at present I am peaceful and intend to make an effort to get on with my studies as before and leave the consequences to God," she recorded.[3]

But Adoniram came home! Then the two of them translated Scripture side by side, dividing up the task. Descriptive linguistics was not yet a formal discipline, so there were many unknowns: grammar, the way words are arranged following a local mental map; phonetics, the sounds of language, with combinations never heard in English; Bible background; cultural interpretation. Should they aim for the common spoken language or for the elite, elegant and literary language level? There were pros and cons either way. Should they translate as literally as possible, even if the words made no sense and the structure was stiff? Or should they paraphrase and in so doing introduce their own interpretations? Many questions swirled through Ann's and Adoniram's heads as they swatted yet another mosquito buzzing around their desks.

Ann translated Daniel and Jonah and wrote a catechism in Burmese. One day she started wondering about the Thai people in Burma. No missionary knew their language. So Ann learned Thai, translated the Gospel of Matthew and wrote a catechism. She was the first Protestant to translate any of the Bible into Thai.

Today most Bible translators work in teams. Trained local believers are networked with international consultants. Though the Bible has gone into 4,000 languages, there are 2,400 still to go. Many of the older translations also need revision. As a pioneer paving the way, Ann's life illustrates the multifaceted challenges that Bible translators may have to face.

WHY MAKE THIS A PRIORITY?

Why did Ann put so much effort into translating the Bible? Given her diverse responsibilities, why did she make this a priority in her short life?

The Bible is not the foundation of our faith. God is our foundation. Yet how do we know God? How do we discern between warm, fuzzy feelings and the Creator of the cosmos?

We are centered by the never-ending story of the Bible. In Scripture we see what God is like, what he has done for us and what he will do. Scripture connects us with our roots, the people throughout time who have responded to God. Scripture connects us with our brothers and sisters throughout space who at this very moment are opening the Bible on their laps or listening to Bible stories in order to learn how to love God better.

Are there confusing parts in the Bible? Boring parts? Incomprehensible parts? Yes. Those are parts that Bible scholars wrestle with. But those sections need not snag and derail our attention for long, because there is so much more.

In Scripture we are plugged into a supracultural standard that critiques us in order to sharpen and polish and refine us. "The word of God is living and active. Sharper than any double-edged sword, it penetrates even to dividing soul and spirit, joints and marrow; it judges the thoughts and attitudes of the heart" (Heb 4:12).

Scripture also nurtures us:

> As the rain and the snow
>   come down from heaven,
> and do not return to it
>   without watering the earth
> and making it bud and flourish,
>   so that it yields seed for the sower and bread for the eater,
> so is my word that goes out from my mouth:
>   It will not return to me empty,
> but will accomplish what I desire. (Is 55:10-11)

And throughout history Scripture has equipped people—even slaves, women, minorities and other marginalized and subordinated people—to speak truth to power.

God himself identifies with the Word:

> In the beginning was the Word . . . and the Word was God. . . .
> Through him all things were made. . . . In him was life. . . . The
> Word became flesh and made his dwelling among us. We have
> seen his glory. (Jn 1:1, 3-4, 14)

God's Word matters. That is why Ann poured so much of her short life into it.

The happy catastrophe. It matters to me too. When I was a little girl, I would wake up in the morning, stumble down the stairs half asleep and meander into the kitchen. There I would see my dad sitting at the table, reading the Bible and memorizing it. He set an example. When I was thirteen, I decided to memorize a whole book of the Bible. I chose James. That summer it was my task to repaint the interior moldings and windowsills upstairs in our house. As I lugged around a paintbrush and a can of paint, I also hefted around a King James Bible and memorized James. Since then I've memorized other books. If I have any serenity and smile today, it is because my taproot goes down into the Word.

Scripture still sometimes leaves me breathless. I see such honesty, such beauty, such profundity, such ultimacy. *Eucatastrophe* is a word coined by J. R. R. Tolkien, the creator of the *Lord of the Rings* trilogy. He was thinking about fiction, in which tragedy and comedy are two classic plot genres. Tragedy is more significant. The literary power of catastrophe packs a wallop. Yet when God in Christ went to the cross and rose from the dead, a truly happy catastrophe unfolded. Not a comedy but a tragedy that births new life. Tolkien had this in mind when he fashioned the word *eucatastrophe*. That's what I see when I turn to the Bible. A grand cosmic tragedy with innumerable small scenes, but magnificent new life emerging out of it all.

God didn't send us a summary or an outline or a how-to book. He gifted us with a complex compilation of story, doctrine, poetry and prophecy. It takes a lifetime to absorb. Scripture is not a computer manual to be mastered analytically, though rational study is essential. More like an onion, the Bible has layers and layers to unpeel. We mull over it, we inhale it, we savor it. To really get it, we obey it (Jas 1:22-25).

IS CONTEXTUAL THEOLOGY CONTRADICTORY?

When Jesus came, he adapted to a local lifestyle. He ate the food, learned the slang, got his feet dusty on the roads, and suffered political oppression alongside ordinary people. The colonial rulers pounded nails into his hands with the support of local collaborators.

God in Jesus fit into a local culture. God's written Word does the same. A translation accommodates to a language and worldview. Local people absorb it and begin to live it out in their context.

But contextual interpretation is far from easy. Consider this case.

In Zimbabwe a group of Christians were listening to a Bible story. The main character was a king who procured land in a new place and gave out loans. To a man we may call James, the king gave ten shares of the local monetary unit. To Tom he gave five shares. To Joe he gave one share. Then the king traveled on (Lk 19:11-26).

Some time later, the king returned and summoned the three men. "How did things go?" he asked. "Did you make a profit? Did the investment increase?"

James had doubled his money. Tom also had made a profit. The king rewarded them with more.

But Joe had not done a thing.

"You wicked servant!" the king exploded. "You knew I was a hard man, expanding into all sorts of areas. Why didn't you invest the funds so I could collect some interest?" Turning to his assistant, the king said, "Take Joe's share and give it to James."

"But, Sir, James has plenty already," the assistant blurted out.

According to Luke 19:26-27, the story concludes with the king saying, "I tell you that to everyone who has, more will be given, but as for the one who has nothing, even what he has will be taken away. But those enemies of mine who did not want me to be king over them—bring them here and kill them in front of me."

Don't play the king's game. "Isn't that the truth!" the Zimbabweans listening to the Bible story exclaimed. "The rich get richer, and the poor get poorer. Those who have get more and more. Those who lack get less and less. How courageous Joe was to refuse play the king's game.

How noble to opt out of the system."

What? Doesn't the "parable of the talents" encourage us to be good stewards, using our resources to the glory of God? That's how many Christians have interpreted this story.

Yet not only in Africa but also in Central America and Palestine some Christians have seen Joe as the hero. "Notice the context," they say. "Look at how the story begins in Luke 19:12: 'A man of noble birth went to a distant country to have himself appointed king. . . . But his subjects hated him and sent a delegation after him to say, "We don't want this man to be our king."'"

"We've experienced this over and over," say the Zimbabweans and others. "We've suffered invaders from outside. We've endured strongmen who hang onto power in spite of the peoples' protests. We don't admire those rulers. We resent them and look forward to the day when they will be replaced.

"Furthermore, notice Jesus' situation. According to verse 11, his Jewish followers thought that the kingdom of God was going to arrive immediately. They had the wrong idea. To correct this, Jesus told the story. We are not supposed to focus on building a kingdom here and now, Jesus implied. Rather we are to focus on our relationship with him. And Jesus certainly was no model of stewarding talents efficiently so as to increase profits. When he told this story he was on his way to the cross, squandering all that he had because of what he believed."

Can opposite interpretations be true? Here we have an interpretation very different from the traditional teaching on this story. Are both interpretations right? Certainly it is good to steward our resources and contribute to the public good. On the other hand, it is also good not to buy into corrupt systems or to support those who get richer and richer while others are getting poorer.

It seems that both interpretations teach something useful. Should we leave it at that? Does contextual theology mean that Christians in different places and times may interpret a Bible text in opposite ways?

No. Jesus was not a mystic who uttered wise sayings to be interpreted any way we want. Jesus believed some things were important. Some

things were real. Some things were true. When he told a story, he had
a meaning in mind. We may not always be able to discern all that he was
thinking, but we can have confidence that he did not intend opposed
and contradictory meanings.

The Zimbabweans, Palestinians and Central Americans who saw Joe
as the hero studied the story in Luke. When we add the parallel passage
in Matthew 25, different details appear. Interestingly, this version does
not say the king was an outsider or that people resented him. (Commentaries reveal a misunderstanding here. This story is not about a foreign ruler but about a local ruler like Herod who went to Rome to receive his commission.)

In Matthew 25 the ruler calls James and Tom "good and faithful,"
implying virtue as well as profit. Most importantly, Matthew includes a
whole series of stories showing that the kingdom will not come easily.
Here are the stories surrounding the parable of the talents:

- A man who is about to leave on a trip entrusts his estate to a manager.
  The manager abuses the hired help and gets involved in wild parties.
  When the householder returns, he punishes the manager severely.

- At a wedding banquet, five bridesmaids are prepared (with adequate
  oil in their lamps) and five are not. The unprepared girls have to go
  buy more, and in the end they find themselves shut out of the
  celebration.

These two stories precede the parable of the talents. Immediately
following it is this story:

- A king arrives with heavenly and earthly power. All nations gather.
  The king separates the people into "sheep" and "goats." He welcomes and rewards the sheep because they fed the hungry and visited
  the sick and prisoners. He ejects the goats, because they neglected to
  do these things.

Preceding all this, Jesus prepares his disciples for suffering and persecution before the kingdom arrives. He tells them to be alert and dis-
cerning. He concludes this section: "Who then is the faithful and wise
servant, whom the master has put in charge of the servants in his house-

hold to give them their food at the proper time? It will be good for that servant whose master finds him doing so when he returns" (Mt 24:45-46). Immediately following the stories the events leading to the crucifixion swing into action.

What meaning can we draw from this? Overall, the stories commend faithful stewardship. The parable of the talents is part of this series. Joe is not the hero.

Still, the theme of poverty and suffering recurs. Indeed, whether you are a sheep or a goat depends on how you respond to the poor and the marginalized. The Zimbabweans', Central Americans' and Palestinians' concerns for justice are validated. But the parable of the talents is not the primary text for this validation.

Principles of interpretation. To avoid making mistakes, scholars have developed classic principles for the interpretation of texts, sometimes called "hermeneutics." Here are some principles for biblical interpretation.

- Give priority to what the text means in the original language.

- Consider the context in which the passage was written: culture, historical situation, geographical environment, literary style.

- Interpret Scripture by Scripture, seeing the Bible as a unity.

- Interpret progressively in time. That is, interpret the Old Testament in light of the New Testament.

- Consider how the passage relates to God's salvation in Christ. "The most 'entire' context is Jesus. Every biblical text must be read in the living presence of Jesus. . . . Meditation discerns the connections and listens for the harmonies that come together in Jesus."[4]

Although interpretations that contradict each other are not equally true, theologies do vary from place to place because different contexts raise different questions. In response, local theologies develop distinctive emphases. Bible themes that interest people in poorer countries, for example, include "robbers on the roads, streets full of crippled and sick, the struggle to pay gouging tax and debt collectors, demanding landlords, . . . imminent national collapse, . . . personality cults of dictators, . . . judgments on the rich and haughty, . . . sowing and reaping and shepherding, . . . feasts of plenty, and wells that never go dry, . . . deliverance from evil," according to Philip Jenkins in *The New Faces of Christianity: Reading the Bible in the Global South.*[5]

Taken together, all sound contextual theologies, like all good translations, open up a little more of the fullness of God's thoughts. Each one complements and enriches the rest. We can learn a lot about the Bible as we listen to people who are different from us.

AFRICAN THEOLOGY IN CONTEXT

Consider African theology. In the introduction to the *Africa Bible Commentary,* Kwame Bediako says,

> Scripture is not just a holy book from which we extract teaching and biblical principles. Rather, it is a story in which we participate. When David Livingstone preached in Africa in the nineteenth century, he is said to have always referred to the Bible as "the message from the God whom you know." In other words, Scripture speaks to us because Scripture speaks about us. And it speaks about us because we are part of the gospel we preach.
>
> When we turn to Christ as Lord, we are turning over to him all that is in us, all that is about us and all that is around us that has defined and shaped us. Thus salvation encompasses not just our "souls," but also our culture at its deepest level. We need to allow Scripture to become the interpreter of who we are in the specific concrete sense.[6]

When Africans immerse themselves in Scripture, three of the theological themes that often emerge are *community, suffering* and *power.*

COMMUNITY

Justin Oforo was my student at Regent College. "In the West you study the philosophy of René Descartes, who said, *Cogito ergo sum* (I think, therefore I am). You know you exist because there is somebody who is thinking. But in Africa we say, *Cognatus ergo sum* (I am kin to these people, therefore I exist). We know we exist because we are in relationship," Justin says.

In Justin's community of Mwaka in Tanzania, all parents take responsibility for each others' children. And all are aware of their connection with God the Creator, whether they are Christian or Muslim or pagan. People live in relationship, both horizontally and vertically. It is a miracle when a person is converted to Christianity in Africa, Justin says. Yet it is an even bigger miracle when it happens in the West where the community support system is so weak. The concept of the fatherhood of God is easier to understand in Mwaka than in Vancouver, he believes. Even though many forces have torn African societies, the theme of community remains strong. An isolated person is dysfunctional.

Ancestor worship? In *Faces of Jesus in Africa*, Robert Schreiter explores how relationships can help people understand Jesus. He discusses Jesus the ancestor, Jesus the chief, Jesus the elder brother and Jesus the master of initiation.[7]

Ancestors are key relatives, symbols of continuity and custodians of blessing. Traditionally, Africans have prayed to ancestors in times of need. Should Christians continue this?

"Jesus is like the ancestors in that people can take their problems to him and he does guarantee a better future for those who follow him," Nigerian theologian Yusufu Turaki says. "But there is a danger that making him an ancestor may be tantamount to reducing his post-resurrection elevation as Lord of Lords (Phil 2:9-12) and may cause people to lose sight of his status as God."[8]

A better approach is modeled in the book of Hebrews,

> which was written against a religious background similar to that found in traditional African religions. . . . Taking this approach, it can be said that Jesus has come to fulfill our African ancestral cult, and has taken the place of our ancestors, replacing them with himself. He has become the mediator between God and African society. Consequently, African veneration, worship, and respect for the ancestors should now properly be addressed to Jesus.[9]

William Wade Harris was a powerful Liberian Christian who lived
from 1865 to 1929. According to Kwame Bediako, Harris

> cut himself off from his Grebo life and family in a radical conver-
> sion, but he did not live without ancestors or a community. He
> simply changed his family connections to those based on faith in
> Christ. . . . His was a spirituality of vital participation totally in-
> digenous to his African way of being within a community. . . .
> His new ancestors [were] Moses, Elijah, and supremely Jesus
> Christ. . . . That was how he broke through to many people and
> they became Christians.[10]

Puberty rites. Like ancestors, initiations help hold a community together from one generation to the next. These rites mark passage from
one stage to another. Think of Jewish circumcision and Christian baptism. In Africa, puberty rituals that usher adolescents into adulthood
have been important.

But there have been drawbacks. Some rites involve sacrifices to spirits. Some involve sexual experimentation. Some involve female genital
mutilation. Some use a single knife to circumcise a group of young
men. In an era of AIDS this is a time bomb.

Given these negatives, many churches abandoned puberty rituals.
Unfortunately, this created a vacuum. The teaching that occurred during initiations, the networking and the honoring of young people all
contributed to public morality.

Both Baptist and Pentecostal churches in Nairobi now run year-long
initiations for young people. Parents have contributed ideas. Sexuality,
career choice, peer pressure and holiness are some of the topics. At the
end, young men are left on a beach to practice their survival skills for
several days. Young women have another kind of camp. Community
matters, and these initiations strengthen it.

SUFFERING

"Mama, I hurt too. No one ever will be able to replace Daddy." Rose
Galadima stroked the older woman's arm.

When Rose's father died, her landscape changed overnight, like a beach after a tsunami. At the time Rose was a wife, mother and lecturer at Jos Evangelical Seminary in Nigeria. Now, while grieving her own loss, she tried to help her mother find something to hold on to. Through her mother Rose was catapulted into the harsh life of an African widow.

Everywhere she looked she discovered widows scrambling for survival. In Nigeria traffic accidents create many fatherless families. Disease and violence rob others. What does a widow do? She chokes through spasms of grief. If she has small children and lacks marketable skills, she may fall into prostitution. Then comes AIDS. Then orphans.

Rose determined not to accept this as the natural order of things for the widows in her nation. "By God's grace, I will do what I can," she muttered.

"Sir, it's your turn to pay." One and two at a time, short-term housing spots were found for widows and their children. She persuaded a nongovernmental organization (NGO) to provide one week of skill training. She rounded up a meager cache of donated supplies so the women could start tiny businesses.

Then she went to a Nigerian Christian businessman. "Sir, I have come with a request. When my father died, God laid on my heart the widows in our society. I've begun to help them, a few at a time." Rose told the man what she had done. "Last week I helped Esther, Raiza and Rachel. I used all the money I had. This week Deborah, Fala and Lydia have asked for help. Sir, it is your turn. Would you like to know what it will cost?"

She got the funds.

Well over one thousand widows are stable and self-supporting today because Rose would not accept the status quo. Because she had no capital, she went to wealthier Nigerian Christians who did. Rose used what she had: her heart, her brains, her hands, her feet, the direction of the Holy Spirit, and the people of God. By introducing more people to a fellowship of suffering, she reduced suffering.

Suffering is a pervasive theme in African theology because it is so common in everyday life. Knowing Jesus as the model ancestor, chief and elder brother is not enough, some African theologians observe. Healthy people, strong people, settled people can appreciate him in those roles. What about hurting people? Thank God, Jesus is also the nurturer, the healer and the one who suffers with us.

Anne Nasimiyu-Wasike, professor at Kenyatta University, has applied this to women:

> Most African women spend sixteen to eighteen hours daily working to provide their families with food, shelter, water, clothing, medicine, and education. . . . In his own lifetime, Jesus rejected the androcentric culture of the Jewish people. He gave special attention to the marginalized. . . . And most of these people were women. . . . There are several Christological models that emerge. . . . In the eschatological model, Christ is sent by God to an alienated world where the presence of God takes the shape of the Crucified One. Why? . . . In his suffering Christ took on the conditions of the African woman and conditions of the whole of humanity, and in his resurrection the African woman is called to participate in the restoration of harmony.[11]

Men suffer too. Drawn by the example of the suffering Servant (Is 53), some men and women suffer willingly. Ethiopia has a rich Christian heritage, with one of the oldest churches in the world. However, during the 1980s that nation suffered under a brutal communist regime. Many were martyred. One prisoner was a pastor outstanding not only because of his ministry but also because of his NBA size. He was 6' 8" tall. This pastor was so renowned that President Nyerere of neighboring Tanzania flew to Ethiopia in his private jet to intercede for the man's release. It was granted. He was escorted out of jail into the custody of the Tanzanian embassy to be taken in the president's limousine to his jet and whisked to safety.

But the pastor declined the privilege. "No, Sir," he told President Nyerere, "I am not leaving the country. My place is here. If I leave, it will discourage all those pastors who do not have the opportunity to leave. It will also undermine all I have said when I urged Christians not to desert our country in its time of need."[12]

A few weeks later this pastor was strangled to death by government soldiers.

Another Ethiopian, named Assefa, was imprisoned and released, imprisoned and released, and frequently threatened with death. For years he had no home. Sometimes he survived on food gathered from garbage dumps. Yet when political conditions loosened, Assefa became the national director of the student Christian movement in Ethiopia. Throughout the 1990s, almost one fifth of Ethiopia's university students participated in this movement. There were five hundred trained Bible study leaders. Assefa's perseverance produced fruit. Even ordinary villagers would say, "Go to the God of Assefa. He can help."

"Which of these two Ethiopian brothers showed the greater faith: the pastor who was strangled or Assefa? They both walked by faith, but the Lord saw fit to take one and to spare the other," says Lindsay Brown, who recorded their stories.[13] Whether in life or death, both these Ethiopians followed the God who suffers with us.

POWER

In traditional African religion, power has been important. In traditional social structures too, communities have needed big men (or big mamas) who could exert power on behalf of the group. Spiritual, social and material power have been connected.

When Africans learned that Jesus died to conquer the powers of evil (Col 2) and that the power of God is greater than that of any of the spirits (1 Jn 4), this was very good news. Today believers call on Jesus' power for protection, for healing, for exorcism, for food, for reconciliation and for deliverance.

But Jesus' road to power was strikingly different from the usual route. Jesus suffered. Yet the amazing news is that suffering is not the last word. Jesus did not stay dead. His power blasted death. Consider these texts:

[Jesus] humbled himself
    and became obedient to death—
        even death on a cross!

Therefore God exalted him to the highest place
　　and gave him the name that is above every name,
that at the name of Jesus every knee should bow. (Phil 2:8-10)
　　Jesus . . . for the joy set before him endured the cross, scorning
its shame, and sat down at the right hand of the throne of God.
(Heb 12:2-3)

And the classic text on the suffering Servant:

He was pierced for our transgressions;
　　he was crushed for our iniquities,
the punishment that brought us peace was upon him,
　　and by his wounds we are healed. . . .
He was oppressed and afflicted,
　　yet he did not open his mouth;
he was led like a lamb to the slaughter . . .
He was cut off from the land of the living;
　　for the transgression of my people he was stricken. . . .
[Yet] after the suffering of his soul,
　　he will see the light of life and be satisfied. (Is 53:5, 7-8, 11)

"Mr. President, I cannot." Because the Jesus who suffered is our powerful king, African Christians celebrate when they worship. They dance. They expect the Holy Spirit to empower them to do what they need to do. They testify that the joy of the Lord is their strength.

Some carry this into their professions. Procel DaSilva Armando won a scholarship to law school in Portugal. There he became a Christian, developed the habit of reading the Bible regularly and learned to apply it to every part of his life.

He returned to his country of Guinea-Bissau, one of the world's poorest nations, ruled by a dictator who amassed vast riches for himself. Armando rose quickly in the civil service and was appointed deputy to the chief justice.

Before long, he faced a moral dilemma. Because certain statesmen were alarmed by the growth of the Christian community, they lobbied the president to restrict freedom of worship.

The president was persuaded. "Take care of this matter," he told the chief justice.

The chief justice in turn delegated the job to Armando. "Draw up a law to restrict free worship."

What to do? Power belongs to the Lord, Armando knew. Whatever little power he held must serve the Lord. So he declined to do the job. Eventually he found himself called on the carpet in front of the president.

"Why do you refuse?" the president asked him.

"I am a Christian," Armando answered. "I could not frame a law restricting the activities of my brothers and sisters in Christ. You must do with me as you will."[14]

This made such an impression that the president decided not to implement the a law. Since then Armando has had many opportunities to use his power for good in several high positions.

In Nigeria, Jerry Gana has served in politics for more than twenty-five years and is widely respected for his integrity. "I realize the importance of legacy," he says. "I want to help change the political landscape in Nigeria and I believe this can be done through a group of Christians exercising influence. . . . So I am asking God to give me fifty years, as the political situation in Nigeria cannot be changed overnight."[15] Power always has mattered in Africa. Applying Scripture to his context, Gana hopes to channel God's power to bless his people.

HAMMERING ON OUR SKULL

"If the book we are reading does not wake us, as with a fist hammering on our skull, why then do we read it? . . . A book must be like an ice axe to break the frozen sea within us," says the philosopher Franz Kafka.[16] The Bible is a book like that. It hammers, pierces and shapes not only our thoughts but our whole lives.

One Sunday when the apostle John was worshiping alone on the prison island of Patmos, God's Spirit gave him a directive: "Write!" (Rev 1:11)

Write what?

"Write what you see," he was told.

And do what with the manuscript?

"Send it to the . . . churches."

John opened his imagination. Visions came, shaped by the Scriptures that John knew well and framed to fit the believers John knew well. The lion and the lamb. The whore of Babylon. The marriage supper. The city with no need for electricity. The tree whose leaves will heal the nations.

That was not enough, though. One day when John took up his quill, an angel stopped him with a new directive: *Eat* the book (Rev 10:9).

Don't write it. Eat it. This had happened to prophets before, as John knew. Ezekiel and Jeremiah also wrote when times were bad, and they too had been commanded to eat their manuscripts (Ezek 2; Jer 15).

What did all this mean? In his book aptly titled *Eat This Book*, Eugene Peterson explores John's predicament. Peterson begins with a tale about his dog.

"Years ago I owned a dog who had a fondness for large bones." Although he was a small dog, he often appeared on the patio dragging a big bone that he had found in the forest. He "pranced and gamboled around his prize, wagging his tail, courting approval." Then he would drag the bone away to the shade of a large rock and start chewing, gnawing, licking, sometimes growling. Eventually he would bury the bone. But the next day he would dig it up and worry it some more. "An average bone lasted about a week."[17]

"I always took delight in my dog's delight, his playful seriousness, his childlike spontaneities now totally absorbed in 'the one thing needful,' " Peterson observes. Later Peterson discovered a verse in Isaiah that deepened his delight: "As a lion, a great lion growls over his prey . . . " (Is 31:4). The Hebrew word translated "growl" usually is translated "meditate." This illustrates *active* Bible meditation, as active as a dog worrying a bone, savoring it, returning to it again and again.

Wolf down the Scripture, Peterson recommends. Take it in. Let it form you. Then live it. To this end, he commends the spiritual discipline of *lectio divina*, which has four parts:

- *lectio*—reading the text
- *meditatio*—meditating over the text
- *oratio*—praying through the text
- *contemplatio*—letting the text live through you

The last step cannot be controlled, Peterson says. *Contemplatio* is not asking continually, "What would Jesus do?" It is jumping into the river. The text is the flow. Cuban-born theologian Justo González echoes this in his book *Mañana: Christian Theology from a Hispanic Perspective:* "The purpose of our common study of Scripture is not so much to interpret it as to allow it to interpret us. . . . The lamp is a means to an end. . . . The final purpose of interpretation is to discover what obedience requires of us."[18]

This is echoed again in a statement from a global conference of Bible agencies.

> Scripture refers to "the word of God" in at least five different senses. First and foremost, there is the eternal and personal word, the agent of creation, who is God, and who became a human being in Jesus of Nazareth. Secondly, there is the spoken word, since at different times through prophets and apostles God chose to speak his mind, and without this self-revelation of God we would not know him at all. Thirdly, there is the biblical word, for in God's providence what he had spoken came to be written for the benefit of all peoples in all places. Fourthly, there is the preached word, the gospel made known by public proclamation. And fifthly, there is the embodied word, since God's purpose is that it be "adorned" or "made attractive" in the lives of his people who receive and obey it (Tit 2:10).[19]

GOD SPEAKS MY LANGUAGE AND KNOWS MY NAME

One reason the Word hammers us so powerfully and tastes so savory is because it is so particularly ours. God in his sovereignty chose to come close, first in a human body in Jesus, and then through human words transmitted by people like Ann Judson.

Lamin Sanneh grew up in an established Muslim family in Gambia, West Africa. As a boy, he memorized the Qur'an in Arabic. That was not his language, but he was told that it was God's chosen language. Christian missionaries had a different view, however. They translated God's Word into local languages. This intrigued Sanneh.

He saw that missionaries often criticized cultures wrongly, condemning customs they did not understand. Yet when missionaries said, "God speaks your language," they affirmed local cultures whether or not they intended to. When they translated Scriptures, they opened doors to amazing new worlds.

Eventually Sanneh was drawn to Jesus. Today he is a Christian professor of history at Yale. His book *Translating the Message* explores the power of the Bible.

Elizabeth is an internationally recognized bilingual educator who has made her home in the jungles of Southeast Asia for the past thirty years. Wending her way down remote paths to train native teachers, she has to watch out for snakes and leeches. In the evenings she sleeps in village huts. When there is no electricity, she joins the neighbors around the fire, sings Christian songs and tells Bible stories. Watching her accommodation to this hard life year after year, her Marxist colleagues have marveled, "You *live* the values of equality that we *talk about*."

One recent Christmas Eve, Elizabeth found herself at a tribal teachers' meeting far in the interior. As she listened to reports on new reading groups, her mind wandered. *What a wretched time to be working! My friends in the capital are celebrating. And I'm stuck way out here.* Yet as the reports continued and the demand for primers outstripped the supply, her heart lifted.

The next morning she sat by the roadside, hoping to catch the daily truck to the capital. *Maybe I can make it back in time for Christmas dinner,* she thought.

Some of the tribal teachers walked past, heading home. They were so used to jungle trails that even on the paved road they walked single file. "Goodbye, Elizabeth!" they called.

"Goodbye!" she answered. "And make sure that Uncle takes his medicine," she added. "And congratulate Vanni on the new baby."

Majority-culture people standing nearby overheard this exchange. They were surprised, because they despise tribal people. "She knows their names," they exclaimed.

Suddenly Elizabeth didn't care if she missed all the Christmas celebrations. At that moment, standing by the side of the road, she experienced the meaning of Christmas. The Creator of the cosmos, the King of eternity, the Lord of the universe came close enough to know our names, every single one. The Word became flesh. This living Word is the heart of the written Word.

4

PULSATING PASSION

Jesus' People in Latin America

"Spit on your Bible! Throw the Bible down and spit on it!"

"What?"

"Now!" The guerilla raised his gun and aimed at Andres and Enrico, two students who had just arrived for a Christian meeting in Peru.[1]

Throw the Bible down? Or resist? Andres asked himself frantically. *Give in? Or stand still and lose everything?* His thoughts whirled. He felt light-headed. *What good will it do if I die? God sees the heart, after all."* He felt like he might vomit.

But he couldn't drop the book. He couldn't spit on the Bible. Clutching it tight against his chest, he stared the guerilla in the eye. Not because he was brave. He was frozen with fear. At the same time, in a small corner of his mind, Andres felt insulted on God's behalf. Why should the Bible be dishonored? Why should it be treated like dirt?

These guerillas were no surprise. Though Andres never had seen them before, he knew they were members of the *Sendero Luminoso,* the Shining Path movement. Originally the Shining Path had coalesced on behalf of the common people who suffered daily. Poverty, inequality and corruption had propelled the rebels into action. Unfortunately, they directed violence against anyone who held a responsible position in a community. Such people impeded the revolution, the guerillas believed. They had to go. You can't make an omelet without breaking eggs, and you can't make a revolution without eliminating people who stand in the way.

That included Christians. Jesus' people looked forward to the kingdom of God instead of a utopia shaped entirely by humans. Pressing toward heaven didn't keep Christians from improving their communities, however. They started literacy classes and clinics, and helped alcoholics and drug addicts and prostitutes find new lives. They listened to husbands and wives, and counseled them about how to resolve their conflicts. They taught parents how to nurture their children better.

From the revolutionaries' point of view these actions slowed down the revolutionary movement. They inclined people to be more content with the status quo. Ultimately this prolonged the pain of the poor.

When Andres was attacked, the Shining Path already had killed three hundred pastors and many lay workers, especially women.

A lot of students at the university identified with the cause. Some had taken up arms. They had made a list of fellow students who were viewed as obstructions. One by one, they were ticking the names off.

Now it seemed it was going to be Andres' turn. But while he stood frozen, his friend Enrico moved. He tossed down his Bible and leaned over to drool a small blob of spit onto it.

I will be shot and Enrico will be saved, Andres shivered.

Instead, the gun barrel swiveled away from Andres. Bullets tore through Enrico, and he crumpled lifeless to the cement. Then the guerilla sheathed his weapon. Andres' mouth fell open. His eyes bulged. Why was Enrico killed? He had cooperated. Why wasn't Andres the one who was shot?

"You can go free because you stood by what you believed," the guerilla shrugged, as he stomped off into the night.

Terrorists inflamed. In the long history of Latin American conflicts, the Shining Path struggle of the 1980s and 1990s was particularly vicious. Yet out of the ashes and pain, Peruvian Christians created something remarkable

Terrorists burst into a church and shot it up in July 1984. Six worshipers died and fourteen were hurt. Tragically, official forces could be lethal too. Just one month after the July massacre naval infantry burst into another church. While holding the congregation hostage, they took six worshipers outside and shot them. When the believers streamed out, they stumbled over the corpses strewn on the ground.[2]

The Ayacucho region where this took place is a jewel in Peruvian history and culture. Here on the Plains of Quinoa a Peruvian army defeated the Spanish. It was Peru's decisive battle, and it reverberated throughout the continent. In modern times Ayacucho's Easter celebrations have been considered second only to those in Rome and have drawn a lot of tourists.

Yet the people have remained very poor. Indian tribes drawn together by the Inca empire have constituted much of the population. When the Spanish came to dominate Peru in the centuries that followed, the local people were demeaned and neglected.

Abimael Guzmán, father of the Sendero Luminoso, might have remained simply a Marxist philosophy professor in Ayacucho if not for a tragic event. Local education officials had announced a school fee. Citizens rose up in anger, kidnapped a city official and burned a police station.

When the military arrived, the mob looked dangerous. Soldiers shot into the crowd. One hundred fifty men, women and children died, according to local estimates. Some were Guzmán's students. He himself was detained and imprisoned for a year. When he was released, he was no longer smoldering, he was aflame for revolution.

Over the following years as the Sendero Luminoso increased, violence exploded frequently. The Sendero grew strong enough to cause a complete electric blackout right in the capital. For a day the four million people in Lima sat in darkness.

Military rule was declared for the "Emergency Zone." Now armed men from both the right and the left roamed the roads and made demands.

This was the setting in which terrorists gunned down the members of one church, and the navy gunned down members of another in 1984.

Peace and Hope Commission. Evangelical leaders in urbane Lima didn't want to think about violence. What could they do? But a Christian journalist courageously slipped past the news blackout and into the Zone. He interviewed eyewitnesses to the killings in the churches. Sneaking back out, he returned to the capital where he played the interview tapes for church leaders.

No longer passive, they rose to action. Corn, lima beans, flour, oil and medicines were collected for Christians who had fled their homes. Temporary housing in small and simple churches was organized. Impromptu clinics for the sick and the pregnant were established. Long-term care for widows and orphans was arranged. These were the first priorities.

To gather and distribute supplies, church leaders formed the Peace and Hope Commission, so named when one of them was encouraged by Romans 15:13: "May the God of hope fill you with all joy and peace as you trust in him, so that you may overflow with hope by the power of the Holy Spirit."

After an extended emergency session the National Evangelical Council of Peru (CONEP) circulated a declaration to government authorities, media and citizens. It stated the facts. It called for the authorities to act. It also gave a theological framework for what was happening. "Sin, in all its manifestations, causes disunity: self-centeredness, pride, lies, violence, murder—and racism against indigenous peoples. . . . All Peruvians regardless of ideology, uniform, or religion are guaranteed human rights."[3]

The declaration quoted Genesis 1 when it affirmed that God created people in his image.

It quoted 2 Chronicles 7:14: "If my people, who are called by my name, will humble themselves and pray and seek my face and turn from their wicked ways, then will I hear from heaven and will forgive their sin and will heal their land."

It quoted the commandment "Thou shall not kill" and added "neither with ideologies, nor bullets, nor lies, nor hunger." It quoted God's question to Cain, "What have you done? Listen! Your brother's blood cries out to me from the ground" (Gen 4:10).

It quoted Jesus' words, "Blessed are the peacemakers" (Mt 5:9). It quoted great Peruvian thinkers.

Finding free land. Then God gave the commission a dream beyond relief and advocacy. Crammed like rabbits in hutches, the refugees' situation was unsustainable. A new idea began to surface: resettlement. To reduce homelessness in the cities the government offered free land in certain border regions if people were willing to do the hard work of pioneering. Peace and Hope investigated this. They asked uprooted believers, "Are you interested?"

Soon the commission was organizing migrations. They helped the people get land, which sometimes meant negotiating with local jungle Indians. Here the people set up villages—pole-framed houses and a central plaza that doubled as the essential soccer field—and cleared areas for fields. They built a school and a church. Peace and Hope sent Silas Santiago for training so he could treat health problems common in the jungle, like parasites, dysentery and tuberculosis.

It was tough. There were no roads, and paths to rivers were steep, long and sometimes dangerous. Homesickness overwhelmed some of the settlers. Eventually a group of skilled British volunteers helped the people build three pedestrian suspension bridges, two water purification systems, a boat ramp and a warehouse. Plans were underway for a water reservoir and consultation from an agronomist and a topographer to help them survey a site.

Two decades later, under the direction of attorney Alfonso Wieland, the Peace and Hope Commission continues to serve a variety of human needs, from assisting displaced coffee farmers to training women about their rights and opportunities. Hundreds of Christian Peruvian women have run free breakfast canteens for poor children. Thousands of men have formed community "peasant patrols" during periods of heightened danger. CONEP has issued several key public statements, including "Justice and Truth for Reconciliation" in 1995 and "Why Christians Should Reject the Second Reelection of Mr. Fujimori" in 2000.

On the first anniversary of the church killings, the Peace and Hope director, Pedro Arana, sent a pastoral letter to the church members. They must forgive, he told them.

> The Gospel demands more from us, because it has given us more. . . . You must not permit any "root of bitterness" to poison your lives. . . . The Gospel demands that we forgive those who have deprived families of husband, son, of the provider, and of hope for the future. . . . We must forgive because we live from and within the forgiveness of God. . . .
>
> Blessed are the dead who die in the Lord from now on. "Yes," says the Spirit, "they will rest from their labor, for their deeds will follow them" (Rev 14:13).
>
> The eternal God knows these men and their constructive labors, and the Peruvian people also will one day know them.

Without this church's tragedy the Peace and Hope Commission never would have been formed. Because of the sacrifice of six men, thousands have benefited. "As the Scripture says, their deeds have followed them."[4]

CHRISTIANS WHO ACT

Throughout the continent of Latin America, Pentecostals—Christians who emphasize the Spirit—are spreading like wildfire. Like the Peace and Hope Commission, many reach out in service to their communities. *Global Pentecostalism: The New Faces of Christian Social Engagement* by Tetsunao Yamamori and Donald Miller documents this.[5]

Take Renascer Church in São Paulo. A big church, Renascer owns several busses, and every evening and many noon hours volunteers drive them into the poorest neighborhoods to feed people. Although São Paulo is one of the world's richer cities, large slums *(favelas)* fester. Renascer busses head right into those slums.

"Pull over. Here's a good place to stop," David said to the driver when they paused near the open market. Although it was dark, vendors were tidying stalls and stacking produce for the next day. While the bus idled, men and women scuttled out of cardboard box "houses" in the dark alleys and crept near.

Cecilia stepped down among them. "Here's the Word of God for today," she said, and in a clear voice read Psalm 46. "God is our refuge and strength, an ever present help in trouble." Just a few short comments, and she was done.

Volunteers ladled stew out of a large kettle on the floor and passed full plastic cups out the windows. Then they stepped down to mingle. "What's been happening? . . . No job yet . . . Still adjusting from the countryside . . . The price of oil . . . A government raid . . . No water."

"Do you have any water?" one man asked.

"Yes, please!" others clamored.

"Of course." Volunteers handed around empty Coke bottles that they had filled with water.

"How about a blanket?" the volunteers asked. These were passed to those who wanted them.

After half an hour, the bus moved on and the homeless, with blankets around their shoulders, skittered back into their cardboard boxes.

Every night Renascer volunteers feed twenty-five hundred people. Resources come from offerings as well as fruit, rice, beans and other staples that members donate.

This is Christianity in action.

The incompetent assassin. Swimming in huge reserves of oil, Venezuela is potentially a wealthy country. Unfortunately, most Venezuelans have not been able to tap into the wealth.

Venezuelan Juan Pérez Alfonso has been called the father of OPEC. He went to his death bitterly disappointed at the way the influx of oil money had increased the gap between the rich and the poor in his country. "Oil money has done nothing but lead us to waste," he said.

> This oil income, from the very beginning, has been hurting us. If oil were to disappear, it might be better for us. . . . One cannot plant oil. It is impossible. Our solution does not lie in imitating the United States. . . . We must try to produce enough black beans to feed the Venezuelans. For this, we do not need capital. We

need devotion, and we don't have devotion because of all that money. . . . When you receive so much dung from the devil, you can do nothing but wallow in it.[6]

Reacting against the previous capitalist fiasco, President Hugo Chávez has been trying a socialist approach.

Pastor Mario ministers in one of the poor communities in Venezuela. One night, walking home after visiting a sick member, he felt a rough hand clutch him and spin him around. "We don't want you in this neighborhood, Pastor," rumbled a voice.[7]

There was prejudice against Protestants, Mario knew, and even more against Pentecostals, who were thought to be a disorderly sect. It was too dark to see clearly, but to his horror Mario felt cold metal press against the back of his head.

"You've been warned before," the voice continued. Mario thought of the stones thrown regularly at the church building. "Now it is your time to die."

Hearing a click, Mario sagged.

"What? No shells?" the voice shouted in outrage and disgust. Footsteps receded, and Mario was left alone.

When he recovered from the shock, Pastor Mario decided he had to take positive steps. He had to reach out to the community rather than just care for his church members.

Since then his church has created multiple services.

- a community basketball court for children and youth

- a vaccination program

- birth-control counseling

- a food distribution program

- marriage counseling

- movies for children on the streets

- help in the extensive paperwork required to register children with the government

- an NGO that offers home improvement loans

Now the community knows that this church cares for them. They have seen love at work.

The thieves who robbed the thieves. In an even more violent part of Caracas, Pastor Eugenio ministers. From the beginning his care for the community was clear. But one night he was shaken out of a sound sleep, and like Mario, felt a pistol held to his head.[8]

"Get the church keys and unlock the door," the intruder snarled. Once inside, the man ripped out an amplifier and grabbed a guitar. Then he oozed away into the darkness.

In front of the church Pastor Eugenio shook his head and tried to grasp what had happened. He looked up at the smoggy sky and made an attempt to pray.

Around the corner trotted five street toughs, all armed. *What next?* Eugenio thought. *This is not my night.*

To his amazement the young men held out a guitar and amplifier to Eugenio. "Is this your equipment?"

"Yes," Eugenio trembled as he reached out and closed his hand around the familiar smooth wood of the guitar neck. "How did you find it?" Eugenio wondered.

"We saw that thief walking down the street with this stuff. 'Where did you get those things?' we asked him. 'From the church,' he said. 'No way,' we said, and we grabbed the loot back. We want you here, Pastor. You do good work."

Dancing to the Lord. In still another Caracas community a fifty-year-old woman named Marlena has made a difference for teenagers. She lives on a hillside at the end of the metro line. Landslides cause houses to crack and collapse. Unemployment, binge drinking, early sex, early pregnancies, teen gangs, drugs, family violence and spiritism are common.

Marlena's husband beat her until he left, and her son died in a gang fight. Broken-hearted, she found love in a Pentecostal church. After meditating and praying and fasting, she began to open her home to teenagers.

On a typical Friday night, Adolfo thumps out the rhythm on an overturned metal tin while twenty-five teens sing and dance to a wor-

ship song. The room is small, 12 feet by 12. Then sixteen-year-old
Beatriz winds her way to the cloth-draped podium in the corner.
Everybody hunkers down and turns to face her.

"How should we live as Christians?" Beatriz asks. "Listen to the
apostle Paul in Colossians 3: 'Since you have been raised with Christ, set
your hearts on things above. . . . For you died, and your life is now hidden with Christ in God. . . . Put to death, therefore, whatever belongs
to your earthly nature: sexual immorality, impurity, lust, evil desires
and greed. . . . You used to walk in these ways, in the life you once
lived. But now . . .' " This teen girl shakes out several pages of notes and
zooms back and forth through biblical cross-references.

Snacks and relaxation are followed by singing and dancing, this time
more vigorous. For hours it continues. That's Friday night at Marlena's.
Instead of carousing, participating in orgies and fighting, these teens are
expending their energies in an ethical context. But it is not dull. They
sing, dance, eat, joke and relax together. They experience the life-
transforming presence of Jesus. They speak in tongues through the
power of the Holy Spirit. They welcome the challenge of fasting on
Wednesdays, and all-night prayer meetings once a month. They bask in
Marlena's care for them, her discipline as she sets boundaries and her
love as she welcomes them for the first time or the fiftieth. They turn to
each other like members of an extended family. Because they're not getting drunk or pregnant, they have money and energy to spend on school
and jobs. The lifestyle change is dramatic.

"Religion seems to bring order to their lives at the very time that it
allows for ecstatic release—which may, indeed, be the unique genius of
Pentecostalism," comment researchers Yamamori and Miller.[9]

Other research shows that when Latin Americans become Pentecostals or *evangelicos*, many learn to read.[10] The Bible becomes *their* book,
and they want to access it themselves. Furthermore, participating in
Bible discussion groups "stimulates people not only to learn to read and
write but also to structure coherent and convincing ideas and communicate directly with individuals and with larger groups."[11] As well, believers learn new social skills. Peasants and poor urban dwellers may

lack strong positive groups. But in the church, "participating almost daily in meetings, they become integrated into community life. Eager to share their faith, they walk long distances and build relationships that extend beyond the local community."[12]

Intriguingly, in this region of machismo the evangelical faith also seems to enhance women's power. Social scientists like Elizabeth Brusco, Lesley Gill, Cornilia Butler Flora, Carol Ann Drogus, Cecilia Loreto Mariz and others have been surprised to discover "that despite the evangelical rhetoric of patriarchy, there are ways that the spread of evangelical Protestantism may actually support women's moral autonomy."[13]

One explanation is that when the Bible is taken seriously, it stands above everybody. Therefore a woman may critique a man, even her husband, on the basis of what the Bible says.

> It is precisely the *crente* [believer] woman's strict observance of a subordinate role, as well as her knowledge of biblical pronouncements and her feeling of being inspired by the Holy Spirit, that gives her the right to "show the man the error of his ways." Her observance and knowledge, furthermore, often erode her husband's ability to dismiss her challenges.[14]

Pentecostals are not the only Christians whose life in Christ propels them into loving service. But Pentecostals are a major force. On the negative side, some Pentecostals have a reputation for legalism. No make-up for women, not even short hair. Others focus on their own members' growth, like Pastor Mario before he saw the light at the end of a pistol. As on every continent, too many Christians are complacent. Still, the number of simple churches that reach out in service to their communities is striking.

The first time I flew home from São Paulo I couldn't believe my eyes as I peered down through the plane window. A cluster of skyscrapers loomed below. Before long there was a second cluster, followed by an interval of lower buildings. Then came a third, small city. Then a fourth. And fifth.

"Impressive. But of course São Paulo is a lot bigger than Seattle," I muttered to myself. After all, I knew the statistics. São Paulo and Mexico City are the two biggest cities in the world.

Masses of buildings emerged on the horizon. And more. And more. Unconsciously I tugged my seatbelt. Minutes passed. Still more edifices streamed beneath me. My chest tightened. "Hold it. Stop! This is over the top," I mumbled. "I can't compute this many people in one place."

Relentlessly new skyscrapers kept appearing.

I was propelled to prayer. "Oh thank You for all those churches down there, the house churches, the storefronts and the megachurches. Nobody could plan for this place. It's too huge for any human design for ministry. Only your Spirit can serve all the needs, moving through people at the grassroots."

And that is what the Spirit is doing.

CHRISTIANS WHO THINK

When Rios Montt became president of Guatemala in the 1980s, a British Christian enthused, "Isn't it wonderful that an *evangelico* has been placed in power?"

"No, it is a tragedy that he has been appointed, because he does not have a Christian mind," a Guatemalan Christian answered. "Corruption continues, and he appoints relatives to positions of influence and power. So his election as president has actually turned out to be a scandal for the gospel."[15]

Christian action without a Christian mind can be a dangerous thing. As *evangelicos* earn respect for their social contributions and rise in power, thinking becomes even more crucial.

Latin American socioeconomic realities. In the 1960s many large entities, both public and private, tried to jump-start Latin American economies. The United Nations dubbed it the Decade of Development. President Kennedy inaugurated the Alliance for Progress. Both the Catholic Church and the World Council of Churches participated. Ambitious projects were begun. Monies poured in. At the end of the Decade of Development, however, the poor were still landless and hungry.

Development may have benefited the well-to-do. They owned land.

They could spend a little for equipment and supplies. They knew how to fill out application forms. They were acquainted with lawyers. But the bulk of the population did not prosper.

When the world economy hiccupped, a new problem emerged. Latin American nations had been encouraged to take out loans. Soon they were buried under interest payments, and their debts ballooned.

Other problems were daunting. Drugs nurtured corruption. Traffickers sometimes wielded more power than governments. Underneath this unhealthiness festered old wounds from European colonization, from periodic American invasions that had overthrown governments in several countries, from *ladinos'* mistreatment of *indios*, and from the sad history of African slavery on a massive scale. "Strong men" appealed to the populace irresponsibly, promising what they could not deliver. Pentecostalism spread like wildfire, but hybrid spiritist movements spread even faster. Many frustrated young leaders in the universities turned to Marxism under the guise of "scientific socialism."

From 1962 to 1965, Catholic churchmen met in the pivotal meetings known as Vatican II. Out of this historic gathering, a paradigm shift emerged. Priests went back to their communities and switched from Latin to the languages of the people. In widely diverse ways they adapted their ministry to their communities. Some began small group Bible studies. Others initiated social action spurred by Marxist theory. There were those who joined guerilla bands and took up arms under the rubric of "just war" against institutionalized "structural violence." Still others gave their blessing to indigenous animistic practices.

In 1969, *evangelicos* convened the first Continental Congress on Evangelization (CLADE). At the request of leaders afire with zeal to apply a Christian worldview to the realities of time, CLADE birthed the Fraternidad Teólogica Latinoamericana. Through publications and gatherings, the Fraternidad continues to provide a forum for serious thinking. Several more CLADE conferences have followed the first.

"Where Is the Latin American Church Going?" This question is the title of a recent paper by Pablo Deiros, who is president of the Seminario Internacional Teológico Bautista in Buenos Aires.[16] It is the kind of

question Christian thinkers must ask as they try to serve their region responsibly. The second half of Deiros's paper's title is a warning: "What Dangers Do We Face?" He raises ten potential dangers: triumphalism, success, subjectivism, syncretism, Constantinism, sentimentalism, populism, fetishism, emotionalism, authoritarianism.

Consider the cluster of triumphalism, success and Constantinism. Some Protestant churches in Latin America are huge and proud of it. When I was in Guatemala, a woman led me around her church complex with great enthusiasm. "Here's our sanctuary," she beamed. "It has fourteen thousand seats. And just over there is our church parking lot, with space for five thousand cars."

Yet she could not grasp why I was training Guatemalan missionaries for the Muslim world. "*I've* never met a Muslim," she said. "They're so far away. What do they have to do with us?"

Local success was the limit of her horizon. She was complacent in her Christianity. In countries like Guatemala, with large numbers of evangelical Christians, triumphalism, success and even Constantinism are dangers. When Christianity became the official faith of the empire under Constantine (d. 337), it became routine, a public form rather than a personal commitment. Power can sap passion, Deiros would warn my Guatemalan friend.

Subjectivism, sentimentalism and emotionalism are other dangers. Many believers rely too much on their feelings, Deiros asserts. People say, "I feel this is the will of God," without bothering to test their inclination by Scripture or by doctrine or by consulting mature believers. Some view doctrine negatively. They find it stifling and imprisoning. Doctrine feels like dead weight. Duties and disciplines do not interest them much either. Yet if you renounce your obligation to think, you may fall into spurious practices, Deiros suggests. "To 'feel good' is not synonymous with 'walking in Christ' or 'walking in the Spirit.' " Jesus lambasted those who said "Lord, Lord," but didn't obey him.

Fetishism means attributing magical powers to an object or rite. This could be an animist or spiritist object, but it could also be the Bible, baptism, the Lord's Supper, a hymnbook, oil, water or certain words or phrases repeated over and over, like "The blood of Jesus covers me."

None of us is without sin, Deiros concludes. We all struggle. To err is human. Yet to consciously continue in error is dangerous. We are not rocks or robots, but thinking beings. God expects us to reflect on our lives, our community, our place and time, and consider how to express his grace and his lordship right where we are.

Pentecostal joy versus liberation anger. When the subject of Latin American Christian thought arises, many think of liberation theology. Gustavo Gutiérrez published *A Theology of Liberation* in 1968. A stream of liberationist works has flowed steadily ever since.

Liberationists point out that Jesus began his ministry by announcing that he would preach good news to the poor, freedom for prisoners and release for the oppressed (Lk 4:18-19). This was not just metaphorical for Jesus, nor is it for Latin Americans. Liberationists call us to look at life from the perspective of the poor. If we do, we will see that charity and relief work are not enough. The *causes* of social problems must be confronted. People who love God and their neighbors must work to change the structures that perpetuate injustice. To do this, we must learn how social systems operate.

Some liberationists go too far, particularly if they lean heavily on Marxism. Orlando Costas is one who has raised points for dialogue that evangelicals continue to pursue with liberationists.[17] For example, the poor are not only sinned against but also sinners. The rich too are made in God's image. As well, the context does not shape the biblical text completely. The text confronts the context in surprising, authoritative ways. Furthermore, people have souls and long for God sometimes even more than they long for bread. Jesus is our ultimate allegiance, not Marx or Che Guevara. His kingdom is our goal, not the classless society.

In their study of global Pentecostals, Yamamori and Miller have suggested one other significant contrast. Liberationists emphasize critique, they say, while Pentecostal evangelicals emphasize harmonious hope:

> In many ways, Pentecostalism operates with an entirely different set of guiding principles than those of Liberation Theology. The imagery of Pentecostals tends to be organic in tone, emphasizing harmony and purity. In contrast, Liberation theologians tend to

use metaphors that conjure images of opposition, conflict, and struggle, reflecting its Marxist orientation. These differences are important because metaphors reflect the fundamental roots of social movements, as well as having a controlling effect on people's behavior within these movements.

The organic image of Christians being part of one body in which Christ is the head, with each individual being called to fulfill his or her particular role and function within the body, tends to motivate people quite differently than does a structural model that begins with the root assumption of exploitation in which one class is pitted against another.

In the latter case, Jesus is a revolutionary prophet. In the former instance, he is a king who rules over a well-ordered and harmonious kingdom. Violence and revolutionary rhetoric are inappropriate within most Pentecostal circles, whereas they are at the heart of some expressions of Liberation Theology. According to the Marxist paradigm, the utopian kingdom will occur only after a revolutionary struggle. For Pentecostals, the kingdom of God is realized as people purify their conscience in obedience to God and follow his guidance and purpose for their lives.[18]

Some liberationists will feel slighted by this description, pointing out that liberation theologians differ significantly among themselves, as do *evangelicos,* and both continue to produce new ideas. Yet Yamamori's and Miller's contrast provides food for thought.

Tomorrow's thinkers. The thinkers of tomorrow are on the university campuses. In *Shining like Stars: The Power of the Gospel in the World's University,* Lindsay Brown introduces some of these future leaders.

Take students in Peru. With scarcely a passing glance, the faculty association at the university in Cuzco rejected Christian students' request to make a presentation. "What can we learn from students?" they asked.[19]

"So they turned us down," Rogelio wrinkled his brows. "What do we do now?"

"Go up to the next level," Patricia suggested. They approached the rector of the university. This time they were more indirect. "Sir, is there some way in which we can serve this university?"

"Certainly," he answered. "The toilets are very dirty. They haven't been cleaned in a long time. Would you scrub them?"

Gulping, Patricia and Rogelio assembled their crew and tackled the toilets. It took them forty-eight hours, but the bathrooms sparkled across the campus. Even before that, everybody was asking, "What kind of group is this?"

News drifted back to the rector. He was so impressed that he assigned lecturers to help them the second day. They had wanted to meet with the faculty. Now they met them over the grime in the toilets, with their sleeves rolled up, serving the community.

Lots of students wanted to hear why they did what they did, and it was easy to share their faith. They did it dramatically. Five students carried big crosses around the campus. Four crosses had a nameplate and a photo: Mao, Che, Lenin and Marx. The fifth cross was empty.

When a huge crowd had gathered, Rogelio spoke to them. "You see these crosses we are carrying around? You see the paintings of the four leaders? They were great men. Now they are dead. The fifth cross is empty because Jesus died and came back to life. That's what we want to talk about." A lot of students began to follow Jesus that day in Peru.

In Guatemala, as Christian students prepared to commemorate Columbus's five-hundredth anniversary, they invited students from Ecuador, Costa Rica, Panama, Nicaragua, El Salvador and Honduras to help them. Together they created a Christian extravaganza. Through dramas, films, music, public talks and personal conversations, almost all seventeen thousand first-year students learned something about Jesus. Eighty-five professed new faith. A nine-month discipleship training course followed. "What convinced me of my need of Jesus Christ?" one new believer reflected. "It was the combination of Bible study and your friendship."[20]

In Bolivia, there were only a few *evangelicos* on the campus in Cochabamba. For six months they prayed. Then, like the Guatemalans, they invited help from students across the continent. Dynamic witnesses arrived from eight countries. For the medical school they hosted a film discussion on abortion. For language students they displayed a Bible translation exhibit. After six weeks nearly all twenty thousand students on the campus had heard the gospel and hundreds had believed. Nothing like this had happened here before. The little group that began the project were reenergized, and most of them continue to volunteer in Christian service today.

In Ecuador the faculty of law at the National University was a cradle of freethinking, with a strong Marxist flavor. Christian students conducted a forum there. "Consider not just the historical Jesus, but the Christ of faith. How would you respond if he was your classmate?" they challenged.

One law student named Eduardo had been losing sleep, agonizing over issues facing Ecuador and issues facing him personally. Although he didn't think God existed, in desperation he had groaned out a silent prayer for help. Later he told the Christian students, "You were sent by God so I could meet him myself."[21]

In Mexico City medical students were banned from holding Bible studies on campus. They could not find a meeting place until they discovered the hospital morgue. Capitalizing on this weird location, they sent out invitations: "You are invited to the morgue for a social discussion. The topic will be 'Evidence for the Resurrection.' " Here among the dead some seekers found new life.[22]

Universities across Latin America resonate with young people passionate about their countries' futures. Christian students are there too, offering a framework for thinking about their societies—and backing it up with action.

THE FIRST PEOPLES OF LATIN AMERICA

Suddenly, where nobody had been standing a minute before, skinny men in fatigues with hard black eyes and acrid smelling bodies shifted their feet but held their guns steady. Bruce blinked.

"Come." One man stabbed to the left with his rifle.

So Bruce disappeared into the wet green maze that entangled the rebels of Colombia. Emerald leaves settled back and covered the spot as though he had never been there at all.

For twenty years this American had been living with the Motilone people in the jungle. He was a maverick. In the beginning no mission board would take him because he was too young and didn't have enough education. "Go to college," they advised. But he had heard God call him to the Motilones.[23]

This tribe had a fierce reputation. Very isolated, their main contact with outsiders was with the explorers who worked for oil companies. The Motilones killed them in order to use the explorers' helmets as cooking pots. When Bruce trekked into Motilone territory, they speared him in the leg. He had to beat a retreat, following rivers to find his way out of the unknown.

But he went back. Two decades later many Motilones followed Jesus, and there were schools, clinics, agricultural and business cooperatives, and a couple hundred young tribal members who had returned from their education in the city to use their professions with their people. These included agronomists, business specialists, nurses, foresters and even attorneys.

In this book the Motilone represent the indigenous peoples of Latin America.

Descendants of Spanish and Portuguese colonists and African slaves are a big part of the continent's population. Aboriginals often have been shoved to the margins, demeaned and exploited.

To their credit, missionaries zeroed in on the tribes because they believed passionately that *every people* deserved to hear the good news in words they could understand. Every tribal person is created in God's image. Jesus died for tribal peoples as much as for anybody. Missionaries also were drawn to tribes because tribal social structures were easier to grasp than city social structures, tribal people responded well to the gospel, and tribal cultures were just plain interesting.

Smoked grubs make a good sauce. Now Bruce was being kidnapped by the hard rebel movement that held hundreds of hostages, sometimes until they died.

Waking up the next morning in the crude guerilla camp, Bruce took a good look at his captors. By and large, these were poor boys from the city. They didn't know how to live in the jungle, which meant they often went hungry. They were just making do as best they could, fired by ideals for a better future.

"Should I help cook?" Bruce asked. "I know the edible plants and the protein sources. I've lived here for years."

Meals improved dramatically. Sun-dried banana skins can be ground into flour. Smoked palm grubs make a tolerable sauce. Leaves and bark yield medicine for diarrhea and asthma.

Then Bruce discovered that most of his captors were illiterate. They had never finished school. So he took on another challenge. "Would you like to learn to read?"

Soon he was teaching a class for an hour and a half every day. While learning to read and write, the guerillas explored history, geography, political science and ecology. In this context, Bruce spoke of Jesus the liberator.

To discourage friendships forming between prisoners and guards, Bruce was moved from one camp to another. As he arrived at the new camps, rebels welcomed him enthusiastically because the jungle grapevine had spread the good news: they would eat better and learn to read too.

Crushing his chest with logs. Yet because he refused to go back and persuade the Motilones to ally with the rebels, he was tortured. He was turned over to thugs. Crushing logs, each weighing about 100 pounds, were placed on his chest, then rolled back and forth. Three or four times a day this happened. In these torture sessions, Bruce felt his insides collapse. His ribs broke. He urinated blood, and vomited even more of it. Although he could hardly walk or even breath after this abuse, he was forced to march on.

He lost consciousness. A blood transfusion was urgent or he would die, the camp medic decreed.

Guerillas fought for the privilege of donating blood to Bruce. A young man named Camilo was chosen.

"Do you know who I am?" Camilo asked Bruce later. "When my father committed suicide twenty-four years ago, my mother was left alone with several children. You Motilone neighbors sent us food. That kept us alive for two years. Nobody ever asked for payment. So I have given my blood to keep you alive."[24]

Several months after his capture, Bruce was released. For years he had dreamed of a network that would unite Colombia's fifty aboriginal peoples. Before he was abducted, he had been helping economic cooperatives in fourteen small language groups. His kidnapping was the catalyst that united the rest. Lobbying together for Bruce's freedom, Indians presented a solid front to the government, the media and the rebels. Today the tribes continue to work together, using that network to increase their power base and efficiency.

They have even dared to stand up to drug lords. Because the rebels infringe on tribal lands in order to grow coca for cocaine, the united Indians issued an ultimatum to the guerillas and traffickers. "You have until December to clear out. After that, you will be at war with all 500,000 of us."[25]

But drug traffickers still threaten. Bruce knows fifty people who have been executed by FARC (Revolutionary Armed Forces of Colombia). Some Motilones are tempted to grow coca. Unquestionably, the situation is precarious. "They have to sustain a status quo with the drug traffickers, with Chávez of Venezuela, with the ELN (National Liberation Army), EPL (Maoist People's Liberation Army), and the FARC," Bruce says.[26] Yet because the Indians are the only ones who know the jungle trails, they hold the upper hand in relation to the drug lords regarding what happens on their own land.

As other tribes have gotten acquainted with the Motilones, they have asked not only for practical help in medicine, agriculture, education and business, but also for teaching about the Spirit that has blessed this tribe. Enthusiastically the Motilones have commissioned thirty three-person teams to serve neighboring peoples holistically.

On another front, when Bruce was released, hundreds of guerillas slipped out of the murderous movement. They had learned that there were alternatives. Many of them now follow Jesus and work for justice nonviolently.

Aboriginals forgive Portuguese. Large tribes like the Quechua and Aymara in the Andes region and Mayan peoples in Guatemala have strong churches and fervent believers. In the jungles of Brazil, over a thousand Indians from a dazzling variety of tribes gather annually in conferences to worship and fellowship. In 2008, fourteen hundred delegates convened.

Recently these Brazilian Indians reenacted the deadly Portuguese conquest. Some of the leaders stood on the platform wearing feathers and loincloths. In a solemn ceremony the aboriginals formally forgave the Portuguese. After that, the whole audience was invited to be reconciled. Individuals sought out people against whom they had grudges and forgave them. Then communion was celebrated.

Tribal Christians continue to suffer from racial prejudice and resource competition by outsiders, and from resurgent animism inside their communities. Discrimination may be present even in Christian organizations, though often only the indios are aware of it.

Two of the great moments of my life were visits to the Museum of Anthropology in Mexico City and the Museum of the Nation in Lima, Peru. In both I was rendered speechless when I viewed small artifacts of great intricacy as well as immense monuments' reconstructions. Such originality. Such finesse. Such evidence of God's gift of creativity showered on all people. Yet also such cruelty, such lust, such oppression and exploitation expressed in these aboriginal objects. Clearly the early peoples were human beings, created in God's image and also sinners—our true brothers and sisters.

Why Should Latin Americans Be Missionaries?

"Why should Brazilians be missionaries?" Professor Ana Santos asks.[27] She gives seven reasons:

1. Size: Brazil has 45 million evangelicals.
2. Culture: Brazilians are extremely relational.
3. Ethnicity: Brazil's society is multiracial, with immigrants from nearly all the continents.

4. History: Brazil suffered colonization instead of colonizing others.

5. Politics: Brazil is neutral in world politics and has offended very few nations.

6. Economy: Brazil's economy is in the top ten and growing rapidly.

7. Biblical basis: Jesus tells Brazilian believers to go into all the world and make disciples.

Propelled by the passionate love of God, Latin Americans spill across borders, not only to indios but also to other countries. Almost ten thousand Spanish- and Portuguese-speaking missionaries serve around the globe.

Antioch Mission trains and sends Brazilians. The story began in the 1960s. Thirty single people who were active in ministry in Parana state asked Pastor Jonathan Ferreira dos Santos to teach them Bible and practical skills in a community surrounded by prayer and service. Ferreira invited the women to live with his family and rented a house for the men. However, the group determined to construct a proper school building. The city donated a piece of land, and after class every day students and professors cleared the forest and laid bricks. By the time they had built the school with their own hands, there were one hundred students.

"When I arrived at the school in 1971, I was amazed at the vitality of prayer, at the practice of preaching in every available place, at the miracles, and at the togetherness of a student-run school. Students prayed together, often all night or early in the morning. They all participated in church planting teams. They prayed for the sick and oppressed and possessed. They fasted. They worked in the garden, cleaned toilets, cut the grass, ran the office and kitchen teams, and monitored the dormitories. Class-bound theory was offered within this active community context," says Barbara Burns, an American professor who has spent a lifetime of service in Brazil.[28]

Nowhere on this school's radar screen was overseas mission. While a few visiting professors had encouraged it, the idea had not caught fire. Then one morning a student who was skeptical about mission was praying. Suddenly he began to cry. Kneeling on the cement, he asked God to forgive him for not seeing missions in God's plan. Others knelt and cried too. Soon whole classes were pouring out to join in the repentance and renewal. Support for missions swelled.

To Africa with love. One of the first graduates to go as a foreign missionary was Clesius. He traveled to the African country of Mozambique, where the people speak Portuguese as they do in Brazil. Clesius had a heart for drug addicts. He settled in and laid the groundwork for ministry. Then a Marxist revolution exploded, and Clesius was jailed.

"Thrown into prison? Clesius? No. How could that be? He's a good old boy. He'd never hurt anybody. He *agrees* with a lot of the Marxists' concerns!" The campus rumbled with conjectures.

Underneath were bigger questions. *Was Clesius really doing the will of God? Then why didn't God protect him? We've seen miracles. Why did God let Clesius down now?* The whole missions emphasis came under review. *Were we right to send Clesius to such a place? Maybe we should have kept our focus on Brazil.*

People were shocked into praying. A small group gathered every day to pour out their hearts for their friend. That was not enough, they soon realized. They must pray not just for one Brazilian rotting in jail, but for Mozambique, for Africa and for the world. As they joined hands and made a solemn commitment, Antioch Mission was birthed.

> Antioch Mission is an evangelical, interdenominational association . . . with the purpose of announcing the glory of God among the nations and of making disciples of our Lord and Savior Jesus Christ, inspired by the work of the Holy Spirit in the New Testament church in Antioch, which, having been born through missionary effort, became a missionary church. The Antioch Mission desires to help evangelical churches fulfill their missionary responsibility in the world, participating in the spiritual and material support of those sent.[29]

These words come from the mission's constitution.

Today Antioch operates many services, including a seminary offering an M.A. degree in missions. It is networked with other missions in the Association of Brazilian Cross-Cultural Mission Agencies (AMTB), the Association of Brazilian Missions Teachers (APMB) and an association of mission departments in the churches (ACMI).

Spreading hope, shaping citizens. Brazilian Antonia "Tonica" van der Meer also worked in Portuguese-speaking Africa. Her field was the nation of Angola. She remembers,

> I became close to people who had lost most of their family members, who had been raped in very cruel ways, who were hurting inside and outside, and who had very little comfort—no sheets, no soap, very little and poor-quality food, often no medical supplies for broken bones, no relatives to visit them, no hope for the future. Sometimes the situation made me physically ill and unable to sleep.[30]

As she visited, she gave small gifts, a bar of soap to one family and a pint of oats to another. People responded. "They didn't demand that I solve all their problems. But in response to my caring, many believed." Joyful smiles replaced dead stares. These poor people also delighted in giving. "They understood that they were still able to serve others and were not just social parasites."

João was a Marxist radio journalist. He and Tonica had weekly dialogues, and he came to follow Jesus. Two years later Angola relaxed press restrictions. The government offered evangelicals a two hour block of time free of charge on Sunday mornings on the country's only radio station. João became director of that program, sharing the good news with millions.

Marco was a government nurse. He traveled around the country promoting a program that helped people avoid the disease known as "sleeping sickness." One day his car crashed in an isolated area. Thrown out onto the road, he lay for hours unable to move until some sympathetic but ignorant people came along. These well-intentioned passersby grabbed him up and loaded him into their truck, then drove for two hours on a bumpy road to the nearest hospital.

Marco was paralyzed from the waist down.

When Tonica and her friends visited people in the hospital, they met Marco. Eventually he came to faith in Jesus. Today he runs a small clinic that hosts a worship service on Sundays. One hundred fifty people have believed. Marco's wheelchair has become a station of hope.

Sonia and Rubem studied under Tonica. Then they went to the mountains to a tribe that never had heard the gospel. They learned the language with a translator and adapted to the culture. Today, while there is no Bible in that language, there are so many Christians that they send their own missionaries to neighboring tribes.

Tonica also started a "chain of honesty" to help believers stand against corruption. If they could travel or do business honestly, they would, but if they could not do it honestly, they would skip the activity. Believers learned to keep each other accountable.

Besides formal missionaries, some Latin Americans travel internationally to work. One million Latin Americans cross the Atlantic to labor in Spain. Once there, some plant churches. Brazilians do the same in Portugal. This is happening on such a big scale that it is changing Europe's religious landscape.

Other Latin Americans go north across the Rio Grande to merge with the forty million Spanish speakers in the United States. The National Hispanic Christian Leadership Conference, based in Sacramento, California, serves thousands of Spanish-language churches. By 2050, Hispanics are projected to grow to 29 percent of the U.S. population. "Many Hispanics sincerely believe that God has led them here for a purpose: to play an important role in a revival of the Christian faith in this country."[31]

MORE IMPORTANT THAN WHAT WE DO FOR GOD

A network known as COMIBAM connects mission movements throughout the continent (www.comibam.org). "COMIBAM has seen great success motivating people. Now we face the second stage," says Carlos Pinto of Ecuador. "Mobilization is not everything. We also have a responsibility for our missionaries. We need to focus on member care, theology, and sustainability."

"Let's not forget humility," adds Tonica van der Meer. Some people "feel good when they can construct great palaces for worship costing millions of dollars or when they can invite a famous preacher. . . . They feel great, successful, and important. . . . But God is not the manager of a successful mission business. . . . Maybe we are becoming like the church of Laodicea, believing we are rich and prosperous while we are really very poor."

We can get so busy in the work of the Lord that we neglect the Lord of the work, she says. If that happens, and our spirits dry out, "we can only offer our own poor good works, which often create dependency and new problems. More important than what we do for God as missionaries is our own continuing relationship with him. . . . May God be gracious, and may his Holy Spirit help us to see our true identity."[32]

These are good words for every believer in Latin America, from the high Andes to the jungles to the biggest cities on earth.

5

SPIRIT

I AM WRITING THIS AT A CAMPGROUND IN OREGON. The Pacific thunders, a comforting, never-ending rumble in the background. Sunlight sneaks through green fir branches and dots a hillside blanketed in ferns. Every year I come to this campsite to clear my head, to get back in touch with the basics, the simple rhythms of light and dark, morning cold and noon heat, the balance of friendliness and privacy in the campers' community, and my own balance between beach hikes and doing nothing at all.

I am a child of the Pacific Northwest, and fiercely loyal. On a broader scale, I am a resident of the Pacific Rim, and I've had the privilege of spending time in a great many of the jewels in the necklace that circles this vast ocean. But always I come back to these particular tall trees, these mountain ranges sliding down to the sea, this shore. Even after so many years camping and hiking and boating and just staring, just inhaling, the beauty of God's created universe still takes my breath away.

There is a character in Fyodor Dostoevsky's *The Brothers Karamazov* named Alyosha who felt this way.

> His soul, overflowing with rapture, was craving for freedom and unlimited space. The vault of heaven, studded with softly shining

stars, stretched wide and vast over him. From the zenith of the
horizon the Milky Way stretched its two arms dimly across the
sky. The fresh, motionless, still night enfolded the earth. The
white towers and golden domes of the cathedrals gleamed against
the sapphire sky. The gorgeous autumn flowers in the beds near
the house went to sleep till morning. The silence of the earth
seemed to merge into the silence of the heavens. The mystery of
the earth came into contact with the mystery of the stars. Alyosha
stood, gazed, and suddenly he threw himself down upon the
earth. He did not know why he was embracing it. He could not
have explained to himself why he longed so irresistibly to kiss it,
to kiss it all, but he kissed it weeping, sobbing, and drenching it
with his tears and vowed frenziedly to love it, to love it forever
and ever. "Water the earth with the tears of your gladness and
love those tears," it rang in his soul. What was he weeping over?
Oh, he was weeping in a rapture even more over those stars which
were shining for him from the abyss of space and he was not
ashamed of that ecstasy. It was as though the threads from all those
innumerable worlds of God met all at once in his soul and it was
trembling all over as it came in contact with other worlds.[1]

Nature is not all loveliness, of course. It can be cruel. Think tsuna-
mis and earthquakes and volcanoes. Even when everything is gorgeous,
nature can be cold. All its beauty can break your heart if your relationships are in ruins or you have no outlets for your vocational gifts or
you're just lonely. All those snowy peaks and azure tropical waters can
leave you aching.

In any case, natural beauty may be slipping away. Polluters spew
and spill, developers clear-cut and pave, and trespassers ooze through
legal loopholes.

Generations have trod, have trod, have trod,
And all is seared with trade; bleared, smeared with toil;
And wears man's smudge and shares man's smell; the soil
Is bare now, nor can foot feel, being shod.[2]

Those who love nature sometimes despair. Yet there are glimmers of hope. One morning early in 2006 I opened my newspaper and learned that after years of patient negotiation, Canadian indigenous peoples, loggers, fishermen, businesses, government bureaucracies and ordinary residents had designed a win-win land arrangement: the Spirit Bear Conservancy. Full of big bears, ribboned with steams rippling with salmon, this vast reserve stretches from the sea to the mountains.

I read this news story and my heart leaped, and my thoughts flew to friends in Borneo where the rivers run brown because of illegal logging and mining far upstream. My mind bounced to friends in Brazil and Burma whose resources are being raped. The Spirit Bear Conservancy stands as a model for my friends. Multiple groups with conflicting interests—including the bears and the salmon, who had humans to speak for them—developed an amicable shared arrangement.

Then my thoughts leapfrogged to Loren Wilkinson, a colleague on the faculty at Regent College, a Christian graduate school in Vancouver, Canada. Loren and his wife and adult daughter had spent a night in jail a decade before. I was at the faculty meeting where he was asked to explain himself.

This Christian family had placed their bodies in the path of mammoth logging equipment, Loren told us, in order to protect part of the Canadian coastline, a region known as Clayoquot Sound. With other protesters they were hauled off to jail. There in the middle of the night, as the group traded ecological songs, Loren and Mary Ruth introduced praise songs and hymns about God's good creation.

The lumber companies paid attention. The various interests—tribal and business and government and community—sat down and listened to each other. All this loosened the ground for later arrangements like Spirit Bear Conservancy.

Why did Loren risk his body and reputation and family? Why did Alyosha hug the ground? Why do I go camping? Because God's creation calls us. It provokes our awe. It compels our reverence. Nature is not God, but it is one of his very good gifts and deserves our attention.

In chapter two we explored the power of the Word. In this chapter we explore the power of the Spirit. These are the two classic touchstones of orthodox theology. Both are essential. The Word without the Spirit is dry and dead. And the Spirit without the Word? You can't tell what spirit you're following. You're likely to end up in Bizarreville.

Nature points to the Spirit, because God's Spirit was active in creation at the very beginning of time.

> In the beginning God created the heavens and the earth. Now the earth was formless and empty, darkness was over the surface of the deep, and the Spirit of God was hovering over the waters.
>
> And God said, "Let there be light," and there was light. (Gen 1:1-3)

The lines quoted earlier—"Generations have trod, have trod, have trod"—are from a poem by Gerard Manley Hopkins, who lived and wrote from 1844 to 1889. The full poem celebrates the Spirit's care for nature.

> The world is charged with the grandeur of God.
> It will flame out, like shining from shook foil;
> It gathers to a greatness, like the ooze of oil
> Crushed. Why do men then now not reckon his rod?
> Generations have trod, have trod, have trod;
> And all is seared with trade; bleared, smeared with toil;
> And wears man's smudge and shares man's smell; the soil
> Is bare now, nor can foot feel, being shod.
>   And for all this, nature is never spent;
> There lives the dearest freshness deep down things;
> And though the last lights off the black West went
> Oh, morning, at the brown brink eastward, springs
> Because the Holy Ghost over the bent
> World broods with warm breast and with ah! bright wings.[3]

The Spirit "broods" over this world. The Spirit nurtures it. That began when the world was unformed. It continues even now, in spite of the fact that the world is such a mess. The whole creation groans, writes the apostle Paul, "[but] the Spirit helps us in our weakness. We do not know what we ought to pray for, but the Spirit himself intercedes for us with groans that words cannot express" (Rom 8:22, 26). When Jesus taught his disciples about the Spirit who was to come fully after he left, the main word he used to describe the Spirit was *paraklete*, which is translated "comforter" or "counselor." The Spirit does a lot of other things, but first of all the Spirit creates and cares.

People are hungry for the Spirit. A generation ago, people trusted science. Now we crave more.

Recently a woman from my city traveled through Egypt. "The highlight for me was the mosques' daily call to prayer," Sara confessed. (That shocked her companions, who were fed up with the blaring intrusion into their sleep.)

"At home, I don't pray on a schedule," Sara explained. "I have stepped away from organized religion. But my psyche so yearns for life's spiritual dimension that I continue to seek the connection. Having mundane activities interrupted with the muezzin's audible cry to God was a showstopper for me."[4]

"My psyche so yearns for life's spiritual dimension . . ." Many people feel like Sara. A columnist for *GQ* magazine, Elizabeth Gilbert, recently authored a bestseller titled *Eat, Play, Love*. Through her words a spiritual quest reverberates.

Describing a New Year's Eve worship service at a Hindu ashram where she spent three months, Elizabeth wrote,

> I'm trying to become a vocal mirror for the voices of the lead
> singers, picking up their inflections like little strings of blue light.
> They pass the sacred words to me, I carry the words for awhile,
> then pass them back, and this is how we are able to sing for miles
> and miles of time without tiring. All of us are swaying like kelp in
> the dark sea current of night. The children around me are wrapped
> in silk, like gifts. I'm so tired, but I don't drop my little blue string

of song, and I drift into such a state that I think I might be calling
God's name in my sleep, or maybe I am only falling down the
well shaft of this universe. . . . As the minutes pass, it feels to me
like we are collectively pulling the year toward us. Like we have
roped it with our music, and now we are hauling it across the
night sky like it's a massive fishing net, brimming with all our
unknown destinies.[5]

By the end of her stay Elizabeth felt she had learned forgiveness and
contentment, and had experienced spiritual power and a brief blissful
"union" with all that exists.

People around us, like Sara and Liz, hunger for spiritual intensity.
Where can it be found? Do we design it ourselves? Or is there a real
God who will fill us with his presence?

A CHRISTIAN MYSTIC

Sundar Singh wrapped himself in a yellow cloth, took up a walking stick
and wandered from place to place. Where people lingered, he would pause
and talk about Jesus. He had a deep impact. Many believed. Lives changed.
Eventually he disappeared into Tibet. Nobody knows where his body lies.

He had no organization, no agenda, no credentials. He simply practiced the presence of God and spoke about God to those who wanted to
hear. The Spirit of God blew through him.

Sundar's Sikh family was loving, intelligent and god-fearing. Like
Muslims they believed in one God, a holy book and no castes. Like
Hindus they believed in reincarnation. They sent Sundar to the best
school in the region, which happened to be run by missionaries.

In school Sundar learned that Jesus said he was "the way and the
truth and the life," and that "no one comes to the Father except through
me" (Jn 14:6). This disturbed Sundar greatly. He could see that the
teachings of the Bible contradicted his family's religious beliefs.

Yet when he meditated on his own historic Scriptures, the words did
not come alive. When he practiced yoga, his stress was not relieved. He
even went into the forest to consult a guru. He came out with a little
wisdom, but not much more.

The message of Jesus threatened his precarious equilibrium. When Sundar was fifteen, his beloved mother died. Grieving and confused, he lashed out in rage.

"Look! Look what Sundar is doing!"

"What's he holding?"

"Teacher's Bible."

"He's tearing pages out!" Crowding close and then edging away, Sundar's fellow students shook with shock.

When he had ripped half the Bible to shreds, Sundar ran to the school garbage fire and tossed the rest of the book into the flames.

Horror was too mild a word to describe Sundar's father's state of mind when he was informed. "Are you crazy?" he said to his son. "What did your mother teach you? Books—no one ever damages a book. And spiritual things—we respect them. What's gotten into you?"

Although he was punished, Sundar remained confused. Where was the Spirit? All his life he had been taught to seek it. Without God, there is no significance. Yet God eluded him.

Suicide or Savior? Thoughts of suicide flitted through his mind. Why not end this hopeless ache? On the third morning after he had burned the Bible, Sundar got up at 3 a.m. and prayed. "Are you there, Creator of the universe? I am asking you to show me a sign. Otherwise I will lie down under the morning train, and seek my answers in the next life."

At 4:30 the room began to shimmer and then to glow. Out of the mist a figure emerged. Was this a Hindu avatar? No, it was not Shiva or Vishnu or any other recognizable god. Then a voice spoke. "Sundar, how long will you mock me? I have come to save you because you have prayed to find the way of truth. Why then don't you accept it?"[6]

There were blotches of blood on the figure's hands and feet. Clearly, this was Jesus. Overwhelmed, ashamed, incredulous, awed and joy-filled, Sundar bowed and prayed. The figure faded, but joy remained strong.

"Wake up, Father!" Just like a little boy, Sundar catapulted into his father's room to share the amazing vision. "It was Jesus!" he blurted out.

His father patted his shoulder. If he took this seriously, it would shatter everything. How could a person worship Jesus and be a Sikh? Today there are Christian Sikhs, but Sundar's father couldn't imagine that. Still, he wasn't upset. *He's just lost his mother. Patience is what he needs*, the man thought.

"Three days ago you were ripping the Bible to shreds, and now you announce that Jesus is Lord? Sleep on it, boy," Sundar's father said kindly.

In the days that followed, Sundar pondered. There was no doubt in his mind that Jesus had visited him and penetrated to his core. Sundar had encountered the Ultimate or, more accurately, God had found him. What next?

"I am your Lord. You are my follower." This message reverberated in his heart. Unless he was going to betray God and turn his back on the reality he had experienced, he had to let people know about Jesus.

So he did.

Like dynamite, everything exploded. His schoolmates turned on him. Their parents turned on his teachers. The teachers barely escaped with their lives to the next city. School closed down.

Sundar's father took him in hand. "My dear son—light of my eyes, comfort of my heart. . . . Consider your family. Surely you do not want the family name to be blotted out. Surely this Christian religion does not teach disobedience to parents."[7]

His father promised him a bride immediately, along with 150,000 rupees. His uncle promised him a chest of gold.

"I am not an unreasonable man, my child," his father continued. "But if you refuse me, I will know that you are determined to dishonor your family and I will have no alternative but to disown you." His father stroked Sundar's uncut hair. This was a Sikh man's pride.

Sikh means "lion," his father reminded him. "Don't behave like a jackal. Be a lion."

Sundar considered it all.

Then he cut his hair.

With tears and anger, his father led him to the door and ordered him out, never to return.

Nothing but stories. Sundar slept that night under a tree. It was cold. Up to that point, he had not lacked anything. Now, following Jesus, he learned to live with nothing.

Although he enrolled in a Christian school, he found it too comfortable. Spiritual life was too routine. God was too packaged. On his sixteenth birthday he disappeared into the jungle. Thirty-three days later he reappeared, dressed in the yellow cloth of a wandering truth-seeker. For the rest of his life, he just walked and told stories and prayed.

From time to time Sundar visited a Christian boys' boarding school. He lived in a cave nearby, and students trekked out to listen, sometimes sitting up late into the night.

His visits made a difference. Behaviors changed. One boy entered the low caste dorm to take care of a sick student and stayed there until he was well. No one in the school had ever done this kind of thing before. Another boy found a leper dying in a field. He loaded the contagious man on his back and carried him for two miles over a mountain track. When they graduated, such boys chose service careers instead of pursuing prestige and wealth.

"What was the attraction that made such a wonderful change?" commented a teacher.

Nothing that was merely second-rate could possibly have effected it. No mode of living, half in comfort, half in self-denial, could have worked such a miracle. Indeed, those of us who did our work surrounded by too much outward comfort did not impress the young people. We did not think it possible for us to change our style of living, though we often talked the matter over. But Sundar Singh's life could stand the test. It was reckless in its self-spending. He had counted the cost. The Cross was not preached only, but lived—and that made all the difference.[8]

Sundar walked with God and opened himself to the Spirit. "Prayer means diving into the ocean of reality and finding pearls of divine truth," he said.

As a diver holds his breath while he is diving, so a man of contemplation and prayer shuts himself in a chamber of silence, away from the distractions of the noisy world. Then he is able to pray with the Holy Spirit from above, without which it is impossible to lead a spiritual life. . . . To hear God's voice, we must wait for him in silence. Then, without voice or words, he will speak to the soul in the secret room of the heart. . . . The gift of ecstasy God has given me is far better than any home, and far greater than any hardship I might endure.[9]

Yet the Spirit always drew him back to serve the people.

" 'He's back! The Sadhu has returned!' The news ran like wildfire through the dingiest alleys." So one biographer describes Sundar's arrival in a town. "The children—the dirty toddler with the bloated stomach; the girl with the maimed foot; the boy with the scarred face; the scrawny offspring of the lepers, shunned even by the Untouchables—they heard the cries. Sundar Singh was back—and he was there again for them. And so they hurried—running, scuffling and limping—to his cave. It would be impossible to imagine a happier band of children."[10]

PENTECOSTAL POWER

In the burgeoning populations of Asia, Africa and Latin America, many people are brought to Jesus by Pentecostals. These churches emphasize the Spirit, though not the silence that Sundar treasured. When Pentecostals worship, they open up their emotions and throw their whole bodies into the activity. They sing passionately, they sway, they shout, they dance, they cry, they may even collapse into the arms of others who will pick them up and support them. When the service is over and they walk out the church door and down the streets to their own neighborhoods and businesses, they expect the Spirit to walk with them, and they call on him to heal, to exorcise evil powers, to protect from dangers, to right wrongs, to guide, to reconcile and to strengthen. The Spirit also propels them to reach out to the needy.

Daniel Ruffinati is a Pentecostal like this. But he did not begin adult life that way. Far from it.[11]

"What are you in for?"

Daniel turned away and tried to shrug off the question.

"I mean, what's your crime?" Marcos persisted.

"Armed robbery," Daniel mumbled.

"Good. I don't like to hang out with murderers."

Urine and vomit smells jolted the nose in this Argentinean ward. Ten feet away a scrawny man banged his head softly against the wall over and over. *Tap, tap, tap, tap, tap, tap, tap, tap, tap, tap.* Another man was busy taking off his clothes so he could get naked as fast as possible. He did that every day.

"Yeah, I heard you tried to blow up a bank," Marcos barreled on, ignoring the bizarre scene around them.

"I'm schizo, man," Daniel grunted in exasperation, "So are you. That's why we're in the prison psych ward."

"Can you read?" Marcos was not deterred. "Me, I'm blind. Well, you can see that plain enough. But I've got a Bible and I'm looking for somebody to read it to me."

That's how Daniel got started. Beginning in Genesis, he read many pages aloud every day. After four days, Marcos's interest moved on. But Daniel was hooked. He kept reading.

One day he hit Deuteronomy 13 and learned about the danger of worshiping false idols. "You've been focused on false gods, too," said a still, small voice. "But you have a choice, just like the Hebrews did. You can choose to go on the way you have been. Or you can turn your life over to your Creator."

Daniel kept reading. Sixteen days later he raised his eyes from the last page in the New Testament and realized that he was a different man. During the month that he had been reading, he had begun to experience a strange and powerful joy. He had quit smoking. He had quit taking mood-altering medications. He had started wearing clean clothes. And he had made several vows based on what he had read.

Before long he was preaching to Marcos, the head-banger, the naked man and other cellmates. Some believed. Together they cleaned the jail.

They cared for sick prisoners. Violence declined, especially rapes. Soon half the jail was attending Christian meetings. The authorities welcomed the peace and order. This went on for two years, while Daniel served the rest of his sentence.

Although a dozen doctors had seen Daniel over the years and concurred with the diagnosis of paranoid schizophrenia, those schizophrenic elements disappeared. Doctors were amazed.

In the fifteen years since his release, Daniel hasn't forgotten his fellow inmates.

The Christian Assistance Service for Prisoners and the Mentally Ill was born from his own pain. With his wife, Maria Elena, Daniel goes into prisons and especially into the mental wards. He tells the inmates his own story. They can see the results as he stands there in front of them. He represents alternate possibilities.

Every week Daniel and his wife take mental patients out of the hospital on picnics. They run job-skills workshops in jails. They provide support for women prisoners who have babies while they are incarcerated. They transition released prisoners back into society.

This kind of work burns people out. But Daniel and Maria Elena are refreshed week by week by the empowering presence of God's Spirit. That propels them back into the hard places. While the Word of God was pivotal in Daniel's journey of faith, it would not have been enough to sustain him without the Spirit.

WALK IN THE SPIRIT

Non-Pentecostals, too, practice the presence of God and depend on his power. Take the Mangalwadis. In their first years of marriage Vishal and Ruth lived in a wretched, lawless, desperate village in India. One day a scream ripped through the afternoon doldrums.[12]

"Snakebite!"

A cobra slithered near the water pump. Ramkali was the first woman along the path. When that striated body reared, she gasped. Before she could think, the snake's head shot forward like lightening, and fangs pierced Ramkali's ankle.

Shanti was the next woman along the path. By then the cobra had slithered away. Ramkali was on the ground, moaning.

"Help!" The call stabbed the air. Villagers swarmed. Ramkali was hoisted up and trundled to her shack. "Call the sorcerers! Quick!"

Rites and incantations began, but Ramkali swooned into unconsciousness. The government doctor happened to be in the area. He had no antivenin, but he administered glucose intravenously.

"What more can we do?" Ramkali's husband wrung his hands. "Is there anyone else who can help?"

Vishal approached the village chief. "We don't know sorcery, but we can pray."

"Please do."

Two Christians joined Vishal, as well as one Muslim who was learning about Jesus. Together they gathered around the bed of the woman who was almost dead. Fifty people circled them in the shadows, looking on. They began to pray in Jesus name. Within ten minutes Ramkali opened her eyes. Three days later she was well enough to walk three miles to Vishal's home to thank him and the God who answers prayer.

Pentecostals emphasize the Holy Spirit, but so do many non-Pentecostals, like Vishal.

He faced not only cobras but also political snakes. When he lived in the village, politicians from two parties threatened to kill him. So did the highest police officer in the region. "But through the power of prayer, we were able to withstand," he says.

As Vishal did community development work and human-rights advocacy, he depended on God. "I believe in human planning, strategy and action because man is significant. He affects not only machines but society and history as well. Bur I also believe in prayer because God is Almighty," Vishal says.

> It is necessary that we stand in the supernatural power of the Holy Spirit, because the battle between good and evil ultimately is supernatural. The modern man ignores the supernatural, diabolical dimension of evil; therefore he is unable to understand or to deal with the social dimension of evil . . .

Faith is power because it produces hope and generates action in a stagnant society. Faith gives staying power in the midst of opposition—the power to stand, to serve, to fight, to suffer, to die and to overcome. Most supremely, trusting or praying releases power because our dependence on God moves Him to act.[13]

When J. I. Packer has lectured on the topic of the Spirit in his systematic theology class at Regent College, he has raised five questions to help students evaluate whether they are walking in the Spirit as fully as they might be, whether they are being good stewards of the Spirit's potential. These address churches and Christian communities as much as individuals. Here are the questions:

- The issue of reality in church life: Is orthodoxy enough?

- The issue of restraint in evangelism and pastoral care: Do we allow the Spirit room to work?

- The issue of radicalism in church order and structures: Do our structures serve or stifle the Spirit?

- The issue of repentance in the church: Why is the Spirit quenched?

- The issue of revival or renewal as a meaningful hope for the church: What expectations do we settle for?[14]

WISDOM FOR BABIES
Aisha and Faridah are middle-aged sisters, born and raised Muslim and now living in Muslim communities. Both follow Jesus. Aisha has brought about twenty people to Jesus, and Faridah has started a chain that includes about fifty disciples. These sisters demonstrate how the Spirit gives wisdom to believers with very little training.

Aisha cooks for a foreign family, and Faridah irons their clothes. Every week, after the household studies the Bible together, the two women take the Scripture pages they have studied, go to a local copy shop and make copies for all the people they expect at their worship services later in the week. Every weekend they head home to their villages where they will lead Bible studies and prayer and praise meetings.

Early in the mornings when Faridah is in the village, men who drive motorcycles with sidecars hover around her door. They are coming to ask for prayer. Accidents can happen. Sensing that God is with Faridah, they request her to talk to God for them, to plead with him for protection for their driving that day.

Faridah has developed prayers that teach theology. First she prays the Lord's Prayer over the drivers. Then she prays a trinitarian prayer that she has devised.

> In the name of God the Creator, the Sustainer, the Judge, the Holy, the Loving, the One True God who comes close to us in the person of Jesus. . . . I ask blessing on these drivers this day.
>
> In the name of Jesus the Messiah, the Word of God, who had a virgin birth, who died for our sins, who rose in power, who will come back to judge, who can protect us from the powers of darkness, who calls us to be his disciples. . . . I ask blessing on these drivers this day.
>
> In the name of the Holy Spirit . . .

Every morning Faridah teaches through her prayers.

After people believe and evidence sustained commitment, the women baptize them, pouring water on them three times, once to mark forgiveness of sins, once to mark the righteousness Jesus gives and once to announce that sin no longer has dominion over them.

Recently a group of believers wanted to be immersed. They chose a park with numerous swimming ponds. For three weeks they baked and sold pies to earn the park entrance fee. The foreign family loaned their car with a full tank of gas and a driver, and the candidates set off.

Once in the park, the group searched for an isolated, unoccupied pool. (They did not want complete anonymity, however. They detained a passerby, handed him a camera and asked him to record the moment.)

Entering the pool and standing in a circle, they prayed and recited Scripture. Then all together they sank down until their heads were covered, then whooshed up out of the water, raised their arms into the air and called out "Praise the Lord!"

Ten men from this chain of disciples have moved across the country for a year to work in a big construction project. They take turns returning home, one each month, to visit their families and to bring the month's salaries to all the wives. The wives send back ten copies of all the Bible texts they have studied. Now the church is growing on the opposite side of the country.

Jesus told his disciples not to worry about what to say in tight situations because the Spirit would give wisdom (Mt 10:19-20). Later Peter and John amazed Roman officials who saw that the two were unschooled (Acts 4:13). The Spirit enlightens nobodies, according to Paul (1 Cor 1). Stories like Aishah's and Faridah's are being played out in a thousand places in our time.

FRESH FOR THE FAITHFUL

"Choose Jesus or choose your family!" Mannu's parents threw down the gauntlet. She chose Jesus and never saw her parents again. The pain aches to this day.

Mannu had been living in India, but one year after she was married she and her husband relocated to Nepal. At that time it was illegal to witness to Hindus. Evangelists faced a six-year prison sentence. In spite of the threat, they immediately began a church in their living room. Some of the first believers were neighbor women whom Mannu taught to sew. They believed and brought their husbands. Today the Patan church has more than two thousand members.

Mannu's husband was arrested but freed on bail while his case was pending. Eight years later his case finally came to court. He was sentenced to six years in jail, followed by banishment. His lawyer advised him to activate the banishment at once, rather than go to jail. He did.

But Mannu stayed and appealed the case to the king. If the appeal lost, she would be imprisoned in her husband's place. She had peace about that. It was more important for her husband to stay out of jail, because his ministry was more pivotal, she felt.

She felt that God had given her Jeremiah 42:10-12:

If you stay in this land, I will build you up and not tear you down;
I will plant you and not uproot you, for I am grieved over the
disaster I have inflicted on you. Do not be afraid of the king . . .
whom you now fear. Do not be afraid of him, declares the LORD,
for I am with you and will save you and deliver you from his
hands. I will show you compassion so that he will have compassion on you and restore you to your land.

After a year, their superior called her to Bangkok and told her, "If you
want to live separately from your husband, you must quit the
ministry."

Mannu explained the verse in Jeremiah, and said, "Give me three
more months. I'll pray, and if I don't receive further direction, I'll join
my husband in India."

In those three months a national revolution took place. Her husband
returned and in time received awards from the Ministry of Education
for Nepali textbooks he had written while in exile.

When Mannu first learned of her husband's arrest, their children
were in boarding school in India. She traveled to the school, took the
three apart into a corner and talked to them about the joy and the suffering that comes with serving the Lord. Then she told them their father
had been taken.

"How come Daddy gets all the privileges?" was her oldest daughter's
response.

Since then, that girl has graduated from Vellore Medical School and
returned to Nepal to provide medical care for her people.

The Spirit gives power not just for healings or exorcisms or un-
trained believers, but also for faithful believers who need endurance.
Decade after decade, the Spirit blows freshness through each day.

TEST THE SPIRITS

"Fang doesn't have a nose anymore! It's been chopped off!"

"No!" Huey reared back in horror, her eyes growing huge.

"I've just seen him,"

"What happened?" Huey whispered.

"The Eastern Lightening cult grabbed him. When he wouldn't join, they—Oh!" Siu sobbed.

"Thank God he came back at all, then. A lot of people just disappear. Their bodies turn up later, with arms or legs chopped off. But others are brainwashed, and join the cult."

Chinese cults. The Eastern Lightening cult in China attacks Christians, especially those in "house churches." Sometimes it is violent. At other times it sends young women to seduce Christian leaders, including missionaries. In 2002 Eastern Lightning kidnapped thirty-three leaders of the China Gospel Fellowship network. After several weeks they were released, but in such bad shape, emotionally as well as physically, that it took months of prayer before they were functioning again.

Clearly Eastern Lightening is an evil body. Other cults may be harder to discern. When the gospel is spreading and the church is growing, individuals and groups will express the faith in their own unique ways. Some strange beliefs and behaviors may take root if leaders are not trained and groups are not free to fellowship with others because of political persecution.

But when does a group move from being weird to being heretical?

Chinese Christians asked this in relation to a movement called the Three Grades of Servants. This body has about a million members. In the 1990s the Chinese government classified this group as an evil cult. Reportedly members were required to confess their sins to Xu Shuangfu, the founder. He was the "supreme servant," and members were divided into three grades under him. Those who tried to leave sometimes received death threats, according to accusers.

Were these accusations true? In 2003 a group of house church leaders asked Xu to face a formal inquiry into his practices. He agreed to meet them.[15]

When he arrived, he brought books and videos from his church, and spoke humbly.

"If my church is in error and really a cult, then please come and rebuke us and show us the error of our ways so we can repent!" he said.

"Please be brothers to us in this way. If you do not point out our errors, how can we ever change and walk with Jesus like you?"

After extensive investigation a press release signed by "preachers from the house churches of China" was released in 2006. It affirmed that Three Grades of Servants was not a cult but an independent denomination, and that its leader had a good and consistent testimony. "Though some of the (Three Grades of Servants) internal titles for preachers and management methods might be different from those of the conventional churches, this does not hinder their firm belief in Jesus Christ as the Savior," the document stated.

In November 2006 Xu was executed by the government after severe and prolonged torture.

What the Chinese churches did is an example for all of us. Not all spiritual power is from God. "Do not believe every spirit," 1 John 4 begins, "but test the spirits to see whether they are from God, because many false prophets have gone out into the world."

How do you test? The next verses tackle that question. "This is how you can recognize the Spirit of God: Every spirit that acknowledges that Jesus Christ has come in the flesh is from God, but every spirit that does not acknowledge Jesus is not from God. This is the spirit of the antichrist."

Jesus—fully God, fully human—is the key. The Chinese house church leaders kept that focus when they evaluated Xu. Was he setting himself up as a little god, almost replacing Jesus? No, they concluded. Therefore his movement was a church, not a cult.

African Instituted Churches. Africa is home to tens of thousands of indigenous congregations. Some are parts of huge denominations, like the Cherubim and Seraphim, the Church of the Lord Aladura, the Zion Christian Church or the Kimbanguist movement.

"How 'Christian' Are African Independent Churches?" is the title of an article by Dean Gilliland.[16] He asked this question because some of these so-called churches practice paganism. Charms, magical formulas and fortunetelling are more familiar to their members than the story of Jesus. Some leaders even present themselves as divine.

How do Africans Christians discern? How do they "test the spirits"? They do it like the Chinese house-church leaders. They ask:

- How central is Jesus? Do members use his name merely as a magical mantra, or do they listen to his teachings and obey them? Do they understand what his death and resurrection mean?

- How central is the Bible? Are members studying it, committing its teachings to their hearts and expressing them in action? Or do they consider the Bible merely an object with esoteric power?

- How central are baptism and the Lord's supper, two sacraments that Jesus commended?

- Are heretics disciplined? Or are deviations allowed to flourish unchecked?

- What direction is the movement heading? Is it becoming more Christ-centered and more biblical? Or less so?

Hindu-background oral learners. In India there is a farming region where approximately two thousand little churches took root between 1997 and 2003. The church planters taught agricultural, health and technology skills as well as Bible. Nearly all the training was oral because that is how the local people learned.

Bible stories were told in sequence in the evenings after the agricultural teaching was finished. Villagers who showed interest were invited to join groups that listened to more Bible stories broadcast over FEBA radio. Then they discussed what they had heard. The same core Bible stories were made available on cassette tape.

Today, with thousands of illiterate believers, there is danger of heresy. "The locals are now addressing aberrant doctrinal beliefs through [Bible] stories."[17] They have found that lay pastors trained this way maintain more orthodox doctrine than literate pastors in the same people group who are trained in seminaries.

Heresy can happen anywhere. In the West our idols may be money, sex and power. To avoid "blaspheming the Holy Spirit," we have to test the spirits, wherever we are (Mk 3:29; 1 Jn 4:1).

WHEN YOU ARE NOURISHED

What exactly is the Holy Spirit? Part of the Trinity, we are told. This is one of the hardest concepts humans ever have had to grasp. It took theologians three centuries to find words to describe it. Scholars talk about three personal centers within one essence. None is subordinate to the others. "There are not three roles played by one actor or three relationships to us sustained by one agent, but three coequal and co-eternal entities within one entity, each being God in just the same full sense as the other two."[18] All three are present in creation, in redemption and in sanctification.

At the core of the Trinity is love. God is love. Even before anything was created, God loved. But who? From the beginning the three persons of the deity existed in relationship, and love flowed between them.

The Spirit is God's empowering presence with his people, in the words of Gordon Fee. First of all, the Spirit initiates radical transformation. Early in his ministry Jesus advised a good man named Nicodemus, "You must be born again" (Jn 3:7).

"Be a fetus?" Nicodemus wondered.

"No. Be born of the Spirit," Jesus explained.

Next, the Spirit gives us the assurance that God has adopted us (Rom 8:15-16; Gal 4:6; Eph 1:13), helps us grow morally, protects us from sin and evil, gives us hope for the future, connects us with other people, fills us with love, and makes us more like Jesus (2 Cor 3:17-18). The Spirit also guides us. While God is a mystery far beyond, the Spirit who knows God's mind can channel wisdom to us (1 Cor 2:4; Rom 8:26-27)—not just facts, data and information, but multilevel, holistic understanding framed in relationship (Rom 8:15-16, 26-27; 1 Cor 2:4; 2 Cor 3:17-18; Gal 4:6; Eph 1:13).

The Spirit bestows *gifts* like supernatural healing. Daniel Ruffinati in Argentina was liberated from paranoid schizophrenia miraculously, and Ramkali in India was cured of a snakebite. The Spirit also nurtures *fruits* like "love, joy, peace, patience, kindness, goodness, faithfulness, gentleness and self-control" (Gal 5:22-23). Daniel and Maria Elena have demonstrated these fruits, working gently and joyfully with mentally troubled criminals. Vishal and Ruth Mangalwadi have showed love, peace, patience and faithfulness in their dealings with potential murderers.

Such benefits are not just for our personal salvation or private improvement. In 1906 the foundational Pentecostal theologian Minnie Abrams published *The Baptism of the Holy Ghost and Fire*, in which she developed a "missiology of divine love." When someone receives the baptism of the Holy Spirit, she taught, "the fire of God's love will so burn within you that you will desire the salvation of souls. You will accept the Lord's commission to give witness and realize that he to whom all power is given has imparted some of that power to you, sufficient to do all that he has called you to do."[19] In particular, "speaking in tongues" is intended to propel a person to mission, a natural response to experiencing God's love, Abrams said.

Hudson Taylor demonstrated this "burning sufficiency." The Overseas Missionary Fellowship—which began as the China Inland Mission—today has over a thousand members. However, in the early years its success was dubious. There was no supporting organization. Interior China was unmapped. Violence flared in spurts throughout the region. "Walking in the Spirit" was something the founder, Hudson Taylor, learned to do in order to survive.

When a donor named Macartney visited Taylor on the field, Macartney was amazed.

> Here is a man almost sixty years of age, bearing tremendous burdens, yet absolutely calm and unruffled. Oh, the pile of letters! Any one of which might contain news of death, of shortness of funds, or riots or serious trouble. Yet all were opened, read and answered with the same tranquility. . . . He knew nothing of rush or hurry, of quivering nerves or vexation of spirit. He knew there was a peace passing all understanding, and that he could not do without it. . . . Yet he was delightfully free and natural.[20]

Macartney said to Taylor, "You are occupied with millions, I with tens. . . . Yet I am worried and distressed, while you are always calm.

Do tell me what makes the difference."

Something happened, Taylor answered. He hadn't always been peaceful. When the mission first began to grow, he felt overwhelmed, as though the weight of the world was on his shoulders. Would he make a mistake that would cost people their lives? And sometimes the work was pure drudgery.

Then he learned to draw nourishment from the Spirit of Jesus, moment by moment, like a branch drawing sap from the stem of a vine (Jn 15).

"My dear Macartney," Taylor concluded, "the peace you speak of is in my case more than a delightful privilege, it is a necessity. . . . I could not possibly get through the work I have to do without the peace of God 'which passes all understanding' keeping my heart and mind."[21]

Energy flows when you are nourished. Christians around the world demonstrate that. Sundar trekking in Tibet, Daniel in Argentina, Vishal in India, Faridah in her Muslim country, Mannu in Nepal and Hudson Taylor in China discovered that God's Spirit empowers people. Yet this life, this energy, is not something we can control. We cannot package it. As Eugene Peterson wryly observes, Moses did not take a photo of the burning bush to show people back home. Isaiah did not record a CD of the singing seraphim. The apostle John did not reduce his visions of Jesus to a bunch of power points.[22] These people were bowled over by God's presence. There was no way they could domesticate the Spirit. "Our 'God is a consuming fire' " (Heb 12:29).

IF YOU ASK HIM

It is morning in Oregon. Scarf around my mouth, mittened hands in my pockets, I stroll down the beach. Mist shrouds Haystack Rock. Gulls whirl and cry. Puffins, their bodies short and stubby like bumblebees, steamroller through the air, wings whirring.

Combers roll in endlessly. Foam breaks like lace. Thirteen hours away, where this water laps on the opposite shore, my Asian friends are settling into sleep. What a wonder this world is. There is so much beyond what I am able to grasp. I glimpse edges, touch fringes. And yearn. Not for measurement but for mystery. Not for best practices but for beautiful presence. Not for standards but for Spirit. For the reality beyond.

"If anyone is thirsty, let him come to me and drink," Jesus said. (Jn 7:37)

No eye has seen,
    no ear has heard,
no mind has conceived
    what God has prepared for those who love him. (1 Cor 2:9)

How much more will your Father in heaven give the Holy Spirit to those who ask him? (Lk 11:13)

6

AXIS OF HOPE

Jesus' People in the Muslim World

Even as a teenager Hanif Avarsaji was passionate about poetry. Rhythm pumped in his blood. Lines shimmered in his brain. If you love poetry, Iran is a good place to be. These people treasure their poets. For love, for social commentary, for expressing our longing for God, what is better than a poem?

In school Hanif immersed himself in Persian literature, including the great poets like Hafez, Saadi and Fardousi. At religious festivals he listened to recitations in honor of the day. Little by little, he began to experiment with creating his own poems.

One day Hanif was invited to recite in the mosque. People liked it.

"His words are fresh—"

"And the thoughts are penetrating. You can tell that he has studied and meditated. Let's invite him again."

Soon Hanif became a regular fixture at mosque events. Every ceremony required an original one-hundred-line poem which Hafez wrote and recited from memory within the space of five minutes. This required a rapid-fire delivery.

Looking for opportunities, eventually Hanif migrated to California. Immediately the local Shiite mosques drew him into their orbit. Again he was in demand as a poet. "Within two months, all the Iranians here knew me," he says.

In other circles Hanif encountered Iranians who had become followers of Jesus.

"What is this?" he wondered.

"Come and see," they answered and invited him to a Bible study.

Although he attended a few times and even dropped into an Iranian church for a couple of services, Hanif was not impressed by the teaching.

"They're friendly people. And they seem to be ethical. And god-fearing. But it's nonsense to think that Jesus is God," he said.

To make ends meet while he was still learning American ways, Hanif worked at Taco Time. One day the pastor of the Iranian church walked in. He was a tall, dignified man.

"What's he doing here? He looks completely out of place in Taco Time," Hanif mumbled to himself. "Well, he's in my section, so I'd better take his order. Anyway, he won't remember me."

"May I help you, sir?" he asked the pastor.

"Yes, Hanif," the pastor answered.

"You remember me?" Hanif blurted.

"I remember you. I know your name. That's why I came into Taco Time. I just wanted to tell you that God loves you."

Something like electricity coursed through Hanif. He was so overcome that he rushed to the supervising manager. "I have an emergency! I have to leave!" He whipped off his apron and fled home.

All that afternoon Hanif talked to God. He had received a Bible at the Bible study group. Now he opened and read it. "I felt there was something right about Jesus," Hanif remembers. "Maybe he could be God after all." In the evening he fell on his knees and opened his heart, and Jesus came to him.

Persian rap videos. Today Hanif is in charge of TV programming for youth on a Christian station that is beamed into Iran via satellite seven

days a week, twenty-four-hours a day. This did not happen immediately, however. There were a lot of spiritual bondages to cut through.
Vices. Bad relationships. Not only did Hanif have to shed old sins, he
also had to learn the gospel, the great story recorded in the Old and
New Testaments and the doctrines and the history of God's people. He
enrolled in Bible school in California.

Hanif brought his mother and brother to Jesus, but he was rejected
by the Islamic community.

"You're not welcome here," said his former friends when he dropped
in at the mosque to see them.

Meanwhile, the Iranian pastor had been observing Hanif. "Would
you be interested in writing for our TV ministry?" he invited. "The
salary is tiny, but the opportunity is huge."

Hanif accepted at once and began to develop the youth
programming.

Questions boil just under the surface among the youth in Iran.
Will I get a good job? Will I find true love? Should I try drugs? Why
are there quarrels in my family? Why is Islam so rigid and negative?
Why not experiment with drugs? Will Iran be attacked? Where can
I find happiness? And back to drugs, which blight the lives of many
Iranian teens.

Hanif never speaks badly about Islam. He talks reverently about
God and shows the beauty of Jesus. Some Muslim parents, desperate
for positive influences on their children, require their teens to watch
Hanif's programs. The teens get interested and continue watching on
their own.

What do they see? The studio looks like a tastefully designed living
room. Since Iranians are very stylish, the room is decorated appropri-
ately. In this comfortable room Hanif takes calls beamed from Iran. If it
is a repeat caller, Hanif refers to their earlier conversation and asks, "Did
God make any difference in that problem we discussed last time?" Then
Hanif prays. Discussions of contemporary issues, lots of music and chat
rooms are supplemented by e-mail follow-up. And the youth of Iran are
ushered into the presence of Jesus.

When I visited Hanif in his office, I saw his first two Persian Christian rap videos. One opens with a man lying on train tracks. Every couple of seconds the camera shifts to a different angle. Poetry pounds and throbs. Is there a meaning to life? The viewer ponders the train tracks. Then a lovely woman emerges out of a mist, singing beautifully and simply about Jesus.

The second video opens with a man in the throes of withdrawal from a drug. Jesus comes to him in a vision. Just a few minutes long, the videos are compelling. Training as a mosque poet has prepared Hanif to introduce thousands—maybe millions—of Iranians to Jesus through sharp rhythms and words.

Hanif is a Christian outside of Iran. What about those inside? Consider Nadia and Ferouz.

"TO STAY AND BE A LIGHT": NADIA AND FEROUZ

"Mama, who will take care of us if you go to jail?" Eight-year-old Nadia trembled. Men in uniforms had knocked loudly on their front door. When Daddy answered, they had grabbed him by the arm. They said he was a bad Muslim because he worshiped Jesus.

He had been "arrested," whatever that meant, and now he was sentenced to prison. Nadia knew she wouldn't see him for a very long time. And he might be hurt.

But Mama too?

"The children will be placed in a Muslim home," the court decreed. Nadia and her siblings were separated. She arrived at the foster home as a little girl still playing with dolls. The years passed. Her body changed. She began to notice fashions. And boys.

Nadia wished she could talk to Mama about her feelings and go shopping with her for grown-up clothes. Where was Mama? Still in prison? If she got out, would she be able to find them? Nobody told Nadia anything.

In the home where Nadia lived now, she was supposed to join the family in prayer regularly, holding her hands above her shoulders, falling to her knees, touching her forehead to the floor, reciting prayers to Allah in the Arabic language, a tongue foreign to Iranians.

Where was Jesus in all this? If he really cared for her, Nadia thought, why did he allow this to happen? Why didn't he rescue her and bring their family back together? Why did Mama and Daddy think Jesus was so important that they were willing to lose everything for him?

As she grew to be a young woman old enough to make her own choices, Nadia began receiving offers of benefits if she would convert to Islam. "Nadia, there is very good scholarship if you join the Muslim youth association . . . a lovely summer camp in the mountains . . . a painting workshop conducted by a terrific artist . . . concerts . . . new software upgrades. All you need to do is recite the creed publicly: 'There is no God but Allah, and Muhammed is his Prophet.' "

Would that be so bad? For concerts and camps and computers? But Nadia remembered her father and her mother. She remembered the Scripture verses that were sealed in her heart. "My parents did not suffer in vain," she determined. "They stuck to their commitments. They knew how to value something. I'm not going to throw that away."

Then she met Ferouz. Christian friends introduced them. He was intriguing and mysterious in some ways, but he radiated a kindness that made her feel warm and protected, and a steadfastness dependable as a rock.

"What do you want to do with your life, Nadia?" he asked her one day.

"To serve the Lord," she answered.

"Let's do it together," he smiled.

So Nadia and Ferouz were married and learned that the love of God nurtures magnificent human love too. Every morning they caught busses for their jobs, and every evening they came home to tea and someone who cared just for them.

"Do you remember Shirin?" Ferouz asked one evening as he reached for another handful of pistachio nuts.

"Who?"

"You met her at my school picnic last year. The third-grade teacher."

"Hmm. Yes, maybe. Tall, slim, graceful, with a longish nose. Is that the one? Kind of shy, but with a pretty smile?"

"Yes, that's her." Farouz agreed. "I'd like you to invite her for tea. Her husband has left her. She's struggling."

"Of course," Nadia said.

In the workplace and the neighborhood, people found that they could talk to Ferouz and Nadia. The couple listened, and then they prayed. People were comforted and encouraged. Naturally the pair talked about Jesus, the source of their energy and hope. Some friends believed.

With these young believers Nadia and Ferouz read the Bible, helping them understand God's majesty and love and plan for us. They probed Jesus' stories and actions, and marveled at his death and his resurrection. They traced the great sweep of believers through the Old and New Testaments. People learned to pray, to face troubles, to build godly habits and to make wise decisions.

"So many are desperate for something more. What a privilege it is to be able to share Jesus with them," Nadia commented.

One night uniformed men knocked loudly on their door.

"Oh God, is history repeating itself?" Nadia cried.

It seemed so. Nadia and Ferouz were pulled apart.

"You will come with us," said the officer, as he gripped Ferouz' arm. "The woman will go with those other officers. The rest of you," he directed his squad, "spread out and search this place thoroughly. Look for any incriminating documents."

In their court appearance the judge was harsh. "You have broken the law of the land," he thundered. "You have introduced a foreign religion and induced Iranians to turn away from their true faith. You have led them into apostasy. This is a crime worthy of death."

Ferouz and Nadia were jailed, he in one prison and she in another.

In time, for unknown reasons, they were released.

"We are free from prison, but we are not free from persecution. They still have a file against us stating that we work with foreigners to blaspheme Islam and the penalty is death," Nadia says. "Miraculously until today we are alive. We do not know what the future holds but we believe God has chosen us to stay and be a light in this Iranian city."

WHEN THEY MURDER

One fifth of the world's people are Muslims, ranging from Javanese to Uzbeks to French to Nigerians. Since it is impossible to describe them all, we will focus in this book on one group, the Iranians, also known as Persians.[1] Some elements in the Iranian Christians' story are common to believers in other Muslim societies. Yet ultimately every people's story is unique and deserves attention on its own.

Reliable sources estimate that there are more than 800,000 followers of Jesus inside Iran. But following Jesus is costly. Some believers are fired from their jobs. Others are imprisoned. Even when they live in distant countries, some Iranians have been grabbed by masked men, shoved into cars and whisked away. In recent years numerous prominent pastors have been killed, including Mehdi Dibaj, Haik Hovsepian-Mehr, chairman of the Council of Protestant Ministers in Iran, and Tateos Michaelian, head of the Bible Society of Iran.

Muslim regimes do not foster religious freedom. Certain minorities like Jews, Baha'is and some ancient Christian groups are tolerated because these people never have been Muslim. It is conversion out of Islam that is prohibited.

Of course there are converts whose Muslim families accept them. And there are countries with so many new believers that no government can keep tabs on them. But resistance to conversion is increasing worldwide. It may be harder for a Muslim to follow Jesus now than it was twenty years ago.[2]

For example, the Malaysian government supported religious freedom until the mid-1990s. Since then Malaysia has hosted compulsory "reeducation" camps for Muslims who call Jesus Lord.

Consider Lina Joy. She was in love. Her fiancé was a Christian. It was not legal for them to marry in Malaysia since she was born Muslim, even though she had been worshiping openly as a Christian for many years. She asked the government to register a change of religion on her ID card so she could marry. Her case wound its way to federal court. In 2008 the high court judges rejected Lina Joy's request, ruling that a person "cannot, at one's whims or fancies, renounce or embrace a religion."[3]

Why this persecution? Are Muslims crueler that other people?

In Iran, rallies roar "Death to Israel! Down with the Great Satan, America!" Participants raise rifles and shake them in the air. Iran has armed Muslim movements in the Middle East like Hezbollah and Hamas. Because of this violent ethos the International Atomic Energy Agency has slapped sanctions on Iran for not complying with mandates on nuclear power. President George W. Bush dubbed Iran as a key member of the "axis of evil."

However, Iranians see the picture from another angle. "What about British imperialism throughout half of the twentieth century because of lust for Iranian oil?" they ask. "What about covert U.S. action that led to the replacement of Iran's legitimate ruler with the Shah (to help safeguard the British oil business)? Or U.S. support for our enemy Iraq in the 1980s Iran-Iraq War when a million Iranians lost their lives? And keep in mind," they add, "that modern Iran never has invaded another country."

Clearly the picture is complex. Muslims do value godliness, family, loyal friendships, modesty and honor. Iran's calendar dates back twenty-five hundred years to the reign of Cyrus the Great. His empire was the largest the world had ever seen. Civilizations even earlier than that were renowned for their order and humaneness. Water was piped a hundred miles from the mountains to the cities through underground tunnels to reduce evaporation. Good roads, a pony express mail system, standard weights and measures, widespread use of coins, and a coherent law system facilitated orderly living. (However, an early secret service—"the eyes and ears of the king"—hinted at the triumph of control over free-thinking.) Medicine, architecture, art and poetry flourished. Trade along the Silk Road passed through Iran. Foreigners who conquered Iran, like the Greeks and the Arabs, made use of the workable systems already in place.

Along with cultural and civil richness, Iran displays natural beauty. "Mountains stand so near you would almost think, as you walk on the roof at sunset, that by throwing out your hand you could touch the snow patches clinging to their steep sides," says one visitor.

With such a great heritage, why persecute Christians?

"If 'Islam' means 'submission to God,' how could converting *out* of Islam be an improvement?" a Muslim might answer. "If somebody stopped submitting to God—in other words, if he stopped being Muslim—would that make him a better person? Or improve his life? Or improve the society where he lives? Of course not. In the long run, even those who are tempted to leave the Muslim faith eventually will see that the good life means submission to God. So we don't want to introduce freedom of religion. It leads to ethical relativism and eventually moral garbage spread throughout the community."

With the best of intentions, Muslims squelch conversion. It is not allowed—and yet it happens and keeps happening.

AXIS OF HOPE

A new tier of leadership is developing among Iranian Christians from Muslim backgrounds. This makes sense in a situation where the old tier is likely to be incarcerated. Just a few years ago, the government arrested ten top leaders and made them sign an agreement that they would not baptize. Others were ready to take up the responsibility, so baptisms continued.

Big churches are not the goal. After Iranian believers heard about runaway Christian growth in China and weird heresies that developed when people believed faster than they could be taught, they committed themselves to small fellowships. When a group reaches twenty-five people, it may divide. Both groups are expected to grow. For example, two people who began meeting together a few years ago have seen their tiny fellowship give birth to more than twenty groups.[4]

Christian theological seminaries are not allowed. However, there are several training programs run by Iranian believers outside the country. These not only teach Bible, theology and practical ministry skills, but also offer a lot of prayer and counseling for believers under stress. Pent up emotions are released in a trustworthy context. Graduates return to Iran, and the effects reverberate.

Anyone can download the Persian New Testament from the Internet. A slim, printed copy in modern Farsi language fits easily into a shirt pocket.

As well as the Bible, Iranians have published over six hundred Persian-language Christian books in recent years. These are available through their own distribution networks such as the one run by Iranian Christians International. Numerous original music CDs have been created too.

Some Christians in Iran are not converts from Islam, and the government allows them more freedom of worship. These are members of historic Armenian and Assyrian churches. Other Christians are converts from the Jewish population that has resided here since the time of Esther. Because these people never have been Muslim, they are not considered "apostates" or heretics when they confess Jesus. They are not abandoning "submission to God" because they never have been submitted, from a Muslim point of view. Muslims can attend Armenian churches *providing they are not baptized*. Baptism is the watershed that symbolizes a move from Islam to Christendom.

Twenty years ago pastor Haik Hovsepian encouraged Armenian churches to worship in Farsi, the language that all Iranians speak, one of the oldest spoken languages in the world. When Persians poured into the churches, the government issued an ultimatum: All Persian believers must be reported.

The churches made a united response. None would report new believers to the government.[5]

Sadly, government intelligence agents infiltrated a network of fifty churches in 2008. The agents posed as sincere seekers who were responding to satellite gospel broadcasts. Church members were rounded up and forced to sign documents limiting their future association. Now groups keep more distance from each other in order to maintain security.

There are several networks of believers. Internationally, these include ELAM and Iranian Christians International. Inside Iran, young leaders recently took a three-day retreat to build strong ties and defuse misunderstanding and competitiveness before they arise.

Some Iranians feel called to take the gospel crossculturally. These missionaries are being sent to Afghans, Turks, Kurds, Uzbeks and tribes within Iran.

Clearly the church of Jesus among Iranians may be suffering, but it is also sophisticated. Iranian congregations are planted worldwide. There are at least three in Korea. This international presence adds strength. Seminaries and publishing houses, mission-sending programs, a corpus of indigenous worship music and TV broadcasting networks like Hanif's all are indications of maturity. They mark a church that is taking responsibility for its own future.

Believers like to quote Jeremiah 49. This contains a prophecy about Elam, a region and a reign that are a noble part of Iran's heritage. The text predicts violence and disaster. "I will scatter them to the four winds, / and there will not be a nation / where Elam's exiles do not go" (v. 36). But it ends in hope. "I will restore the fortunes of Elam / in days to come, / declares the LORD" (v. 39).

Jesus' people in Iran represent not an axis of evil but an axis of hope. They see the beauties as well as the sins of their country, and can envision its potential in the future. They pray God's blessing, God's protection, God's conviction of sin, God's transforming power and God's raising up Iranians to bless the nations just as their ruler Cyrus did so long ago (Is 45).

How Did the Gospel Come to Iran?

God has been in Iran all along, of course. God created the Iranian people and endowed them with the capacity to create the unique cultures of Persia. In Iran, as everywhere else, God communicates through nature, conscience and dreams and visions. He "gives light to everyone" (Jn 1:9 TNIV). He "wants all people to be saved and come to a knowledge of the truth" (1 Tim 2:4 TNIV).

Beyond this "general revelation," Iran has been blessed by witnesses to God's "special revelation" of himself. Daniel, Esther and Nehemiah lived there. As we saw in chapter one, these well-placed believers told emperors about the true God, and some of those emperors publicized God far and wide throughout their domains. Cyrus the Great helped God's chosen people return home from captivity. The wise men at Jesus' birth probably came from Iran and may have worked in the same department as Daniel had a few centuries earlier.

Iran received another influx of witnesses immediately after Jesus' time. In spite of Cyrus's offer, some Jews decided to stay in Persia rather than returning to Palestine. They continued to make pilgrimages to the temple in Jerusalem. Some of them were present when the Holy Spirit descended in power on the day of Pentecost, as described in Acts 2. Iranians participated in that flaming event—Parthians, Medes, Elamites and Mesopotamians.

It is hardly surprising that even before A.D. 500 there was a body of Christian literature in the Persian language. Cities like Herat and Meshed had bishops. One of the greatest missionary movements in all history went right through Iran, the Nestorian passage along the Silk Road, partly powered by Persian Christians.

Catholics arrived in the 1200s and Protestants in the early 1800s. Louis Esselstyn was one of the Protestants, a persevering man who would not give up. When Louis first traveled to the holy city of Meshed, a mob chased him. An unknown rescuer shoved him into the post office, locked the doors and later helped Louis slip away.

Twenty years later Louis came back. By this time he had lost most of his hair, grown a long red beard and spoke Persian fluently. He hiked in at the head of a mule train loaded with boxes of Persian Bibles. Once settled in Meshed, he made himself at home in the bazaars, joking, chatting and selling Bibles or just reading and discussing the contents. Some people kissed the Scriptures reverently as they received them.[6]

Where did Louis's Bibles come from? A man named Henry Martyn is responsible. In 1806 Henry went from England to India. Six years later, at the age of thirty-one, he was dead. What a waste! Or was it? In those six years Henry studied three languages in order to translate the Bible. While working on his Persian translation, he lived in Iran. There he finished the New Testament. Because of Henry's work, Iranians could read the New Testaments that Louis hefted into their bazaars.

Neither Henry nor Louis saw much fruit. As far as we know only one Iranian professed Jesus as Lord during all Louis's decades of witness. But they laid a foundation so that today people like Hanif and Nadia and Ferouz can have the Word in words they understand.

FIVE THOUSAND MILES ON THE BACK OF TRUCKS

"Can you eat anything and sleep anywhere?"

"Yes, I think so."

"Then I suggest that you consider Persia."[7]

It was 1918. William Miller was twenty-five, a Princeton graduate who felt called to be a missionary. Someone working in Iraq directed his attention to Iran. Over the next forty years William would travel fifty thousand miles across Iran, east and west and north and south, by foot, by cart, by donkey, by whatever means was at hand, in order to provide Bibles or simply to talk with interested people about Jesus. During one six-month period he witnessed in twenty-nine towns, riding five thousand miles, mostly on top of trucks hauling supplies.

When there were no trips and no visitors, William wrote. A basic compilation of Sunni Muslim doctrines had been translated into English, but there was nothing comparable for Shiite Muslim doctrines. Many Iranians are Shiites. While learning Persian—already having studied Arabic—William translated a book of Shiite doctrines from Arabic to English. The Royal Asiatic Society published it. Both Shiite and Western scholars benefited. Then William began writing in Persian, beginning with a commentary on Romans.

During the nineteenth and early twentieth centuries, missionaries like William set up clinics, hospitals and schools for girls as well as boys. During this period both Britain and Russia built roads across Iran. Britain wanted oil, and Russia wanted a water port. By 1944 the Anglo-Iranian oil company was reputed to be the biggest in the world, with forty thousand employees. Missionaries served refugees during the conflicts that erupted and remonstrated with foreign powers when their troops and citizens behaved badly, advocating for the Iranian people who could speak neither English nor Russian.

Sometimes missionaries shared the gospel in big multilanguage meetings. The first night might be in Armenian, the second in Persian and the third in Syriac. These languages were spoken by populations who had come to Jesus in different eras. Syriac was the religious language of the Assyrian Nestorians.

Most of all, Christians distributed Bibles. They were convinced that the Word of God has power. Sometimes they opened bookstores, tea rooms or market stalls where people could talk about the Bible. They sold it at low cost, occasionally just bartering a Bible for whatever small object a person offered. Eight or ten Christian men might eat together while studying the Bible, then split up two by two and go to homes and businesses to offer Scripture. Especially at Easter and Christmas, they would say, "This is our great festival. Would you like to read the story?"

How did Iranians respond? Consider Gasem.[8]

Wrapping the cheese. At the end of the work day Gasem often stopped by the bakery. "Please give me a loaf of pebble bread," he would request.

In this kind of bakery, dry fuel is piled on a pile of pebbles and set on fire. When the stones are hot enough, the baker brushes off the ashes, then lobs a hunk of dough as long as a bath towel onto the rocks. To bake the second side, he turns the bread over with a wooden paddle. When the bread is done, he brushes off the little stones that stick to it. This is pebble bread.

Next Gasem would buy goat cheese from the grocer. Then he would head home where the teapot was boiling and the family was waiting. They spread a large cloth over the carpet, laid out their cheese, bread and tea, and sat down on the floor to enjoy their supper.

One evening when Gasem unwrapped his cheese, his eye was caught by words on the paper covering it. As he read the page, he was drawn into a story about a man who hired people to work in his vineyard. No matter how early or late they were hired, all received a living wage (Mt 20:1-16). *How generous!* Gasem thought.

The next day he found another story on his cheese wrapping. By the third day, he was asking the grocer to wrap his cheese in a page from the book.

"Why not buy the whole thing?" the grocer offered.

So Gasem acquired a New Testament (minus several pages!) He knew God had given Jesus a sacred Scripture and was delighted to have his own copy. But where could it have come from? He pondered. He had never seen this book anywhere else.

"Probably from that foreigner who used to pass through here. The one who died in the famine," his brother suggested. That foreigner was Louis Esselstyn.

Thoughtfully, the brothers looked at the crumpled pages of the book.

"There is another American missionary here," Gasem's brother added. "He works at the hospital. Why don't we go see him?"

They did. They received the gift of a complete New Testament and weekly Bible studies. All their family members came to follow Jesus and were baptized.

Many dreams, many Paths. In William Miller's books, *Tales of Persia* and *My Persian Pilgrimage*, he introduces many Iranians who were touched by the Bible. Hasan looked for the truth in three countries, although he was enslaved by opium. The Bible helped him kick his drug habit. Saeed mocked Christians but was drawn by the story, and became a remarkable Christian doctor. Merat was a policeman who went wrong and was sentenced to be executed. Faithful Christian friends helped save him, and the Word came alive. Jalily was a successful businessman who heard the Word through his son's school, responded and became a Bible distributor himself. Behzad was a renowned artist who created miniature mosaics. After the Word touched him, his art was enriched by biblical motifs. Hasan received a Bible from his Iranian schoolteacher and compared it carefully with the Qur'an before he believed. Nusrollah had a dream that helped him understand the Scripture. Mehdi received the Bible as a six-year-old. His mother took it away from him. Many years later, when they were moving house, he found it, read it and believed.

Ahmad's story tugs at the heart. His family was multicultural, his father Iranian and his mother Spanish. His father had lived a corrupt life, and his mother had died young. But Ahmad remembered that when he was a little boy his mother had sung to him about Jesus.

When Ahmad met William Miller, he was eager to know more. As soon as he heard the good news, he believed. They met daily for Bible study. One day Ahmad was sick, so William visited him at home. There he saw Ahmad's mother's books, including *Pilgrim's Progress* and a Bible.

Written in a very fine hand in the Bible was an inscription that Ahmad could not decipher.

"Look at this," Ahmad said. "My mother wrote these words. But I can't read them. Can you?"

"Yes," William said. "Listen. Twenty years ago, when your mother was dying, she gave you to the Lord Jesus. She wrote, 'I hope my little one read this holy book and our Lord save him. Amen O Lord, I give my son to you. . . . I hope he becomes a good Christian.' "[9]

Developing mature leaders. Tehran bakes in the summer. Yet just ten miles from the city, the peak of Towchal stretches up 14,000 feet. This is part of the Alborz mountain range. During the hot season, urban dwellers escape here on day trips or longer vacations. There are villas with pools, flowery gardens and places to picnic and hike. Many people enjoy sleeping in tents.

A summer Bible school, the "Garden of Evangelism," was developed in one of these villas. Students earned certificates after they studied for nine months. The study was spread over three summers, for three months each summer.

"What did the students learn in this school?" Miller asks.

> They learned the Bible in the Persian language. They learned how Christians had taken the good news of Christ to all parts of the world. They learned how to explain to Muslims and Jews the truths that Christians believe. They learned also how to lead a meeting and how to deliver a talk. And they also learned how to keep their rooms clean . . . and how to wash dishes. They learned, too, how to live together in peace and love and how to forgive one another. Perhaps this was the hardest lesson of all![10]

They also played volleyball and hiked and climbed to promontories where they could sing and pray as they watched the sun go down.

Women's work for women. Not only men like William Miller but also women like Sarah Belle Sherwood spread the good news. Sarah arrived single in 1883, married in Iran and worked there until 1919.

On an evangelistic trip on horseback, lasting seventeen days and passing through twelve villages and two cities, Sarah encountered women's dreams. One woman took Sarah to the tiny enclosure where she milked sheep and goats. Four of her five sons joyfully caught and held the animals, "while the baby wandered about among them, throwing his arms around the neck of this one and that one and kissing them." Later in the evening the village woman brought a "little bride" to visit who was nine years old and had been married for two years.

Although no woman in this village could read, Sarah's goat-owning hostess confided that she had sent her oldest son to school where he had topped his class of 102 pupils. "My sons belong to God," she told Sarah. "He gave them to me to train for Him. When I say this, the women laugh at me and say, 'What kind of talk is this?' But it is true, is it not?"[11]

Daughters belong to God too. So missionaries started schools for girls. The women teachers had great hopes for their students. One wrote in 1880,

> There are several girls who have expressed a wish to become Christians. Oh how entirely helpless I feel in this work! Only the Holy Spirit can take of the things of the Spirit and make them felt by these hearts. Words cannot express the anxiety I feel to have these girls become not only Christians but such devoted, reliable Christians that they will be able to do the most possible good to the greatest number.[12]

They did not expect these girls merely to keep house. As the young women married "kind Christian husbands," their teachers believed this would give their graduates "a scope to work more effectually."

Although Mrs. L. C. Van Hook ran a school, she wrote, "Our daily work is to tell the story of the cross to those with whom we are thrown in the simplest possible manner." Sometimes this happened during informal visits, when a woman could offer a prayer or read a little bit of the Persian Bible. Sometimes it was during a planned group Bible study.

Sometimes it occurred in more unusual contexts. One rainy season 150 local women asked the missionaries to accompany them up the mountain to pray against landslides. Rain had been heavy, and streams were engorged. There was a small "prayer house" up the trail. "After the local women prayed, they wanted us to pray, and all gathered around us. There, on that mountain side, the rain falling slowly and gently, Miss J. stood and boldly preached 'Christ and him crucified' to this waiting company of 150. Then we sang, and she prayed. It was an impressive hour."[13]

Why recount all this history? Because we stand on the shoulders of others. Wherever we are in the world, crosscultural and local witnesses have written chapters in our story. In the early 1970s, for example, a group called Operation Mobilization sent summer teams to Iran to stir up interest in the Bible. These teams talked to so many people that eventually thirty thousand Iranians enrolled in Bible correspondence courses. It was a blip in history. By 1979 the fundamentalist revolution had erupted and religious freedom was no more. Nevertheless, the Bible had been introduced to many. Who can say how much this may have fertilized the movement to Jesus which is occurring today?

CALLED TO WITNESS, NOT CONVERT

Jesus calls Muslims—Iranians, Arabs, Indians and Pakistanis, Indonesians and Uzbeks—through visions, dreams, healings and exorcisms, through Bible stories—especially stories of Jesus—through prayer for their needs and through friendship.

Christians don't convert people. Only God converts. Christians *do* witness, however. (So do Muslims. They call their witness *da'wah*.) We will trace four themes in Christian witness among Muslims.

Jesus is Lord. Muslims think it blasphemes God to say he took on human form. Jesus is a great prophet, but not God.

Yet the Muslim scripture, the Qur'an, speaks of Jesus as the Word of God *(kalima)*, the Spirit of God *(ruh)* and the Messiah. It speaks of his virgin birth, his admirable life, his miracles and his role in the final judgment at the end of history.[14]

Many Muslims are intrigued by Jesus, and the more they learn about him, the more they want to know. Through Internet, radio, TV, correspondence courses, videos, CDs and face-to-face Bible studies, witnesses who focus on Jesus cannot go far wrong.

Jesus died for us. This statement points to the second big difference between Muslims and Christians. Muslims believe God would not allow his holy prophet Jesus to die the shameful death of a criminal. So, although the Jews wanted to kill Jesus, God rescued Jesus and stuck somebody else on the cross. Some Muslims think it was Judas who hung on the cross. Others think it was an angel.

There is a festival that can help Muslims understand Jesus' death. All Muslims celebrate the *Eid al-Adha* every year. This feast commemorates the day when Abraham offered God his son, but God provided an animal instead so that Abraham's son was saved. Muslim families kill a goat or sheep ritually, distribute meat to the poor, invite friends and enjoy God's good gifts in the larger context of his care throughout history. The fundamental meaning of this event is the same for both Muslims and Christians: God himself will provide a sacrifice. This foreshadows God's offering his own Son in our place. Many Muslims glimpse the truth when it is set in this framework.

Some believers celebrate Good Friday at the time of this annual feast, instead of the day when it falls in the Western Christian calendar. To them it makes sense to connect these events. It also provides a springboard for natural witness.

Jesus' people worship like Muslims. Some of Jesus' people in Central Asia circumcise their baby boys in church. Why not? A baby must be dedicated to God. Circumcision is a sign. The loveliest place to do this is the place where we worship.

These circumcisions become venues for witness. To take part in the event, Muslim relatives and friends crowd into the church for the first time in their lives and join the feast that follows.

Contextualizing worship raises many questions, however. These reverberate among Christians who are witnessing to Muslims. Should Muslims who follow Jesus continue to pray five times a day, reciting the traditional Muslim prayers to the Creator? Should they join in the month-long fast of Ramadan? Or recite the Qur'an, the Muslim scripture? Or worship in the mosque, intoning the creed "There is no God but Allah, and Muhammad is his Prophet"? Or go on pilgrimage to Mecca? Or continue to call themselves Muslims, emphasizing their submission to God? Should Messianic mosques be planted within the Islamic community?

Too much contextualization poses several dangers, which may be classed as doctrinal, communal, sacramental and generational. Consider the importance of doctrine. Believers who are occupied with Muslim worship practices may not develop a mature and balanced biblical worldview unless they have a sustained source of teaching outside of Islam.

Second, consider the importance of Christian community. Muslims emphasize community, *ummah*. Jesus emphasized this (Jn 13; 17). Jesus' people are called his body, his house, his family, the branches of his vine. Believers need to know and love each other. We were never meant to live as lone believers.

Third, consider the importance of the sacraments. How vital are baptism and the Lord's Supper? Many Muslim-background believers consider these extremely significant. Can Jesus' followers experience these sacraments and remain Muslims?

Fourth, consider the next generation. Children need multiple adult role models to show them what it means to obey Jesus as Lord. How will the next generation of believers develop?

Beyond these considerations, deep contextualization may not work for everybody because people have widely different personal histories. Some believers' journeys have led them to identify more with the larger Christian community. This is simply the way their stories have developed. They don't feel at home with Muslim forms. Instead, they feel excluded when worship forms are contextualized radically.

Certainly all of us should treasure our people's way of life. While idolatry and exploitation are woven through Muslim cultures, this is true of other cultures too. Local believers everywhere have to decide what to affirm and what to reject. Meanwhile, regardless of contextualization theory, Muslims keep coming to Jesus.[15]

Jesus was a Middle Easterner. Jesus is closer to Arabs than to Western-ers. He spoke a language related to Arabic. Some of the very first Chris-tians were Palestinians. Tragically, Muslims today do not connect Jesus' followers with this heritage. They connect Jesus with those who attack them. They think of the Crusades, Western colonization, the Iraq War, Christian support of Israel against Palestinians and threats against Iran as part of the "axis of evil."

On the other side, many Christians think of Muslims as terrorists, when in reality this applies only to a few. We need a 180-degree para-digm shift. We need to appreciate Muslim cultures in our hearts. In many countries Muslims introduced monotheism, literacy and ethics based on what they thought was the law of God. During the Middle Ages, Muslims pioneered medical, mathematical, scientific, architec-tural and engineering breakthroughs. They kept the wisdom of Greece and Rome alive throughout Europe's "Dark Ages."

As for family values, while outsiders can tell horror stories about polygamy and child marriages and honor killings, Muslims criticize the so-called Christian nations for neglecting the elderly, promulgating pornography, leaving singles without spouses, ogling women, condon-ing widespread promiscuity and the like.

In view of the wrong things Christians have thought and said about Muslims, we must cultivate humility. This includes admitting freely that Jesus was a Middle Easterner, closer to an Arab than an American.

IF YOU SEARCH FOR ME

One day when Simin was four years old she heard screams.[16] She scram-bled up the stairs on the outside of her house and ran across a series of connected flat roofs until she looked down on a yard where people were washing a baby. They wrapped it up and traipsed off in a procession. She crept down the nearest stairs and followed.

Soon she was barreling back into her own house. "Grandmother, why do they take people and put them in a hole in the ground?"

"Because people die. Where have you—"

"Why do they die?"

"Fate. When it's their fate, when it's their time, they have to go. We all have to—"

"When they die, where do they go?"

"Ah, there's the mystery. They say there is a bridge ten thousand times finer than human hair. If you are good enough, you will be able to cross it when you die. Then you'll be in paradise. But you, with all your naughtiness, you're more likely to end up in hell—"

Hell. Simin began to have nightmares.

When soldiers came to enlist her cousin in the army, she thought that they were demons who had come to take her to hell. She fled out the back door and stayed away all day.

In the evening she went down to the river to wash her face and hands. There she saw a man floating on the water. He had an unusually kind face.

"What are you doing here?" he asked her.

"Washing my hands," she answered.

"Why don't you do that at home?"

Simin explained that she was afraid.

"What are you worried about?" the man smiled. "I am the one who decides who goes to heaven and who goes to hell. And you are going to be with me."

Peace flowed over Simin. For many years she treasured that glimpse of something more, so different from her grandmother's picture of the supernatural. As a young woman, Simin immigrated to the United States and entered nursing school. But she never stopped asking, "Is there really a God? What is he like? Can we know him?"

When she dissected a cat in anatomy class, she marveled at its intricate design. "Who made you?" she kept asking.

"There is no god," her professor advised her. "Evolution has produced us. So enjoy. You're young. Life is before you."

"Even a blind person knows there's a god," Simin retorted. "But I want to communicate with him!"

She took long walks into the hills, asking, "Where are you?" Once she even questioned shoppers as they walked out of a supermarket. "Excuse me, Ma'am. Do you know God?" But she didn't find anybody who did. Finally she wrote God a letter.

Do you remember when I was talking to You in my anatomy class? I'm from Iran. I'm a young girl. Everybody thinks I have so much. But I don't have anything because I don't have You.

God, I'm tired of running my life. Would You make friends with fools? If You would, here is one. I'm very lonely. All the things that other people on earth enjoy don't do anything for me. But I confess I'm nothing but trouble for You. . . .

I don't know what mailman to give this letter to. Yet if You're powerful enough to create the human body, You're powerful enough to see me writing this letter.

I don't know what to call You. Some call You energy. Some Allah. Some Buddha. You tell me who You are. I know You must have a personality.

Simin waited. There was no response. She became discouraged. What was the point of living? Suicide began to look better than meaninglessness. One day she cried out, "Oh God, either take my life and use it, or let me take it."

Suddenly a big wind whooshed around her even though she was indoors. All at once she was overwhelmed by her inadequacy to negotiate with the Creator. She bowed over. Then bliss pumped through her. It seemed that God said, "You are being born again." All night long she bathed in this incredible presence.

In the morning her doorbell rang. A woman handed her a paper. Opening it, Simin read, "Here I am! I stand at the door and knock. If anyone hears my voice and opens the door, I will come in and eat with them, and they with me" (Rev 3:20 TNIV).

Simin raised her eyebrows. "Who said this?"

"The Lord Jesus Christ," the woman answered.

No! No! No! Simin shouted inside. *I'm never going to give up the Muslim religion. If this is what You wanted to show me, God, I shouldn't have started looking for You.*

The woman invited Simin to go to church. Having had such a bliss-ful experience of God's presence the night before, Simin felt obligated to testify to everybody, even Christians. So she went with the woman. During the open microphone period in the worship service, Simin shared her experience.

"Simin, would you like to be born again?" the pastor asked her quietly.

"I *am* born again! Didn't you hear what I said?"

"But do you follow Jesus? There is no other way to be born again except through Jesus. He is the way, the truth, and the life—"

"No, Jesus is only a prophet as far as I know. And you people ought to fall down in awe and reverence and worship God, not a man."

When the service ended, someone gave Simin a Bible. Though she intended never to return to the church, she read the Bible. Ten days later a letter arrived from the church, asking standard questions for new visitors.

I'd better let these people know there's no way I'm going to become a Christian, Simin decided. So she answered all the questions with negatives.

"Are you interested in learning more about the Christian life?"

"No!"

"Would you like someone to pray with you?"

"No!"

And so on.

Planning to mail the letter, Simin scooted across the bed where she had been sitting while she wrote. As she moved to get up, she had a vi-sion. Bare feet walked toward her. She saw the hem of a garment with a Jewish design. The vision put its hand on her face and said, "Go to sleep. The Lord is with you."

Drowsiness overcame her. She fell back on the bed and slept sweetly until morning. When she awoke, bits of the vision came back.

"God, who was that Jewish man in my room last night?" she asked sleepily.

"The Lord Jesus Christ. The Lord Jesus Christ. The Lord Jesus Christ." Voices murmured it over and over. Unearthly music swelled.

Simin rolled out of bed and fell flat on her face. "O Lord Jesus, forgive me," she cried. "I don't know if you know my background. I'm from Iran. I'm a Muslim. It's so hard for us to think of you as God . . . "

She went back to the church, asked for the microphone and told what had happened to her. That was twenty years ago. Since then she has demonstrated great gifts in evangelism and in healing. Today she is an elder in a two-thousand-member church. Her favorite verse is Jeremiah 29:13, "You will seek me and find me when you seek me with all your heart."

A FATHER'S PRAYER ON THE DEATH OF HIS SON

Iranians are coming to Jesus. Many are paying a high price. Bahram Deqani-Tafti was gifted with potential and brimmed with the love of Jesus. He had just returned to Iran from study in England when he was murdered. At his funeral his father offered this prayer:

O God, we remember not only Bahram, but also his murderers.
Not because they killed him in the prime of his youth and made our hearts bleed and our tears flow.

Not because with this savage act they have brought further disgrace on the name of our country among the civilized nations of the world.

But because through their crime we now follow thy footsteps more fully in the way of sacrifice;

The terrible fire of this calamity burns up all selfishness and possessiveness in us;

Its flame reveals the depth of depravity and meanness and suspicion, the dimension of hatred and the measure of sinfulness in human nature,

It makes obvious as never before our need to trust in God's love as shown in the cross of Christ and his resurrection.

Love which makes us face our hate toward our persecutors,

Love which brings patience, forbearance, courage, loyalty, humility, generosity, greatness of heart,

Love which more than ever deepens our trust in God's final victory and his eternal designs for the Church and for the world,

Love which teaches us how to prepare to face our own day of death.

O God, Bahram's blood has multiplied the fruit of the Spirit in the soil of our souls.

So when his murderers stand before You on the Day of Judgment, remember the fruit of the spirit by which they have enriched our lives, and forgive.[17]

7

CATASTROPHE

"What is the punishment for child marriage?"

A tiny whirlwind of dust swirled. Women sitting on the ground covered their noses with their saris but kept right on chanting out the answer. "Punishment for child marriage? One month in jail for the parents and all concerned."

"What are basic needs?" the drill continued.

"Food, clothing, health treatment, education, housing, rightful work, and rightful rest," the women recited.

"What are the fundamental rights of women?" "What must police consider before making an arrest?" Questions flew and answers swarmed back. Another legal workshop for women was underway thanks to the Bangladesh Rural Action Committee.[1]

Village educators have conducted over one hundred thousand of these "legal literacy" courses. Two million poor women have graduated from them. The trainers are local women who receive some pay for surveying land, a skill which they learn during the course. When they conduct the workshops, however, they are volunteering their services free of charge.

Dowry issues top the list of legal problems facing women in Bangladesh. Brides who do not bring enough dowry may be tortured. Divorce complications are another problem. Mutilation by acid is a third. A woman who gets out of line may have acid thrown on her. It will burn and dissolve her flesh. Leaders of women's associations in some neighborhoods have been disabled by acid, simply because people objected to women organizing. Rape, trafficking of women, very early marriage, inhumane punishments and dire poverty are other blights. Women here need to know their options so they can develop coping strategies.

The BRAC legal workshop is a course lasting twenty-two days. It puts tools into women's hands. What can they do about an acid attack, for example? There are hospitals where they can receive free treatment. There is an Acid Survivors Foundation. And there is legal action, which recently saw three acid throwers sentenced to death. In the workshops, women learn Muslim and Hindu law regarding family and inheritance, as well as bits of civil, criminal and land law. They also learn how to do local arbitration, which can solve many conflicts when women know their rights.

FACING TROUBLE

Trouble takes us unaware. A woman leaves the vegetable market planning to ask about her children's homework after the evening meal. Suddenly she is drenched in acid, burning, blinded. Boys play soccer. Out of nowhere a tsunami roars in and swallows them all. A family is planning a holiday when they learn that one of them has cancer. Trouble takes us by surprise. We go about our work, our fun, our love and our petty squabbles. Then, in the blink of an eye, an abyss opens under our feet.

What should we do? Facing a sudden catastrophe or, on a broader scale, facing the systemic evils of racism, poverty, injustice, disease and ecological disaster, how should Jesus' people respond? When newscasters broadcast photos of a tidal wave or a famine, our churches often will send money. Yet the larger catastrophe is the silent hunger, sickness and death that go on year after year. To a significant degree these evils are preventable. This is the huge material-physical disaster, whether or not it is covered in the news.

I have lived through devastating typhoons in the Philippines. But those storms didn't scare and sear me as much as one Christian woman I met in a fishing village.

"I'm in pain," she grimaced as we threaded our way between bamboo houses.

"What's the problem?" I asked.

"Urinary tract infection."

"Can't you get medicine?"

"Yes, I'm saving money from our catch every day. So, in twenty-five days I'll have enough for the pills."

My sister. Subject to an indignity of pain and waiting that I would never tolerate. After all, I have my rights. This little incident crystallized something for me. Catastrophe is not always big drama. Sometimes it is just the routine suffering that could be stopped and isn't.

Today I live in the same city as Bill Gates. He and his wife Melinda have given away $40 billion to reduce global poverty. Taking early retirement, they plan to devote their own efforts directly to this struggle. Their foundation researches solutions and delivers them.

Most of us who follow Jesus don't have great wealth. But we do have some discretionary funds. Equally important, we have education and connections. How can we put these to work to serve the poor and oppressed?

Here are some key principles.

Know when to do charity, when to do development and when to do advocacy. If people are bleeding from injuries or dying of thirst, that is not the time to conduct a small-business seminar. Those people need survival help right away. In the long run, though, most of our energy should focus on long-term development rather than short-term charity.

Production is not the deepest problem, however. There is enough food in the world to feed everyone adequately. On a global scale, obesity is more pervasive than malnourishment. The root problem is unequal distribution. Advocacy toward a more equitable spread of resources, infrastructure and opportunities is needed at local, national and international levels.

Sustainable development is best. Programs are not much good if they are not affordable. Nor will such programs be sustained over the long term. Subsidies should be small. Even if it means no Internet in the office, fans instead of air conditioning, motorcycles instead of jeeps, or generic medicines or even local medicinal plants, a sustainable program is worth these inconveniences.

Value-added development is best. Selling crops or vegetables or lumber doesn't earn as much as if those products receive some processing. Sunflowers can be crushed into oil. Grains and lentils and peas can be ground into flour. Wood can be carved.

Participatory development is best. "We did it ourselves!" is the best praise for a project. This requires spending a lot of time with people and listening to them. They may want projects different from the ones that outsiders envisioned.

God designed us to have good relationships with him, with others, with creation and with ourselves. All of these are marred by sin, but the self-concepts of the poor and the nonpoor are warped differently. The poor may be twisted by shame, while the nonpoor may enjoy a false sense of superiority, a mistaken belief that their success is entirely the result of their own efforts.

To combat this distortion poor people need to be asked repeatedly: What do you think? This needs to happen when community problems are being identified, when projects are being designed and when evaluations and modifications are made. Participatory development contrasts with "blueprint development" in which preplanned programs are unloaded on a community like a bunch of McDonald's franchises.[2]

Integrated development is best. "Minimalist" programs can grow fast. They simply loan money and make sure it is paid back. Their focus and procedures are clear. They don't get bogged down with other concerns. However, while they can reduce the vulnerability of the very poor, they don't go far enough. To maintain significant improvements, a more holistic strategy is needed. In his book *Ending Global Poverty* Stephen Smith advocates eight simultaneous components of a successful development project. These include

1. health

2. basic education

3. credit and insurance

4. functioning markets

5. phones and Internet

6. nondegraded environment

7. personal empowerment to gain freedom from exploitation

8. community empowerment for participation in the wider world

The women's legal workshop described at the beginning of this chapter is part of an integrated development model.

On the negative side, such components often add costs and therefore retard sustainability. When Christian projects include evangelism or discipleship in their goals, they face similar problems. Structured witness and discipling activities can add 15 percent to overhead costs, according to one research study.[3] Tough-minded businessmen who want projects to grow quickly in order to achieve economies of scale, do not like this complexity. In the long run, however, integrated development yields more wholesome, balanced communities as neighbors move up the economic ladder together.

Christian development is best. Non-Christians can do excellent development work. Yet "there is a God-shaped vacuum in the heart of every human being which cannot be filled by any created thing, but only by God the Creator made known through Jesus Christ."[4] If humans need God, then development is not complete until they meet him. That happens through Jesus. "There is no other name under heaven given to men by which we must be saved" (Acts 4:12).

Furthermore, conversion unleashes motivation. When people start following Jesus, when they experience a conversion—what Jesus called a "new birth"—their morale rises. They feel more valuable when they believe that God created them and Jesus died for them. They feel empowered when the Holy Spirit flows through them.

If the church is operating properly, new believers feel cared for. They find a safety net with local Christians. Beyond the immediate community, they discover that there is a people they can call their own, extending throughout time and space. They learn that they are in a kingdom that will never be destroyed.

In gratitude they want to give something back, to encourage and contribute to others, to offer more to God. They are ready to learn and eventually to lead. They use their profits for less selfish goals.

Jacob Loewen, a Christian anthropologist, was talking with a non-Christian friend who had pioneered one of the earliest successful development programs. "Would you have changed anything if you could go back and do it over?" Loewen wondered.

"Yes," his friend sighed,

> I would have included a dose of good old-fashioned religion. From an economic point of view, my program was a smashing success. But from a human point of view? Before we began, they harvested enough potatoes to get drunk for ten days. Now they harvest enough to get drunk for three months. When planting season rolls around they're still drunk. Yes, I would have done something different. I would have included religion.

The Christian component of development can make a difference.

FOOD SECURITY

"Another baby." Women lifted their heads as weak mewling cries wafted out of a thatch-roofed house down the lane.

"Is that her twelfth? Or thirteenth?"

"Thirteenth." A turbaned matron squeezed a wet cloth above the wash trough. "Didn't the radio say we have children faster than anyplace else in the world?"

"And most of them sick. Malaria. Worms. Kwashiorkor. Not enough food—"

"So thirteen is not too many. Some have to stay alive long enough to work the farm."

The women shrugged, hefted wet fabric and bent over their scrubbing while the infant's cry petered out.

Where these women lived in southwest Uganda there were no roads and therefore no ways to take crops to market. The landscape was hilly. As people cut trees for fuel, landslides increased. More arable soil was lost. Actually, things seemed to be sliding downhill in almost every area of life. Yet the region was densely populated.

Today, due to agricultural help in an integrated development program, life is improving. Seventy-five thousand villagers are eating better. Some of the program leaders are pastors, and some of the committees are based in churches. The project is sponsored by an agency named Africare.[5]

In this program a village begins with "participatory visioning." Villagers draw diagrams of how their land is used now. Then they sketch ideas showing how it could be used better. They create a time schedule for improvements, with steps. They list indicators by which to measure progress.

Then they choose a local development committee. A road to a market center is something almost everybody wants. So they pitch in with ideas, labor and money. Africare supplies some of the resources.

Next, a few people visit the market center to see what sells well. Generally people in this region plant sorghum, which is edible but not profitable to sell. After the market visit, each village chooses a cash crop suited to their terrain, skills and interests. For some, the crop is potatoes. Villagers plant on a schedule so that some are harvested every two weeks. Uganda will no longer need to import French fries!

Other villages choose apples. The 7,500 foot elevation is high enough for this fruit. However, apple trees need winter if they are going to produce, and there is no winter at the equator. The villagers "trick" the trees by pruning off all their leaves. Now they get two apple crops annually, and can sell apples for a price much higher than sorghum.

For protein, some are raising tilapia in fish farms, and others are raising rabbits or chickens.

"Integrated development" is the context. Farmers have learned land-management techniques, like digging trenches for various purposes, capturing water, enriching the soil and reducing erosion. Thousands of tree seedlings have been planted for soil enrichment, erosion control, wood, fodder, medicine and valuable spices.

Through simple dramas as well as practical demonstrations, villagers have learned about nutrition, disease and health, childcare, how to use fuel and stoves more efficiently, and how to increase natural fertilizers.

Behind field projects like the one in Uganda are resource banks like Educational Concerns for Hunger Organization. Thirty years ago I met Martin and Bonnie Price. Martin had just resigned from his position as a college professor. While he enjoyed teaching, he was restless. As a biologist, he knew a lot about growing things. As a Christian, he prayed for the poor. As a creative thinker, he had some ideas about how to connect the two. That wasn't the primary requirement for a basic biology professor, however. Routine teaching duties filled his hours.

Finally he and Bonnie pulled up stakes and moved to Educational Concern for Hunger's plot in Florida. Here they experimented with food plants. Which ones grew well in desert soil? In droughts? In floods? In containers? On rooftops? Which were the most nutritious? Then they made seeds available to Christians and others around the world, adding a request: "Here's the information we've put together about how this plant responds under different growing conditions. After you harvest it, would you send us a report so we can add it to our data bank?"

Now three decades later, the data flows out of practical books, videos, a website (www.echonet.org), training workshops and onsite consultancies. ECHO has become a destination for people who want to learn how to grow food in hard places. Some interns earn college credit.

A recent workshop in Africa focused on nutritious plants that can be grown by patients who are weak from AIDS. Perennials, for example, will keep on producing even when people do not have the energy to cultivate them. As their roots go deeper, they resist drought better. Amaranth is one grain that survives drought amazingly well.

SUSTAINABLE JOBS THAT SUSTAIN LIFE
Unfortunately, all the agricultural advice, tools and seeds in the world won't help a person who has no place to grow food. For millions of urban workers, rural laborers and tenant farmers, what they need is a

job with a living wage.

Muhammad Yunus was an economics professor in Bangladesh. During one famine, as he walked to his university classes, he had to step around people on the sidewalk who were starving.

"There is something wrong with this picture," he said to himself. Later he would comment, "Economics seemed hollow. I was totally disenchanted with what I was doing. I left the classroom and stepped out into the villages."

In one village he met a woman who built bamboo stools. She earned two pennies a day. To buy her supplies, she borrowed from a moneylender. Like many others in his profession, charging between 50 and 200 percent interest, the lender took most of her earnings.

Yunus thought, "If money was available at normal interest rates, this woman would earn a decent living."

He walked on. "I went around this village to look for other people who also were stuck in poverty because they were dependent on loans from traders and money lenders. I came up with a list of 42 such people."

Amazingly, the total credit requirement for all forty-two people was only $30. Yunus pulled $30 out of his pocket and made loans on the spot to all of them.

Then he went to his banker. "How can we circumvent the usurious moneylenders, and serve the poor through banks?" he asked.

But he was stonewalled. "The bankers I met laughed at me. They didn't think it was possible to give out money without collateral. I ran from one bank to another. They all said the same. I offered myself as guarantor for the loans. This was good for a few hundred dollars . . ."

"I went back to the banks showing proof that poor people do pay back. They said it works in your one village but it wouldn't work over many villages. I tried it over many villages."

Finally Yunus said to himself, "Why am I knocking myself out chasing after banks? I'll create a bank." So he did. The Grameen Bank was born in 1983 as a bank for the poor. It has loaned over $6.6 billion to the poor with dazzling success.[6]

A loan can make the difference between malnutrition and health, between illiteracy and schooling, between quiet despair and the confidence to plan ahead. Today thousands of missions, churches and secular and government agencies run loan programs that have made it possible for poor people to start small businesses. Opportunity International is a large Christian program. Hope International is a medium-sized one. Many standard missions have microenterprise departments.

This kind of project is not for amateurs, however. To do it well requires training and experience. In *Christian Microenterprise Development*, David Bussau and Russell Mask confront hard questions: What is adequate capital? How many clients should a loan officer serve? How do you minimize fraud? What kinds of records do you need to keep, and are there standard software packages for this? How do you decide on an appropriate interest rate? When should you write off bad loans? What do you do in a repayment crisis, which eventually hits every organization? Are subsidies bad? How soon should you plan to phase out external help? How do you manage money when banks close because of recurring disasters? What if inflation rates skyrocket so that savings accounts are not viable? What if the system is so corrupt that it is impossible to manage money without outrageous bribery?[7] The Chalmers Center, where author Mask is based, offers online courses in this area (www.chalmers.org).

In some countries you need $100 to open a bank account, and you must be literate and must provide multiple kinds of ID. So poor people put their savings into gold jewelry, land or animals, or invest in a rotating savings association. In Kenya these savings associations are called "merry-go-rounds," in India "chits," in Indonesia "arisans," in the Philippines "paluwagans," and in French-speaking Africa "tontines."[8]

Fifteen to thirty people contribute a fixed amount weekly in such a group. Every week someone "wins" the whole amount as a "prize." The cycle continues until everyone has received the money. Then a new cycle begins.

Another kind of fund is used for emergencies like a funeral, a fire or payment to offset revenge if someone in your group injures or kills someone in another group. This is like an insurance policy for the poor.

You pay into it when you can and receive its benefits when you must.

Clearly poor people are not without resources or strategies for maximizing those resources. Building on those, we can help them create systems that will provide greater stability.

ECONOMIES OF SCALE

Some loans are tiny. Peruvian evangelical students went to a poor community to offer loans and counsel. One local woman asked for help. "I sell boiled eggs as snacks. But I earn very little. How can I make more?"

"Where do you set up your egg stand?" the students inquired.

She told them.

"Move your stand to the corner just outside the high school," the students advised (following the maxim "Location, location, location!") "When the hungry students stream past at the end of the day, they will buy your eggs."

"And keep a salt shaker on your table. Your eggs will taste better," one student added.

Other businesses are much larger, and so are the loans they need. Dann Pantoja is a Filipino-Canadian pastor who lives in the Muslim region of the Philippines. His movement is called Peacebuilders (www.peacebuilderscommunity.org). With others he has pitched tents on a battlefield between the Armed Forces of the Philippines and a Muslim army, helping to pave the way for a peaceful end to fierce hostilities.

Mountain tribal people were not Dann's focus when some of them asked him for help. "We grow Fair Trade coffee, but the middlemen don't care about that. They pay us the same rock-bottom prices as always. Is there anything we can do?"

The next time Dann went back to Canada, he lugged a few bags of the tribes' beans to Stacey Toews, a man who supplies coffee to a network of Mennonite import stores. This is reputed to be the biggest supplier of Fair Trade coffee in North America.

"Let me see what my tasters think," Toews said.

The beans passed the taste test, and Toews ordered them for all his shops throughout the continent.

Back in the Philippines, a Bontoc tribesman on the island of Luzon e-mailed Dann. "We're growing coffee, too. Can you advise us how to price our beans?"

Then came a call from the Ifugao tribespeople, creators of the famed rice terraces. Dann offered seminars. New tribal coffee councils were born. And Dann realized he was in over his head.

With exporters north and south, he needed capital and expertise. He turned to a Filipino congregation with wealthy businessmen. Dann challenged ten of them to invest 100,000 pesos each in this coffee business, with the proviso that 25 percent of the profits would go to Peacebuilders. The businessmen also would provide expertise on international export, since that was their specialty. The laymen agreed, set up a board and invested. Now high quality beans flow across the Pacific, and humble growers receive fair profits.

Some businesses are tiny, selling boiled eggs. Other are more substantial. In between are businesses like pharmacies and schools. With a $1,000 investment, a nurse in Africa can set up a pharmacy to treat the most common illnesses, generating $5,000 to $20,000 annually. With just $500, a literate slum dweller in Africa can build a one-room cinderblock school. With a second loan, he can stock it. Children in such schools often score higher on exams than those in national public schools. Capital and expertise are the requirements for all these businesses, small or large.

TRANSNATIONAL PROBLEMS
MAY NEED TRANSNATIONAL SOLUTIONS

Land and water are basic resources. Many people do not have adequate access to them. One hundred million families do not own the land they farm. Yet change is not impossible. Countries like Korea, Taiwan and Mexico have shown that land reform can succeed.

Water is the most essential resource. While we can live without oil, we cannot live without water. Fresh water resources are diminishing even as populations increase, climates change and economic developments gulp still more water. In Africa, Lake Chad has shrunk to one-tenth of its former size in the past thirty years. That lake supports thirty million people. In Latin America some of the Amazon's tributaries are dying up. One third of the United States experiences water stress. Chinese water shortages are alarming. Worldwide, a child dies from a water-related cause every twenty seconds.[9]

Huge issues like regional water management require coordinated solutions. When problems are transnational, the efforts to ameliorate them need to transcend national boundaries too. There are models. As the year 2000 approached, Christians—from the pope to Billy Graham to Bono—joined forces to lobby the World Bank and the International Monetary Fund to roll back the debts of the poorest nations. They called this the "Jubilee Project," in honor of debt forgiveness in key years in the Old Testament. Because of this advocacy, poor countries' debts were reduced significantly early in the new millennium.

More recently, a network of concerned Christians and others have pressured pharmaceutical companies to reduce the costs of AIDS drugs for patients in needy nations. As a result of this moral suasion, at least forty companies have agreed to allow the importation and even the local manufacture of cheaper drugs.

In 2000, the United Nations created a set of Millennium Development Goals:

- reduce child mortality

- promote gender equality and empower women

- improve maternal health

- eradicate extreme poverty and hunger

- achieve universal primary education

- combat HIV/AIDS, malaria and other diseases

- ensure environmental sustainability

- develop a Global Partnership for Development

To join this effort the World Evangelical Alliance (WEA) inaugurated the Micah Challenge, taking its mandate from Micah 6:8:

What does the LORD require of you?
To act justly and to love mercy
   and to walk humbly with your God.

At the local level the 120 WEA national affiliates are tackling a kaleidoscopic variety of projects in relation to the U.N.'s eight Millennial goals. At the international level Micah Challenge has sponsored global conferences such as one in New Delhi on nonviolent moral leadership and another in Nairobi on "Creation Stewardship and Climate Change." Topics in Nairobi ranged from disaster mitigation to alternative energy to food and water security to migrations and displacements. Micah Challenge also publicizes related conferences like one in Manila on prostitution sponsored by Samaritana, a Philippine ministry.

ON THEIR OWN TERMS

The poor want something better, but it has to make sense to them. Years ago in the Middle East there was a village where children were getting sick. Sometimes they died. The national health department sent a field staff worker to investigate. He observed women drawing drinking water from the pool where their animals wallowed. Tests showed that the children's sicknesses could be traced to water-borne sources.

Since the pool was small, the health worker recommended covering it and installing a pump. This would eliminate the animal pollution.

The people agreed to the project. However, the day scheduled for this construction came and went with no action. Several times it was rescheduled. Each time the people had conflicting activities. Finally the health worker convened them and asked, "Why are you stalling? Don't you want your children to stay well?"

The first villager said, "I've never seen a pump, and I don't know what would happen if we put one in."

The second said, "All the water would flow out and the pool would dry up."

The third said, "Those iron pipes would spoil the taste of the water. Even our animals wouldn't want to drink it."

The fourth said, "We know that life and death are in the hands of Allah. So how can you be telling the truth when you say it is this water that causes our children's deaths?"

The fifth said, "Until a couple of months ago, you had never set foot in this village. What are you really after? What is in this project for you?"

The last man said, "If this pump saves our women so much time, what are they going to do with themselves all day long?"[10]

This kind of response pops up frequently in community development projects.

The poor want help, but they want it in ways that make sense to them.

There is an obscure fishing village in the Philippines where 250 women run successful grassroots businesses today because Christians took extended time to listen and adapt development to local priorities.

A dozen years ago the villagers were suspicious of the Filipino group that visited and offered them help. The agency was ISACC, the Institute for the Study of Asian Church and Culture.

"You're not communists. And you're not trying to convert us. Why are you here?" the villagers demanded.

"Because of the love of Jesus. But we're not in a hurry to turn you into a project. We'll stay and listen."

After two years, listening paid off.

"Community development organizations come and go, come and go. But you're still here," the villagers observed.

While listening and internalizing local rhythms, pains, and longings, the ISACC staff established credibility. Eventually the villagers agreed to work together to set up a small community store that would provide employment during the rainy season, when they could not fish.

The second project was a water system. These fishermen lived on a peninsula almost cut off from the mainland. They had no drinking water. ISACC got a grant for the pipes, and the villagers themselves provided the labor.

Then they tackled land ownership. Other agencies had promised to help them get titles. The first group had swindled them. The second had neglected the case. The cynicism left behind was something ISACC had to hurdle. ISACC helped them wend their way through pyramids of paperwork. They secured an accurate survey. They negotiated delicately with neighboring landowners. In the end they got a community mortgage.

This motivated the villagers to fix up their houses. Previously the fishing community had been an eyesore for the people who lived a little further inland. That is no longer the case.

ISACC was ready to phase out, but the villagers were not eager to see them go. They kept thinking up more projects. Today, however, one of the young women from the village has become their own home-grown grant writer. When she was a little girl she went to school because of ISAAC's encouragement. As a young woman she interned with ISACC. Today she procures grants for her village directly from TearFund of Australia. As a result, 250 women run their own small businesses.

The poor want help so they can earn a better living. But they want it in ways that make sense to them. A theology of incarnation calls us to live among them and listen to them, just as ISACC did.

WHAT SHOULD WE BE DOING NOW?

What do you do when the most powerful tsunami in recent history wipes out your family, your house, your business and much of your city? Sri Lanka—a green jewel of an island once known as Ceylon—felt the cruel lash of that terrible storm in 2004.

Ajith Fernando is a native of Sri Lanka. Standing amid the wreckage of his smashed country, he took up his pen. Like writers in biblical times, he faced disaster with words of wisdom. "What Should We Be Doing Now?" is addressed to his national church.[11] The eight activities it recommends are good advice for anyone immersed in a poor community for Jesus' sake.

A time to mourn. Grieve first, Fernando says. When we want to serve suffering people, we should respect their pain enough to sit down and open ourselves to it. Before we start making plans and giving directions, we should hurt with them. "Mourn with those who mourn," the apostle Paul says in Romans 12:15. Christians don't cry enough, Fernando says. We keep our sorrow inside when we ought to let it out. There is "a time to weep" (Eccles 3:4).

Jeremiah cried,

> Oh, that my head were a spring of waters
> and my eyes a fountain of tears!
> I would weep day and night
> for the slain of my people. (Jer 9:1)

Nehemiah cried when he heard about the troubles in Jerusalem. Many psalms are laments. Lamentations is a whole book of grieving. In New Testament times when a woman named Dorcas died and Peter went to her house, "All the widows stood around him, crying and showing him the robes and other clothing that Dorcas had made while she was still with them" (Acts 9:39). "This type of scene is very common in Sri Lankan funerals but not in Protestant funerals," Fernando comments. He recommends more tears.

A time to ask why? In the Bible great saints wrestled with God and asked why terrible things happened. Consider Job. Consider Habakkuk. We will never have all the answers. Much will remain a mystery. We do know that "after sin entered the world, the universe lost its equilibrium" (see Gen 3:17; Rom 8:20). Therefore natural disasters will happen until God brings into being a new heaven and a new earth (2 Pet 3:13; Rev 21:1). Paul says that "the whole creation has been groaning as in the pains of childbirth right up to the present time" (Rom 8:22).

God groans too.

One of the most amazing things about the biblical teaching about God is that while we groan, he groans with us (Rom 8:26). God is not so distant from us as to not feel our pain. The Bible says he laments and mourns for people who do not even acknowledge him (Isa 16:11; Jer 48:31). How different from the common idea of God is the statement that when his people are distressed God is also distressed (Isa 63:9).

Jesus cried over Jerusalem (Lk 19:41-44) and at his friend Lazarus's tomb (Jn 11:33-35). "We therefore can conclude that God is weeping with the weeping people of Sri Lanka."

"Christians must learn how to groan. If we don't learn this lesson, when there are problems in the place where God has called us to serve, we will run away from God's will and go to a safer place. So as our nation groans over the tsunami, we also groan."

And no matter how urgent the work, we must take time to worship and also to argue with God, "focusing on those eternal realities which give us the strength to . . . launch out into sacrificial service."

A time to work. "Endure hardship . . . like a good soldier of Christ Jesus," Paul advised Timothy (2 Tim 2:3). "Not to work at this time could be a serious error. Amos pronounces woe to those who are living at ease and having fun while their nation is in a crisis" (Amos 6:1-6).

Our God is not tranquil. He acts passionately because he cares. "God so *loved* the world . . . " "Christ's love *compels* us . . . " We "*press on* toward the goal . . . " We "*work . . . with all [our] heart* . . . " (Jn 3:16; 2 Cor 5:14; Phil 3:14; Col 3:23, emphasis added). God doesn't stand on the sidelines. He gets involved. Jesus sweated blood. This is our model.

> Strengthened by the knowledge that . . . we are princes and princesses in God's great kingdom, we have the strength to do things that others are not willing to do. No work is too small for us, for God gives us the strength to be servants. It may be cleaning toilets or dressing festered wounds; it may be clearing garbage. We not only have the strength to do these things, we regard doing them to be a great privilege.

A time to pray. "The most powerful thing that a Christian can do is to pray. . . . In Old Testament times when the nation faced a crisis, godly leaders called the nation to prayer." In the list of prayer items that follow, we are reminded that the tsunami did not wash over a pristine land. Before the storm, civil war savaged the people of Sri Lanka. Buddhists persecuted Christians at the highest levels. The tsunami rearranged the agony. All of these realities frame the prayers

- for God's grace to go to those who have suffered loss of loved ones and property, that those who are deeply traumatized would be ministered to and that those who are displaced from their homes would find a solution to their housing problems
- that those who are in camps would be adequately provided for, and that those, like women and children, who are vulnerable to attack from wicked people would be protected
- that Christians would arise and be sacrificially involved in effective service
- that the church would be revived to truly bring glory to God through our actions and our witness to Christ
- that God would guide each one of us individually about how we are going to be involved in the process of the healing of the land
- for the process of relief and rehabilitation, for groups involved in this, especially Christian organizations and churches, and for the government authorities who are responsible for administering the affected areas
- that corruption, waste and a lack of planning would be minimized
- for our political leaders who make the policies that affect the healing process
- that there would be adequate supplies and funding for the huge task of restoring the nation
- that through this tragedy peace would be restored to our nation
- that God's glory would shine through to our nation as it never has been before

A time to give. "This is the time for the people of God to give of their possessions to help those who have suffered. . . . As large sums of money and supplies are coming from abroad, we may think that we ourselves do not need to give because our gifts will be minute. . . . But we must remember that in the Bible the power of a gift does not depend on the amount of money given."

A time to plan. "So much time, energy and resources are wasted due to lack of planning. So many needy people miss the aid they should get and some get more than they need because of poor planning. Planning is especially needed as we move out of the state where we meet emergency needs and start the reconstruction process . . .

> Churches are gifted with willing and able people, and that could be an important resource to give to specialist groups who have the funds and the expertise for relief and rehabilitation. . . . "Two are better than one" (Eccles 4:9). It would be wise for us to partner. This may be also a time for us to show our commitment to our nation as we join with other groups that are not connected with the church.

A time to be careful. "In the passage where Paul urges Timothy to work hard, he also urges him to be like an athlete who 'competes according to the rules' (2 Tim 2:5). When one is running hard it is easy to stumble and fall. It is sadly true that many who have worked hard at relief have made some big mistakes by breaking some basic rules."

We may neglect time with God, or with our spouse, or our sleep. Then we lose our temper. Then we burn out.

Professionally, too, we must be careful not to exaggerate what we are doing, nor to break the principles of accounting, nor to spend funds extravagantly on ourselves.

A time to comfort. We worship "the God of all comfort, who comforts us in all our troubles so that we can comfort those in any trouble with the comfort we ourselves have received" (2 Cor 1:3-4).

> With so many people traumatized, sad, and needing someone to listen to them, those who have received God's comfort can do much to be agents of healing. Even relief workers are in need of comfort today. What they have experienced is emotionally very draining. So Christians should be looking for opportunities to comfort people. . . . Simply being with and listening to hurting people. . . . Leaving our places of comfort in order to be close to our suffering people. . . . And remembering that the greatest need

of people is to have a relationship with the "God of all comfort."

Grieve. Ask why. Work. Pray. Give. Plan. Be careful. Comfort. These are good words for any catastrophe.

MYSTIC SERVANTS

Jesus' People in the Hindu World

"WILL MY WIFE EVER LIVE WITH ME?" TILAK GROANED. He and his wife were Brahmins, the highest caste. But because he followed Jesus, he mingled with all kinds of people. This set off fireworks in his closest social relationships.

Tilak's pain mirrors some of the struggles of Indian Christians, and his life mirrors some of the solutions.

Who are Indian Christians? Narayan Vaman Tilak is just one. Diversity dazzles in this land. There are languages and tribes and castes by the thousands. The religions of Hinduism, Sikhism, Buddhism and Jainism all began here. One of the biggest Muslim populations in the world exists here. So does one of the oldest living churches. Jesus has been worshiped in India ever since the apostle Thomas brought the good news.[1]

There are states where nearly the whole population is Christian, such as Mizoram in the northeast. Yet other states ban conversions completely, in spite of the fact that the national constitution guarantees that right. Now and then violence flares, churches are burned, and Christians are killed. Meanwhile, India hosts the biggest "unreached" people groups in the world—ethnic groups where hardly anyone knows Jesus as Lord—as well as one of the biggest national mission movements, over two hundred local agencies supporting almost fifty thousand missionaries.

Among Jesus' followers, some are illiterate farmers. Some are software professionals. Some are tribal. But youth dominate the future. Fifty-five percent of the population of 1.2 billion is under the age of twenty-five, and 75 percent is under the age of thirty. "Youth churches" are springing up. In one five-thousand-member megachurch in Bangalore the average member is twenty-four-years-old and the pastor himself is twenty-eight.

Three significant streams in this river of Indian Christianity may be classified as Dharmic, Dalit and dot-com.

DHARMA AND JESUS

Narayan Vaman Tilak (1861-1919) models a Christian who loved his culture. He saw how networks tie families and neighbors together. Traditional exchange patterns distribute resources. Art and music deepen human joy with multiple levels of connotation. Even the Hindu religion contains glimpses of wisdom. A heritage like this deserves respect. The gospel needs to connect with it. Tilak's faith was nourished by the best in Indian dharma (teaching and customs).[2]

From childhood, Tilak was steeped in the Vedas, the Hindu Scriptures. But he was not content to stay in an ivory tower of learning. He wanted to experience the God he had studied. As a young man he followed in the footsteps of many other sincere seekers, wrapping himself in a simple cloth, picking up a walking stick and a food bowl, and leaving home to wander as an ascetic.

In the years that followed he sometimes subsisted on leaves. Sometimes he sat in the middle of a river and recited mantras, powerful sacred sayings, hoping that supernatural power would flow into him. He became known as a sadhu, a holy man.

By the end of his life Tilak also was known as a poet and orator, winning high literary prizes and even credited with the rebirth of Marathi poetry.

Singing and dancing to Jesus. After he became a Jesus follower, Tilak wrote devotional songs. Two hundred sixty of the 798 songs in a standard Marathi hymnbook are his. He led *kirtans,* evenings of exuberant singing in which the performers were immersed in the presence of Christ, seeking close union with him. *Bhakti* is the Hindu term for devotional worship of a god. Tilak became a "Jesus bhakta."

He spoke of the Vedas as his Old Testament, and Jesus as his dharma. He honored earlier Hindu writers and singers for the bits of insight that they had provided. However, he also saw where the gospel differed from his tradition, where Jesus called him out. Therefore he emphasized not detachment *(viraga)* but attachment *(anuraga).*[3] He did not merely sink into contemplation. He created a *darbar,* a religious study community where Jesus' love could flow freely to real people.

Spirituality is the foundation for everything that exists, according to classic Hinduism. We stand in awe at the mystery of the Ultimate. Hinduism reminds us that we are not machines, robots or commodities, but souls born to rise to union with the great soul. Appreciating this heritage, Tilak carried on long correspondences with numerous high-caste seekers and quite a few followed Jesus.

"Since I am an Indian," he said,

> it is natural that I should take pride in our Indian literature and in our Indian *mahatmas* (teachers). . . . The traditional way of union with the Supreme through *bhakti,* which Hindu mystics have conceived and Hindu devotees experienced, may be summed up in the four words *samipata* (nearness), *salokata* (association), *sarupata* (likeness), and *sayujyta* ("yokedness" or union). This has helped me to enter into the meaning of that series of Christ's sayings— "Come after Me," "Take my yoke upon you," "Become like unto Me," "Abide in Me."[4]

Here is one of Tilak's poems, titled "Christ and I."

> As lyre and the musician,
> As thought and spoken word,
> As rose and fragrant odors,

As flute and breath accord,
So deep the bond that binds me
To Christ my Lord.

As mother and her baby,
As traveler lost and guide,
As oil and flickering lamp-flame,
Are each to each allied;
Life of my life, Christ binds
Me to his side.

As lake and streaming rainfall
As fish and water clear,
As sun and gladdening dayspring
In union close appear,
So Christ and I are held
In bonds how dear![5]

The unthinkable. Tilak was not too spiritual to get his hands dirty. When his adopted daughter contracted cholera, he and his wife moved into a quarantine camp to care for her. Soon they were disturbed by shouts.

"No! Don't take it away. Please. We need the milk!" A woman with frantic eyes stepped in front of the milk wagon.

"Pay for it!" shrugged the oxcart driver.

"With what?" We beg you—"

When Tilak investigated, he discovered that corruption poisoned the camp. To ensure fair distribution, he took over the camp administration. Even after his daughter recovered, he stayed. So did his wife.

Then the camp toilet cleaners went on strike.

"Someone is bound to give us a raise," they chuckled as they left. "The situation will become too desperate otherwise."

But there was no money for raises. Tilak and his wife cleaned all the camp toilets, even though it was unthinkable for a Brahmin to lower himself to this. The cleaners were so shamed that they returned voluntarily two days later.

Throughout his life Tilak took the side of low-caste people and women, and worked to expand their opportunities. Once he stood up to preach in a church and saw that the building was full of high-caste people. The low-caste members stood outside, listening in through the windows. Tilak marched down the aisle and out the door to preach in the open air. The high-caste members were forced to come out of the church to hear him.

When famine threatened a boarding school and twenty-two boys were left without a place to live, Tilak and his wife took them in, along with four girls. Although the family had very limited resources, they fed and sheltered all the children for months until the boarding school opened again.

By no means was Tilak a saint. While his grandfather and his mother were poets, his father was a strange, angry man who was possessed by a fierce goddess every Friday. This gave Tilak a shaky foundation as a husband. Even after he became a Christian, he often left his wife, Lakshmi, while he went off on long pilgrimages. As she moved from relative to relative during his absences, she sometimes got stuck with Tilak's scary father.

Worse than that, Lakshmi lamented, Tilak ignored caste boundaries. How could a pure woman like her live with a man like him? None of the relatives thought she should stick it out. The marriage appeared doomed.

But Lakshmi was persuaded to move *next door* to him, and in little steps learned the truth of Jesus and was liberated from slavery to caste. The marriage had a surprisingly happy ending. Tilak invested energy in Lakshmi's education. She became his close colleague and won literary honors herself.

India enriches Christianity. Tilak loved India passionately. "Sons and daughters of India, who love Christ and love their own country, pray that God may raise up apostles in India for the advancement of His kingdom," he wrote.

Pray that volunteers from among us may come forth . . . and give the land once more a long line of Christian *sadhus*. . . . Pray that the Lord may raise up in India, not a society, nor a machine, nor any thing resembling these, but a simple brotherhood drawn together and blended as one.[6]

While Christianity blesses India, Tilak believed that India also could enrich Christianity. Consider Greek philosophy. Originally it was interwoven with the worship of pagan gods. In the hands of Christian theologians the pagan ties were loosed but the kernels of wisdom were retained. The same could happen with Hindu thought, Tilak said. If mined properly, this treasure lode would enrich the whole world.

Unfortunately many Indian Christians today know little about their artistic, philosophical and historic heritage. They are comfortable in the routines that have been developed within their church communities. These may attract lower-caste people, and indeed many Christians come from those backgrounds. But if upper-caste people are to be reached, the best of Indian culture must be appreciated. Tilak is a forerunner here.

However, when Tilak equated the Vedas with the Old Testament, he overstated the case. God introduced himself to Abraham and David and Isaiah in a unique way that is not paralleled in other religions. Nevertheless, the general wisdom found in other faiths is a gift of God. And there may be indigenous ideas that display the gospel particularly well. An Indian Christian theologian named Appasamy has explored the idea of bhakti or religious devotion. Another named Brahmabandhab Upadhyay has explored the oneness of all things in God. A forum for this kind of discussion today is *Dharma Deepika: Journal of South Asian Missiology*.

Tilak's *kirtans*, or contextualized musical gospel presentations, continue today through a Christian performing group known as Aradhna.

DALITS AND JESUS

"Yah, Ram!" Rochunga greeted his classmate and fell into step, heading back to their residence hall.[7] In their minds the young men were savoring afternoon tea. The scent of onion and garlic wafted out of one house as they passed it. A whiff of buttermilk emerged from another.

On the dusty street ahead an elderly man from the sweeper caste tottered along. As the boys neared him, the man swerved.

"You scum!" Ram yelled. "Are you blind?"

"Huh?" blurted the started Rochunga. He stared at his friend. What was the problem?

"Your shadow fell on me," Ram snarled at the old man. "You have polluted me. Lie down. Lie right here. On your face."

Trembling, the old men creaked to his knees, spread out his hands and put his nose to the dirt.

Ram drew back a foot and kicked the old man. It was vicious.

Rochunga was a tribal boy, raised in the hills. He had been lucky enough to win a scholarship to this university. He had not had much experience with caste. When Ram kicked the old man, Rochunga was appalled and stepped forward to intervene.

Four Brahmin boys who had been standing on the sidelines shouted a warning and charged over. "If you touch the Brahmin," they glared at Rochinga, "we'll give you a lesson worse than the one he's giving the sweeper."

Rochinga froze. Ram delivered one more resounding kick and sneered down at the man who was covering his head with shaking hands. "Pay for my trip to the Ganges river so that I can bathe there and purify myself," Ram commanded. The other four Brahmin boys made a threatening half-circle around the body.

"Yes, Sir. Yes, Sir," the old man mumbled. "I am so sorry. Yes, I will pay whatever you ask."

This was fair enough, Ram and his friends believed. The old man certainly had done shameful things in his past life. That is why he was born a Dalit, at the bottom of the caste system. According to the law of karma, good deeds will result in a higher birth station, and bad deeds will result in a lower birth station. Why pity the man? He was part of the dregs of the earth. He had earned punishment and deserved whatever Ram meted out.

When culture wounds. Discriminating on the basis of caste has been illegal since India became a nation in 1947, and many of the more fortunate Indians believe that they "live above caste." They don't want to hear about it. Yet it persists in everyday life. Dalits, who constitute one fifth of the population, are barred from many shops and restaurants and temples. At a sidewalk café they are served in disposable plastic cups that will be destroyed after use. If invited to the home of an upper-caste colleague, again they may be served on disposable plastic dinnerware. Nor can they return the invitation. Upper-caste children will not come to their home to play with their kids, no matter how much the parents may rub shoulders in the office or the university. Certainly no upper-caste family will tolerate their child marrying a Dalit. It is unthinkable.

Many professions can be performed only by Dalits—herding cows, sheep or buffalos; butchering, tanning, making pottery from soil, climbing trees to cut fruit; and all the dirtiest jobs. Such tasks are spiritually polluting, according to Hinduism. This belief erases the dignity of a man's or woman's labor. Any pride they might have felt in a job well done is obliterated.

Dalit women have the toughest time. They exist to be used. Some have been gang-raped. Some have been forced to eat feces to demonstrate their subservience. Dalit children—thousands of them—have been stolen from their parents and raised as temple prostitutes.

Marched naked to the police. Take the case of Guruammal.[8] She owned very little. For food she ate rice, lentils and fermented butter. For work she labored in the fields alongside her husband. It was not their land. They were hired hands. But they were young and treasured each other, and, now that they were expecting a baby, Garuammal greeted each pink dawn with wonder and gratitude and hope. Since her mother lived with them, a babysitter already was guaranteed. Life was not too bad.

Then the police raided the village. Although Garuammal was a bystander, the superintendent of police noticed her. "You must be a prostitute," he taunted as he unzipped his zipper in front of her. He also broke her silver pot.

When a subordinate officer arrived a few hours later, Garuammal told him what had happened. Angry to be singled out for criticism, the superintendent promised that he would exact revenge on her.

Thud! Early the next morning, Garuammal and her family were sleeping peacefully when their door splintered and armed men rushed in.

"You prostitute!" the policemen growled at Garuammal as they beat her with their sticks. "Take this off!" They ripped away her nightgown and dragged her naked out of the house and down the street.

After her bare body had scraped and bounced on the rocks for a hundred feet, a sixty-year-old woman intervened. "Sirs, have mercy. As you can see, she is pregnant."

Whop! The truncheon came down. Bones in both of the old woman's hands were fractured.

Naked, Garuammal was marched into the police station.

"Here," said a man who had just been arrested. He took off his own wraparound cloth and handed it to her so she could cover herself.

When Garuammal's case came before the arresting officers, she begged for help. She told them she was pregnant.

"Hah! You should have thought of that yesterday before you made those accusations. Now you'll have to pay the full penalty."

Garuammal spent twenty-five days in jail. Ten days into her sentence, she miscarried her baby. Nobody helped her. Since she has been released, nothing more has been done. Garuammal understands firsthand the gender-specific injustice that many Dalit women suffer.

What Dalits want. India has the world's largest middle class, but also more poor and illiterate people than any other nation. Seventy percent of the population depend on agriculture for a living. Many are subsistence farmers or itinerant laborers. Almost 50 percent of the population does not have electricity. Forty million are homeless. There is also a deficit of forty million girls because of selective abortion and the killing of female babies. India is a nuclear power with a space industry, yet 450 million Indians live on a dollar a day or less.

Not all Dalits are poor, but many are. How powerfully the gospel speaks to them. Whether it connects with Hinduism doesn't matter much. After all, what has Hinduism ever done for them? Such poor people long for justice, dignity and opportunities for the future.

Christians like Vishal and Ruth Mangalwadi have brought good news to the poor. For them it meant beginning their married life in extremely humble circumstances.

"Okay, I know there's no bathroom," Ruth reminded herself when, fresh from her honeymoon, she picked her way over the uneven ground toward her new home. "But does it have to look like such a *shack?*"

No bathroom and, on closer inspection, no kitchen either. No beds— just string hammocks. No furniture at all. It was a hut set in a community of illiterate brigands who looted for a living. Clearly Ruth was not at Wheaton College anymore. There she had earned an M.A. degree. Her family had wondered if they would be able to find her a husband who would be her intellectual equal. They did: the brilliant Christian writer Vishal Mangalwadi. Ruth would live in this village with him for the next six years, giving birth to both her babies here.

She had come willingly. Vishal and Ruth agreed that the gospel must be lived where the people are. God loves the needy, and his people must love them too. Before they left, there would be a multi-faceted community-development program lifting the local economy. There would be three new churches. One of them was composed of former bandits and thieves *(dacoits)*. On the negative side, Vishal and Ruth's two children "bore the scars of the cross in their lungs" because of tuberculosis. And Vishal spent time in jail for disrupting the system on behalf of the poor.

Prison conversations. In his book *The Quest for Freedom and Dignity: Caste, Conversion, and Cultural Revolution*, Vishal describes some of the conversations in the prison.[9]

"Why should a religious person like you meddle in political matters?" some prisoners wondered.

"Jesus was sent to liberate the oppressed," Vishal answered, and he quoted Jesus' words in Luke 4:

The Spirit of the Lord is on me,
>because he has anointed me
>to preach good news to the poor.
He has sent me to proclaim freedom for the prisoners

and recovery of sight for the blind,
to release the oppressed,
to proclaim the year of the Lord's favor. (vv. 18-19).

True spirituality works for justice, righteousness and compassion, Vishal explained. Jesus touched lepers and healed them. That is why Christians start leprosy hospitals. But people need more than social engineering. Slavery begins in our minds and hearts. Transformation must begin there as well. Through long conversations, Vishal explained why he did what he did. Some of the prisoners eventually followed Jesus.

Justice and opportunity. When Hindu violence flared in the 1990s, Joseph D'Souza was tapped to head the All India Christian Council, serving both Protestants and Catholics. Soon AICC was helping Muslims and Dalits as well.

"There was rioting in the streets, mass rape, devastation, and carnage, all created by Hindu fundamentalists," Joseph says of a massacre of Muslims in 2002. "Who stepped in to help these hapless victims? Along with a few other groups, the All India Christian Council, at considerable risk to its personnel, set up camps in Gujarat and provided shelter and food for the vulnerable displaced Muslims for six weeks."[10]

Later Joseph was invited to speak to Muslim audiences, sometimes addressing as many as seventy-five thousand. "Why are you helping us?" Muslims wondered. Eventually they were asking, "What does the Christian Scripture say about justice?"

As well, Joseph's Dalit Freedom Network has served abused and oppressed Dalits like Garuammal. Some have come to Jesus, and he expects many more, because Dalits are restive. On November 4, 2001, thousands of Dalits left Hinduism en masse. Though most opted for Buddhism, Joseph sees this as a stepping stone to the Christian faith. A half-century ago the Indian leader Ambedkar led similar mass conversions from Hinduism to Buddhism. In many of the villages where that happened, there is now a cross beside Ambedkar's statue, and a church. Quite a few of those Buddhists have become Christians. "Ambedkar brought them half way," Joseph says.

In December 2007, India's National Commission for Scheduled

Castes ruled that Dalits who converted to Christianity or Islam were no longer eligible for affirmative action benefits. Dalits appealed the ruling. As they did, they cited a statement of conscience and support issued two months earlier by the National Association of Evangelicals in the United States. It was the advocacy of people like Joseph that had brought the issue to the NAE's attention.

Do all Indian Christians support this position? No. Christianity in India is two thousand years old. There are many Christians-in-name-only whose families lost personal faith a thousand years ago. They have never even heard that Jesus rose from the dead. There are corrupt church leaders who spend their time suing each other for the property the British missionaries left. There are others who cannot think big enough to empathize beyond their own ethnic group or caste. Every country has plenty of small-minded Christians, and India is no exception. Caste-based Christianity still riddles the church.[11]

Ambedkar himself saw this.

> When I read the Gospels, the Acts of the Apostles, and certain passages of St. Paul's Epistles, I feel that I and my people must all become Christians, for in them I find a perfect antidote to the poison Hinduism has injected into our souls, and a dynamic strong enough to lift us out of our present degraded [low caste] position. But when I look at the Church . . . [m]any of my own caste have become Christians and most of them do not commend Christianity to the rest of us. . . . What sort of people are they? Selfish and self-centered. They do not care a snap of their fingers . . . so long as they and their families get ahead.[12]

What we do right. Yet the Indian church also has strengths. First, it is largely nonviolent. In an era of savage retaliations Christians for the most part have been peaceful. They have suffered without seeking revenge. They have been an example to other religions.

Second, the church has been good for women. "Dowry deaths" are a black stain in India. When a family feels it has not received enough dowry wealth along with their son's bride, they may "accidentally" spill oil on her when she is at the cooking fire. Immediately she ignites. Five thousand brides die this way every year.

Christians do not kill their brides. Nor do they abort or kill their baby girls, like so many families who want sons. Instead, Christians educate their girls. When girls' schools began in the 1800s, men said, "It's easier to teach our cows than our women." Today even Hindu Brahmin women know that they owe their education to Christians.

Pandita Ramabai is one of India's most honored women. Born in 1858, Ramabai came to faith in Christ as a young widow with a child. In time she started a community for displaced women who had no means of support. It grew large enough to shelter nineteen hundred women and orphans at one time. Today the community continues as the Ramabai Mukti Mission.

> The gardens and the fields, the oil-press and the dairy, the laundry and the bakery, the making of plain Indian garments, caps, lace, buttons, ropes, brooms, and baskets, the spinning of wool and cotton, the weaving of blankets, rugs, saris and other cloths, embroidery and various sorts of fancy work, thread-winding, grain-parching, tinning, culinary utensils, and dying furnished employment and jobs for hundreds of girls. Within the last few months, a printing press has been added to the establishment.[13]

This is how Ramabai described her holistic, self-supporting community. Active Christian worship and Bible study permeated this place as well.

Women continue to find affirmation in the gospel. Following the tragic tsunami in 2004, a young Hindu widow attended a training course for counselors. People of all faiths were welcome, but each day began with Christian worship. At the end of the course, the widow asked permission to speak.

"I lost my will to live when my husband died," she confessed. "If not for my seven-year-old daughter, I would have committed suicide. But here in the daily worship I have discovered that God loves *me*. Not only do I have a responsibility to my daughter. I also need to take care of myself because I'm valuable to God too."

Christian theology speaks powerfully when it is lived out. Strict Hinduism does not allow Dalits to read or study their sacred Scriptures, but Dalit Christians can own their own Bibles. Hinduism does not allow Dalits to be priests, but Dalit Christians can become pastors.

"The Tilak movement—Dharmic Christianity—has gone on for 200 years, but it touches only a small number of people," Joseph D'Souza says. "By contrast, emphasis on the rights of women draws many." In his view, justice and opportunity are the heart cry of a great many Indians.

DOT-COMS AND JESUS

India is a country of extremes. Caste is one area. The economy is another. India has seen at least 8 percent growth in GNP for the last fifteen years. There is a surplus of educated English speakers. More people speak English in India than in the United States and Canada combined. Many have an aptitude for engineering. Over half of U.S. Fortune 500 companies acquire some of their information technology from India. Thirty percent of the software engineers in California's Silicon Valley are of Indian heritage.

Since the Indian economy liberalized in the 1990s, the middle class has swelled. Due to an inflow of foreign media, work culture, technology and capital, these Indians' values have shifted. Young professionals, 250 million strong, now inhabit their own special world. Neither dharma nor Dalit issues matter much to them. Money, pleasure, status, dating and promotions are what count.

Yet when these modern Indians marry and have children, both dharmic and Dalit concerns may loom larger. In changing times people sometimes become conservative in select areas in order to try to hang onto their identity. One cause that may appeal is *Hindutva,* fundamentalist Hinduism.

Hindutva exalts the Hindu heritage. Unfortunately it also denigrates other faiths. It teaches that Hinduism is the only authentic custodian of Indian spirituality. Hindus are the true sons of the soil. India is not for the 150 million Indian Muslims nor for the Indian Christians, because those "foreign" faiths rot the culture. Never mind two thousand years of Indian Christianity or over one thousand years of Islam. All Indians are urged to "return" to Hinduism. Some people are forcibly "reconverted."

By the 1990s Hindutva hotheads had turned violent. In 1998 a group of nuns were raped. In 1999 an Australian missionary who worked with lepers was sleeping in his car with his two sons, nine-year-old Timothy and seven-year-old Philip, when the car was set on fire. All three burned to death. In 2002 thousands of Muslims were massacred. In 2008 Christians were forced to become Hindu on pain of death. Hundreds of instances of violent persecution have been documented.

Meanwhile, other dot.com Indians live outside the country. Not all are well-to-do, but even the humblest laborers are globally connected through the Internet. Such international flow is not new. Back in the 1880s, for example, Indians built the first railroad in Africa, the Uganda-Kenya railway. Today among the thirty million Indians abroad, one million live in the United States. One has become the governor of Louisiana, Bobby Jindal. The American Association of the Physicians of Indian Origin has thirty-five thousand members. Worldwide, the diaspora remits $27 billion to India annually. Some of the money funds Hindutva.

Sam George is one immigrant who has founded a Christian ministry to serve Asian Indian families in North America, regardless of caste, creed or nationality. The organization is named Parivar. "The Asian Indian community in the U.S. has done exceedingly well academically, professionally, and hence financially," says George, "but relationally we are bankrupt. . . . Families are in need everywhere. Broken relationships, hurting families, painful pasts, irreconcilable differences, hopeless situations, etc., are destroying families all around us."[14]

To help Indian American Christians understand their teens, and to help teens understand themselves, George has authored *Understanding the Coconut Generation*. (*Coconut* refers to those who appear "brown on the outside but white on the inside.") This clearly Christian book with excellent reviews has been used even by youth programs in Hindu temples.

Christian Indian businessmen in the United States have sponsored ministries in Peru, Mexico, Jamaica, Guyana, Panama, Trinidad and many other places.

As I write this, I glance at a full page ad in the most recent issue of the *Economist*. Sponsored by the Indian government tourist bureau, it features a fit and trim European-appearing woman named Julie whose "country of birth" is listed as the United States but whose "motherland" is India, and concludes, "If you are looking for a spiritual and magical journey unlike any other, visit India. Like Julie, you will find that your search ends here."

This is the dot.com dream. Be modern. Be spiritual. Be global. Be Indian. Have it all.

EXPLOSION OF MINISTRIES

Sarita and Sundar Thapa got married, got master's degrees in theology, came back to what was then the Hindu kingdom of Nepal and birthed a Bible school.

This is a Bible school? I might have wondered when I toured it. Students slept nine to a room. There were no computers. A lot of the food came from the student garden. Two weeks out of four the students hiked in the Himalayas telling people about Jesus, especially at trail rest stops where travelers sat on their haunches, meeting and greeting. Many new churches have resulted from those intentional encounters.

What about classes? What about Bible, theology, pastoral counseling, Greek, youth ministry? The school had academic programs for both pastors and laity. Long-term faculty development and library and curricular resource improvement were on their agenda. Meanwhile, students and faculty were out in the community as much as in the classrooms. They picked up litter on the streets. They offered occasional health clinics. At Christmas time they toured neighborhoods, singing carols.

When they dedicated a small building, they invited the community head man and honored him publicly, presenting him with a wristwatch and a Bible. "You are a very important man," they told him. "God loves you. If you listen to him, he will give you more wisdom so you can govern even better."

They also brought the community right into the Bible school, as I discovered when two small children zoomed down the corridor. "Who are these?" I wondered.

"Oh, we found their mother lying in a field. Her husband had thrown her out. Since she was sick, we brought them here and gave them a corner for their sleeping mats. And over here is the room for our old men."

"Old men?"

"Yes, they were sleeping on the streets, waiting to die. So we give them a room and daily rice and lentils just like the students. Now there are six of them. If they can go out and earn something, they do. If not, they're here."

The school has all-night prayer meetings once a month. Daily community worship morning and evening. A plan for each student to plant three worshiping groups before he or she graduates. This is not abstract education. Heart, hands and head are trained together.

Sarita's and Sundar's center is an example of the congregations and Bible-training centers that are exploding throughout the subcontinent.

In the oldest Christian tradition, the Syrian churches, a revival broke out from 1880 to 1920 after the believers got the Bible in their own language, Malayalam. This generated the evangelical Mar Thoma Church as well as a mission movement that has been alive for a century. In the Punjab, in the northeast, and in the south, many thousands have come to Christ in historic "people movements" where large numbers of related people decided to follow Jesus together. Solid churches have resulted.[15] In Allahabad, just a few miles from the confluence of three rivers at the heart of Hinduism, one hundred thousand believers have been gathering every Sunday. They call this the Yeshu Darbar. Whether in Pentecostal, standard Protestant, Catholic or Orthodox churches, whether in megachurches or in a huge array of house churches, Indians are worshiping Jesus.

Some of the networks that tie Christians together include the Evangelical Fellowship of India, the Pentecostal Fellowship of India, the Church of South India, the Church of North India, the All India Christian Council, the India Missions Association, and EFICOR, an Indian Christian relief agency. Bible-training centers and seminaries are accredited by either the Serampore accrediting system, the Asian Theological Association or the India Institute of Missiology.

BEST PRACTICES IN INDIAN MISSIONS

There are almost fifty thousand Indian missionaries. They face the same problems as any missionaries, though with fewer resources. How do we pay for technology upgrades? Or refresher courses? How do we educate our children when there is no school, a poor school or a school in a different language? How do we pay for medical expenses? Or retirement costs? Or trips to visit parents in a society where that is of paramount importance? How do we pay for our parents' funerals? Or our own funerals? Or our daughter's wedding? Or her college costs?[16]

Which Way Forward Indian Missions? A Critique of Twenty-Five Years 1972-1997 by K. Rajendran is a gold mine for mission planners scrambling for solutions. As General Secretary of the India Missions Association, Rajendran offers counsel on a wide range of issues. Since mission is a universal Christian challenge, all of us can learn from Indian missiologists. We also learn more about India when we see what local missionaries struggle with.

First, ministries must develop accountability, Rajendran advises. The India Missions Association requires these standards of its members:

• a balanced board of about seven people who are not relatives

• a minimum of five fully paid evangelists/missionaries

• the mission must have existed for at least three years

• audited accounts, including the last three years

• a resolution from the board to become a member of IMA[17]

Without standards, ministries will drift, Rajendran says. For example, poverty and simplicity are considered virtues of spirituality, yet these virtues may appear as sloppiness. It comes in the form of second grade material for studies, bad food, poor hygiene, unacceptable organizational methods, dirty room service/classrooms, and in many other ways. It is also expressed by a dire financial status, voluntary work syndrome, and an inability to control laziness . . . Sometimes sloppiness is not because of lack of money but because of over-delegation and poor follow-up of instructions. At other times it results from a lack of training.[18]

Ministries must be accountable.

Second, beware of regional domination. There are many more Christians in southern and northeastern India than in the rest of the country. Most missionaries come from those regions. In their zest to serve, they can trample locals. "South Indian Christian workers in the North lack cultural sensitivity and create difficult personal relationships . . . [and]) impose their alien social patterns and violate local norms and feelings," says historian Roger Hedlund.[19] The alternative? Listen, guard against looking down on the locals, hand over leadership readily and allow those who live in that place to hold veto power.

Years ago Donald McGavran applied the principle beyond the north-south divide.

> For example, the Garo missionaries sent from Meghalaya to evangelize the Garas of Orissa ought to be on probation until they have learned Oriya thoroughly well and surveyed intensively how God has raised up a Gara Church of about 25,000 souls in the Baptist and Mennonite denominations. Or, if they are sent to Tripura to evangelize the Jamatias, they must learn Tripuri thoroughly well and study carefully how the fifteen tribes in Tripuri (both the Zo group and the Tripuri group) have or have not become Christians. Missionaries of the St. Thomas Evangelical Church might well go to the Reddis of Andhra Pradesh with the deliberate purpose of starting Reddi congregations. In so doing, the Syrian missionaries would need to learn Telegu thoroughly

and survey with great care the way in which God has raised up a Church of more than 2 million from among the Malas and Madigas, and has already led more than 50,000 middle-class individuals to Christ in Andhra Pradesh.[20]

Such sensitivity also must characterize those who go to India's 150 million Muslims. More accessible than Muslims in many countries, and with a population larger than most Muslim countries, they deserve a focused ministry. Muslims differ from Hindus not only religiously but also in family, economic and moral customs. They recount the history of India differently. For Muslims, the Taj Mahal is a jewel adorning the heritage of six hundred years of Muslim sovereignty on the subcontinent. They also grieve Hindu-Muslim violence from a different perspective.

Muslims who follow Jesus may need separate worship services. Christians from a Muslim background use a different word for God than those from a Hindu background. They use different words and gestures for greeting. They use different words for offerings. The Hindu-background word offends Muslims because it carries a whiff of offerings to idols. Muslims abhor eating pork, but Hindus abhor eating beef. Muslims wear beards and distinctive clothing. Muslims may be uncomfortable with bhakti worship because they have been taught that music and drama have no place in the house of God. Muslim-background believers also want their sons circumcised in a religious ceremony, but Hindu-background believers may find that repugnant.[21]

Third, prepare for transitions long in advance. Cultivate a second tier of leaders who can step up confidently to ensure the ministry's ongoing vitality, Rajendran recommends. Mentor them. Don't succumb to nepotism, keeping it in the family at all costs. Many ministries have foundered when they have done that.

Fourth, avoid offensive clichés. Avoid stereotyping people in catch phrases like "unreached peoples" or "10-40 window," cautions Prabhu-Singh Vedhamanickam Christia ThambiRaj in his 2008 Ph.D. dissertation. He notes that mission planners set goals, diagram systems and measure results. But if members of a "target audience" happen to overhear snippets of these plans, they may feel manipulated. If they sense they have been objectified, perhaps even commodified, they may get angry. This may spew a backlash. PrabhuSingh is an evangelist, and persecution of Christians in the state of Gujarat is the focus of his research. He reminds us that the people with whom we share the good news are complex—"fearfully and wonderfully made." They are not statistics or categories. We should not talk about them as though they are data but should at all times regard them with humility, aware of nuance.

Fifth, be a passionate saint. India longs for saints, according to Rajendran.

In this he agrees with Tilak, who called for bhakti, the passionate worship of God. E. Stanley Jones, a much-loved missionary, wrote of the same vibrant mysticism in his book *Christ on the Indian Road:*

> India is the land of mysticism. You feel it in the very air. Jesus was the supreme mystic. The Unseen was the real to him. . . . He lived in God and God lived in him. . . .
>
> But Jesus the mystic was amazingly concrete and practical. . . .
>
> He did not discourse on the dignity of labour—he worked at a carpenter's bench and his hands were hard with the toil of making yokes and ploughs, and this forever makes the toil of the hands honourable. . . .
>
> He did not argue, as Socrates, the immortality of the soul—he raised the dead. . . .
>
> He did not argue that God answers prayer—he prayed, sometimes all night, and in the morning "the power of the Lord was present to heal." . . .
>
> He did not argue the worth of womanhood and the necessity for giving them equal rights—he treated them with infinite respect, gave to them his most sublime teaching, and when he rose from the dead he appeared first to a woman. . . .
>
> He did not discourse on the equal worth of personality—he went to the poor and outcast and ate with them. . . .

He did not merely speak on behalf of the physical needs of people—he fed five thousand people with five loaves and two fishes. . . .

He did not prove how pain and sorrow in the universe could be compatible with the love of God—he took on himself at the cross everything that spoke against the love of God, and through that pain and tragedy and sin showed the very love of God. . . .

He did not argue the possibility of sinlessness—he presented himself and said, "Which of you convinces me of sin?"

The merely mystical man is weak and the merely practical man is weak, but Jesus, the practical Mystic, glowing with God and yet stooping in loving service to men, is Strength Incarnate.

It is no wonder that India, tired of speculation, turns unconsciously toward him, the mystic Servant of all.[22]

9

SONG

"WHO CAN WRITE SONGS?" That question reverberated in Barnabas's mind as he scanned the letter in his hand. "The refugee camp is crowded. There are lots of new believers but only a few Bibles. So Alice wants some teaching songs." He raised his head. "Why ask me?"[1]

His wife glanced up. "We're in the heart of Cambodia, not in a camp on the fringe. We're at the center."

Barnabas looked skeptical.

"Pray about it," she counseled.

Barnabas prayed.

"You are the songwriter." That was the answer that came whenever he asked God for help.

"I have no training," he protested when he shared this with his wife.

"You know all the old stories," she reminded him. "Your family was rich in the traditional arts. You were raised with them."

"Musical skills are something different," he objected.

"So learn."

"Training takes money."

"See this?" She pulled a thick gold chain from beneath the neckline of her dress. "Remember my grandmother's necklace? I'll sell it to pay for your music lessons."

So Barnabas studied flute (for melody), guitar (for harmony) and composition, all under the tutelage of three fine national musicians. Then in tea shops he began to create lyrics, using a toothpick as his pen and tea spilled on the table to serve as ink. Eventually Barnabas Mam would compose four hundred Christian songs, two hundred of which are in the Khmer hymnal today.

Through genocide and labor camp. Did he grow up in a Christian family? By no means. When he was a child, there were very few Christians anywhere in the country. Shortly before the end of the Vietnam War, World Vision sponsored evangelistic meetings. Many thousands of Cambodians opened their hearts to Jesus. This was a pivotal event in the life of the Cambodian church.

Barnabas was ordered by his communist leader to spy on these rallies. What he saw and heard—a loving God and a loving community—changed his life.

After Cambodia fell to the communist Khmer Rouge regime, one-third of the population perished, including Barnabas's father and six brothers and sisters. Barnabas was placed in a labor camp for fifteen months. Even there he found a bright spot. Whenever there was a thunderstorm, he would seek out a private place and sing "How Great Thou Art" in Khmer, French and English. Standing all alone, looking out at the rain, he envisioned thousands of Christians worldwide singing with him.

Following the labor camp came eight years in a refugee camp. Through it all, Barnabas wrote songs. Because he had internal hemorrhoids, he often wrote lying on his stomach. In the camp he and his wife also planted fifteen churches, trained fifty Christian leaders, opened an English school and pastored a Vietnamese church. Today Barnabas trains songwriters and storytellers.

All his songs are based on Scripture. Many emphasize God's grace and mercy. Often they relate to a common Cambodian experience. When Barnabas created a child's dedication song, for example, he used the tune from a lullaby that parents have sung to their children for hundreds of years. His song talks about God's loving arms, God's protection and the importance of raising a child in the love of God.

Worth more than flowers. For funerals Barnabas wrote a song based on Psalm 90 titled "We Will Be with God Forever: Human Life Is Worth More Than Flowers." We blossom for a short time, then fade away, this psalm says. We need a God who will preserve our spirits for eternity.

One day a woman asked Barnabas for help. Just before her husband died, he had become a Christian. Now at his funeral monks were chanting in one room, and Christians were singing "Amazing Grace" in the next. This madhouse was not a fitting commemoration for her husband. What should she do?

"Pray quietly instead of singing," Barnabas advised the Christians. Then he negotiated with the Buddhist family members. They agreed to allow a Christian service the following day at a nearby Buddhist temple, the most convenient gathering place.

More than three hundred Christians showed up. Barnabas gave them copies of his funeral song on Psalm 90. Buddhist monks, nuns and laypeople surrounded them. After the service, the Buddhists said, "This song is acceptable. Christianity is not alien to us." A nun prayed and placed her faith in Jesus.

One Christmas eve, while traveling with friends, Barnabas slept on a stack of rice straw outside a house. Since that village had a loudspeaker system, he asked permission to broadcast his new Christmas hymn. This recording included the five traditional instruments that are used in the genre of Bassac music—drums, sitar, a two-stringed violin and a wooden box and stick.

That evening the whole village heard how Jesus was born to bring peace to all Cambodians. The next morning a dozen village elders brought fruit and rice to the travelers. "We were so delighted to hear that Christ is not American or French, but the Son of God who came even for Cambodians," the elders enthused. "We understood the songs. We appreciate that Christ came for us and we want to receive him now."[2]

At the height of the cruel Khmer Rouge terror, an international Christian radio program broadcast Barnabas's songs. A Khmer Rouge official wrote to the station to express thanks. Communist songs stirred up anger and hate, the officer said, but Christian songs promoted love and unity. These songs did not betray Khmer culture, he had decided. They strengthened Khmer culture.

In this chapter we will meet people like Barnabas who use a variety of media—story, song, memorization, action, Internet and print—to witness, disciple and worship.

DO CHRISTIANS NEED TO READ?

Every person needs God's Word. It tells us what God is like. It shows us who we are. It affirms us. It critiques us. It introduces us to our people, our role models, our reference group, our roots. It lays down ethical guidelines. It constructs a frame of meaning through which we understand nature, history, citizenship, childraising and dying. It trumpets celebrations, croons poems, wails laments. It gives us hope. Every person deserves access to the Bible.

To this end the church sponsors literacy programs all over the world.

Yet millions of Christians never will read very well. Even functionally literate people may not read much. What about these brothers and sisters? Are they condemned to second-class citizenship in the kingdom of God? Can they grow to maturity? Or will they always stand on the edge of things, peering in like children with their noses pressed against the window? Can they develop the balanced discernment that Christian leaders need? Or will they never be able to "correctly handle the word of truth" (2 Tim 2:15)? If they are to grow in wisdom as they serve and witness and lead, *must* Christians read?

Oral learners throughout history. Every Christian needs the Bible. But reading isn't the only way to access it. Throughout time and space, most Christians have received Scripture orally.

When Moses taught Deuteronomy, the original audience heard it spoken (and sung, in the case of chap. 32).

When Nehemiah rebuilt the wall of Jerusalem and invited Ezra to reacquaint the people with God's Word, the masses gathered like a stadium crowd and listened to the Word read aloud. Then section leaders explained it, translating it into the people's spoken language, Aramaic.

When Jesus learned Scripture, he went to the synagogue, listened to Scripture read aloud, read it aloud himself, and memorized it. He never wrote anything, as far as we know, except some scribbles in the sand.

During the Middle Ages, the church taught through dramas, stained-glass windows, catechisms, statues, pilgrimages, processions, liturgies and feasts. Visual and kinesthetic elements reinforced oral teaching.

Proto-Protestants taught orally too. When the Waldensians made the Bible accessible in the Provençal language at the end of the tenth century, "much of the preaching consisted in reciting long passages of Scripture in the vernacular. Many could not afford an expensive hand-written copy of the Bible, and the ecclesiastical authorities could too easily rob them of such a book, but they could not erase the words which were treasured in the heart," because memorized Scripture cannot be taken away.[3] Two centuries later Wycliffe's "Poor Priests" walked from town to town across England, reading the Bible but also reciting extensively from memory.

Their memories are their documents. In regions where millions of people still don't read today, Scripture continues to spread orally. Consider the Santal people in South Asia. Literacy is less than 1 percent. They have no written history. Their documents are the elders' memories. When Christians came and shared a flowing stream of Bible stories through dramas, songs, dances and testimonies, a man named Marandi believed. So did his family. They were baptized and shared the good news with other relatives, and they too believed and were baptized.

Marandi formed a team to travel to nearby villages to tell stories and sing and act. More people have believed and in turn formed more teams reaching out to still more villages. The multiplication continues today.[4]

In Nigeria a pastor named Timothy has switched from preaching doctrines to telling Bible stories followed by discussions. After he finishes a story, he invites someone to retell it. Then he asks the others, "Is it correct? Has he got the details right?" Together they go back over the narrative, supplementing and correcting each other, and reinforcing the story in everyone's mind.

Through skillful questioning, Timothy helps his congregation think through the story's meaning and application. In the other direction, as people ask questions, Timothy has seen how little they understood his preaching in the years before he switched to stories. Through dialogue he can clarify many points. But sometimes he leaves people hanging. "As I tell more stories, you'll discover that for yourself." Suspense rises and the listeners are propelled into active inquiry.[5]

Memorizing Bible passages is another useful skill. Many believers come from traditions where sacred Scriptures are memorized and chanted. They feel honored when they are directed to memorize God's Word. This is a learning style that should not be devalued.

In South Asia more than six hundred Muslims have come to Jesus over a thirty-year period through the ministry of two single women. Memorization has been crucial. As soon as a Muslim committed to Jesus as Lord, he or she was required to learn thirty-four verses from the Gospel of John. If the convert was not literate, he or she had to find someone else who knew the verses and could teach him or her. This empowered nonliterates. They felt they owned the message. Some became superb grassroots witnesses.

The literate teenagers received prizes for memorizing whole books of the Bible—maybe a radio for Colossians or Philippians (4 chaps.) or a stripped-down bicycle for Ephesians or Galatians (6 chaps.). Teens immersed themselves in Scripture, and several have grown up to be pastors.

Won't they veer off? But, the thoughtful Christian may object, if people don't read, how are they going to keep faithful to Scripture? Won't they veer off into imaginings and half-remembered teachings?

Of course people need access to the actual Scripture text. Fortunately in any population of significant size, there are natural scholars. Given a chance to read, they will. Every church needs such people, whether pastors or laypeople.

But not everybody in the congregation needs to tap into Scripture by reading it.

In other words, text readers should be sought out, honored and listened to. They are essential. At the same time, nonreaders should not be let off the hook. Instead, they should be held to high standards of accountability for knowing Scripture.

In North Africa seventeen believing men learned Bible stories for two years. Their curriculum was ambitious: A sequence of 135 stories. Along with each story they also picked up some songs and dramatic action to equip them to share Scripture throughout the region.

After two years a seminary professor gave them a six-hour exam. He wondered, Did they understand theology? Did they grasp the nature of God? Could they explain the Christian life? Could they connect the stories with doctrine?

Indeed they could. Given a theological theme, they quickly referred to multiple stories to demonstrate the theme. They answered a variety of theological questions using the stories as illustrations.[6]

Do Christians need to read? No. When a congregation is composed mostly of nonreaders, there are ways to help these worshipers understand and remember Scripture. All Christians need to know the Bible, but print is only part of the package.

SONG

"Daddy, did you become a Christian because of your dad's preaching?"

We were raking the grass together. I was about ten years old. My Dad looked off into the distance over the top of his rake, and said, "No. I think it was because of my mother's singing."

His mother died of tuberculosis while he was in his teens. Before that she was in and out of TB hospitals while giving birth to seven children. Yet she sang. Would I be a Christian today if she had not inhaled breath into those tired lungs and let loose with a melody?

Songs are a precious resource for the Christian communicator. Songs can teach. Songs can help us remember a message. Songs can help keep the message accurate, because rhythm and melody, like writing, stabilize a text.[7] Songs can help us party and also can help us cry, and throughout our lifetimes we will need to do plenty of both. Songs can help us witness and help us worship. Those are seven functions of songs.

People like Barnabas Mam, who have grasped the importance of these functions, pour their lives into vocal music.

Songs in the rain forest. Nobody among the Motilones acknowledged Jesus for several years after Bruce Olson arrived in the jungle, as described in chapter four (see pp. 105-8). Bruce wasn't pushy. He hung up his hammock alongside eighty others under their big thatched roof. He hunted and fished and relaxed with the people. He analyzed their unwritten language until he could speak it fluently. He learned their myths.

Then Bruce's tribal blood brother, Bobi, was drawn to Jesus. While the two men walked the trails and sat around the campfire, Bobi absorbed Bible stories and Christian worldview. His life changed dramatically.

Yet he did not witness to anyone else. Bruce wondered if the gospel would stop here.

One afternoon the Motilones sensed that they were under attack from the tiger spirit. On such a night somebody always died. To chase the spirit away, they climbed up into their hammocks and sang loudly.

Bobi chanted too, raising his voice to the Lord Jesus and asking him to protect the people.

No one died.

A few months later several longhouses gathered for the people's greatest annual celebration, the Festival of the Arrows. During this party an older chief from another longhouse squatted down in front of Bobi and challenged him to a song debate.[8]

"We heard there was a Night of the Tiger in your house not long ago. We heard that nobody died. We heard that you were singing to some other spirit. We want to know more about this."

So Bobi and the old chief climbed into a single hammock twenty feet off the ground and began to swing back and forth. Bobi began to sing all that he knew about the gospel.

Song debate is a genre that pops up in cultures from Kazakhstan to the Philippines to the Amazon rain forest. It is a form through which new information can be handled artistically, often at great length. In Bobi's case the debate lasted thirteen hours.

While the two men sang, people around them were cooking, eating and taking naps. But they also were hearing the good news of the Lord Jesus. At the end of that debate several communal houses decided to follow Jesus together.

Today, although threatened by land grabbers, loggers, oil companies, settlers, drug traffickers and guerilla armies, the Motilone are a savvy, integrated community facing the outside world well together. Nearly all of them follow Jesus.

Songs of the slaves. While songs like Bobi's witness powerfully to non-believers, songs also can strengthen believers in mind and soul and body. Consider African American spirituals. Called America's most significant contribution to world music, they were born in the hell of slavery. Some scholars have criticized spirituals for keeping slaves' minds on heaven so they would not agitate for justice in this world. Others note that spirituals served as signals during escapes, and suggest that that was their primary purpose. Still others view spirituals as white Christianity imposed on slaves who mixed it with bits of African music and poetry.

Others, like Paul Jewett, believe spirituals presented a worldview that enabled slaves to respond to their oppression proactively. "As the name 'spiritual' implies, these songs are ultimately expressions of a transforming inner experience that brings to the human spirit new discernment and hope," Jewett says.

> This is what enabled the slaves by faith to transcend the loss of outward freedom and remain inwardly free. Because of this inner freedom, they could be truly human even as slaves. Even though they were treated as 'niggers,' these early black Christians knew they were not niggers but rather children of God; even though they were treated as things, they knew they were not things but persons. Ultimately this faith in themselves was rooted in their faith in God.[9]

That is not all. They expected God to get involved. God rescued the Hebrew slaves from the Egyptians. He protected the prophet Daniel from the lions. He liberated Daniel's three friends from the fiery furnace. Surely a loving God would not merely free folks in other eras. Surely that was not reserved for heaven. God would transform their condition in this world too.

In his essay "Religion as a Cultural System," anthropologist Clifford Geertz suggests that religion may help people transcend circumstances when they reach limits in three areas: limits of analysis, limits of endurance, and limits of moral insight.[10] That is what spirituals did. While blues presented a poignant analysis of the human condition, especially of the way white people treated black people, spirituals went on to affirm a God who loves his world. Therefore the slaves were *not* "niggers." Therefore they looked for concrete liberation: "Let my people go!" Therefore they sang. They transcended the limits of their endurance as they tapped into an alternate worldview.

> In this light, when one looks at the words of the spirituals with their celebration of freedom and deliverance, so far from saying that the black singers borrowed their thoughts from white Christianity, one might better say that the slaves redeemed the Christianity which their masters had profaned.[11]

Songs that teach. Music is a model for "God's polyphonic people," says scholar Jeremy Begbie. It shows us that we can have unity and diversity at the same time. As recurring motifs sparkle through dizzying variations, music also reminds us that past, present and future are connected. As well, music demonstrates that we need both classic repertoire and improvisation.[12]

In Brazil, Guilherme Kerr is a renowned Christian singer and songwriter. Because he knows how songs can teach, Guilherme does not just compose on a whim. Periodically he has gathered a group of musicians to create songs based on a segment of Scripture.

"We'll say, 'Let's work on the Beatitudes—or the book of Acts—or the Psalms.' "

For three months or so Gui and his friends have gotten together on weekends or odd afternoons to pray and play together, experimenting with their chosen text. The resulting songs have blessed Brazil.

In West Africa, a tribe with just a few dozen Christians asked Roberta King for help. Roberta is an ethnomusicologist, a professor and a participant in the International Council of Ethnodoxologists.

"Can we teach the Bible through songs? Can we learn how to compose these songs ourselves?" the handful of tribal Christians asked Roberta.

Working together, several tribespeople studied local instruments and musical styles. They also studied Bible, focusing especially on the first three chapters of Genesis. Then they began to compose. After two months they had a repertoire of nineteen original songs.

"Now that we know how to put Scripture into our songs, we will keep on doing this," they enthused at the conclusion of the exercise.

In India seven Christian families moved across a state line. Because the new state prohibited Christians, they simply registered as tribals. They were so isolated that for fifty years they did not meet another Christian. When one finally visited, he discovered how they had kept the faith. Every Sunday night they gathered and sang through the Bible, melodies and lyrics that they had developed themselves.

In the southern Philippines, where I was teaching some years ago, there were fellowships in three Muslim-majority people groups. Most of the believers were not literate. Because of political violence, few outside Christians could enter the region.

Ballads were popular among these people, and easily composed. So I proposed a plan. Sponsor a two-week ballad-writing workshop. Bring together ballad writers and Bible teachers from each of the three groups. Commission them to compose two longs sets of ballads in each of the three languages. First, a set of biographical ballads, spanning from Adam to John on the isle of Patmos. Second, a series of doctrinal and topical ballads.

Armed with this body of song, a mother sweeping her courtyard or a fisherman at sea could sing systematically through the major themes of Scripture. They could go through the hours of the day in the company of Moses and Hannah, Daniel and Esther, Paul and Lydia. They would learn systematically through song.

STORY

If songs teach, so do stories. The Bible is not primarily doctrines. It is primarily the stories of people who encountered God and responded, sometimes well and sometimes badly.

Jesus loved stories. His parables remain one of the best vehicles for sharing the good news. And Jesus showed the value of our human story when he stepped into it.

Stories connect us with the ultimate questions we encounter as human beings. At the same time, they delight us with their crafted beauty. They touch us rationally, aesthetically, emotionally, spiritually and even physically as we laugh, groan or tense while we listen. Whetting our curiosity, stories draw us into active learning.

Symbols in stories wake us up, expanding our range of meanings, allowing us to think in new ways. When they draw on a particular people's repertoire of images, they reverberate with connotations and connect us with the community of the past as well as the present. Pondering the parables and proverbs of the Bible can prepare us for local stories.

An African story cycle. Heat shimmered as goats foraged. But under the tree of the elders, a person could sit without sweat. Here the men gathered each afternoon. As a new missionary to north Ghana, Paul joined them to rest and listen and learn.

One day Paul asked, "Can you tell me anything about your ancestors?"

The senior elder was pleased. He beckoned to a young man and gestured with his chin toward a pile of rocks nearby. "Go get a stone and bring it here." When the stone was placed on the ground in front of the old man, he asked, "What about our ancestors? Let us begin with our forefather Jafok."

Men chimed in with bits of the story of Jafok's life—his adventures, his sins, his successes. Eventually the voices quieted. Then the old man prodded, "Who was Jafok's father?"

"Saamo! Saamo sired Jafok," they answered.

"Bring a stone for Saamo," the elder directed.

So a second rock was placed on the ground. In time, there was a line of stones, as the lives of various ancestors were recounted. Finally they stopped with Omeru.

"Did Omeru have a father?" Paul wondered.

"Yes," they answered, "but we can no longer remember who he was."

Over the next several months these ancestral stories were repeated, always with a line of stones ending with Omeru.

One day Paul said, "I think I know who Omeru's father was." He walked to the pile of stones, chose the biggest, and rolled it to the head of the line. "God was Omeru's father," he began.

In time he told the stories of Adam and Noah and Abraham. A longer lineage line stretched out.

"Now I will tell a new story," Paul announced one afternoon. He walked to the beginning of the lines of rocks, grunted, levered up the big God rock and waddled with it down the line. Right in the middle of the lineage he set the big rock. He flexed his back a minute, then announced, "One day God himself was born into a human lineage."

All over the region this story is treasured. Now villagers keep piles of stones in front of their compounds so Christians can tell the story when they pass by.

Stories with actions. Marandi told stories to his Santal people. Timothy told stories to his Nigerian congregation. Paul told stories in Ghana, but he dramatically added stones. Aristotle spoke of three kinds of learning: propositions, poetry and practice. *Practice* refers to learning through actions, such as drama, dance, liturgy, apprenticeships and simple object lessons like Paul's use of stones.

In one Bible story series for Arab Muslim women, each lesson is illustrated with a household object—a broom, a loaf of bread or a bucket, for example. When a woman sees this object in her own home, she is stimulated to remember the story that she heard and to repeat it to those around her.

A weekly Bible study for executive women includes water-color painting. The women gather. One reads the Bible text aloud. All the women paint what they envisioned when they heard the words from the Bible. After they finish their paintings, the leader explains the text.

They put away their easels and return to their high-pressure business. Next week they return for another hour of listening and painting. Some lives have been transformed.

In a big country with lots of Christians but also lots of persecution, a foreign Christian artist was invited to teach a minicourse in one of the top art institutes. For three weeks he worked with ten excellent students. They prepared an exhibit for a festival in a large city.

Their theme was the Hebrew exodus. Every day they discussed the story, using the Bible as a text, wrestling with deep questions as they created their art.

In the Philippines there is an isolated tribe known as the iKalahan. A mostly Christian community, they have successfully developed communal swidden (slash and burn) agriculture, guava jelly production and marketing, and an outstanding large-scale land conservancy.

When their Christian faith was still new, they developed house-blessing rituals.[13] If a family moved into a new house, they invited the community. The elders of the church would preside over a dedication ceremony.

First they would call on God. "Be here with us now as we mark this new house in the name of Jesus."

An elder holding a cup filled with pig's blood would approach the door. Swishing a frond through the cup, he would swipe a red streak across the lintel.

"I mark you, door," he would sing. "Blink closed to difficulties and to evil. Yawn wide to industriousness and to all good things."

Then the group would mount the steps and walk across the springy bamboo porch and into the house. Here they would mark each room and sing to it, dedicating it to God. Finally they would sing to every person in the family.

All through the ceremony the aroma of roasting pork would surround them, reminding them that at the culmination of the dedication the whole community was invited to a feast.

This ritual was not completely new. IKalahan pagans had followed a similar house-blessing ritual. The Christians removed the parts that honored spirits, and kept the parts that praised God.

STREAMING

"Why We Can Count on Geeks to Rescue the Earth" is an article that appeared in *Wired* magazine.[14] Most people think pretty small, the article says. Most of us are preoccupied with friends, neighbors, colleagues and a few sports and media figures. (If we are Christians, we may expand our vision to include an orphan or a mission site.)

But computer geeks think in millions.

Bringing spiritual and physical good news to needy people requires hands-on love, but it also requires thinking big. That is behind the Internet Evangelism Alliance, which serves 1,350 evangelistic sites in 850 languages.[15]

One Europe-based site has three hundred evangelistic chat rooms sorted by language and subject. At any given moment, sixty-seven thousand people are on-line in these rooms. The Arabic chat rooms are staffed by Muslim-background believers.

On a French website, www.connaitredieu.com, seven hundred counselors mentor new believers by e-mail. In a recent eight-month period, 44,044 people indicated a personal decision for Christ through this site. Of these, 19 percent are students, and 2.5 percent are Muslims.

Another French site, www.topcretien.com, has five million visitors per year. They started with one volunteer counselor, but now have eighteen hundred. Follow-up is done through e-mail.

At these sites, Christians start the ball rolling by asking questions about Jesus. After that, interaction is the name of the game. People respond, often by texting on their cell phones. Seventy to eighty percent of the responses to major Arabic outreaches are by cell phone.

One site invites everybody to respond with a yes or no to a weekly question. Respondents vote, just as they do for *American Idol*. For example, "Do you think that Christians should be allowed to preach Jesus in Arab lands?" (Ninety percent responded yes to that question on an Arabic site.) This kind of interaction promotes a sense of audience ownership and relationship with the people at the site.

Whatever the medium people use when they respond—cell phone, e-mail, Skype, letter or visit—it is essential to stay with that medium as long as possible. If you switch the medium, respondents will drop away like flies. And there is no way to hold them. On the Internet, you don't know who they are. Ties are ephemeral. They can evaporate instantly. So you stay with the inquirer's medium of choice until eventually he or she suggests that you move to a medium where you can communicate more comprehensively.

How about discipleship? Beyond evangelism, the Internet helps Christians grow and leaders teach, as we have seen in the chapters on China and Iran. Other media serve these purposes too, like radio, TV, videos and DVDs. Consider the *Jesus* film. Most of the text is from the Gospel of Luke. Now in 1,040 languages, this film has been shown approximately six billion times around the world, with significant impact.

A women-focused adaptation of the *Jesus* film is titled *Magdalena*. As a result of this film, there are groups of women in surprising places who call themselves "Sisters of Magdalena."

Cultural hegemony—one culture dominating another—is a big danger in mass media. Enabling local people to control their own media is a challenge for Christian producers. Internet facilitates that best because the interaction is two-way.

Other media can be adapted locally, however. In one New Guinea tribe, people did not want to read the Bible even after it was translated into their language. Although some of them had advanced degrees, they had gone straight from illiteracy to cell phones and visual and audio media. So the Bible translator created "Scripture DVDs." He used video clips and photos of scenes from village life, including special events and cultural practices like women weaving. The audio tracks are the Gospel of John (three DVDs), Romans (two DVSs), and Colossians and 1 John. These have proved popular. For every hundred printed Bibles sold, people buy five hundred copies of the DVD.

BUT READERS NEVER GO AWAY

Indonesia is famous for visual symbols, puppets and live dramas. Yet when I walk down the street in Jakarta, I see the peanut seller reading a newspaper. I see the elevator operator with his nose buried in a novel.

Burmese vendors spread their wares on sheets laid out on the sidewalks. As the day cools, potential customers stroll by. Next to the vegetable hawkers and tool merchants, booksellers lay out their volumes. Readers squat on their haunches and peruse the pages.

In Africa people "hold small print up to their eyes under tiny bulbs while radio sets blare, children yell, societies dance, and drunks fight, all within yards of them—people will read anything provided it is not frivolous, is related to something significant for them, and that they can make intellectual contact with it."[16]

Readers salt our societies, and their influence is disproportionately large in relation to their numbers because they explore a wider range of ideas than other people do. Print encourages them to think sequentially, to connect cause and effect, to distinguish contradictions. It enriches them with the ideas of thinkers across time and space. All of this equips them to contribute more to community discussions. They can expose the non sequiturs of those raised on sound bytes.

For good Christian writing, local authors are essential. Imported, translated books will not have as much impact. Local writers can capture the kingdom stories that vibrate to be written. They can interview mature local saints who are brimming with God-given wisdom. They can apply the whole counsel of God to their time and place. They can help unbelievers learn about God and his world in ways that make sense. They can help Christians grow to maturity.

Hilmy Nor in Malaysia and Patricia Vergara in Peru are two writers like that. Here are their stories.

CIRCUMCISED HEART

"Here's some paper and a pencil," the interrogator told Hilmy. "Write down any questions you want to ask."

Hilmy worked for an oil company and fraternized in business circles. Yet he was imprisoned for witnessing to his Christian faith. He is Malay, and Malays are not allowed to become Christians.

When his interrogator asked him to write out his questions, Hilmy's "immediate reaction was to scream my heart out on paper. What a surprise to see a poem flowing from my pencil," he comments.[17]

Tuhan ku
Ku jauhi kau
Aku merana
Ku cuba dekati kau
Aku azab sengsara

Tuhan ku

Hanya ada satu Tuhan
Dikau
Hanya ada satu kebenaran
Dikau
Hanya ada satu jalan
Kepada kau

Bimbinglah tangan ku
Bukala mata ku
Lembutkanlah hati ku
Lepangkan fikiran ku
Dedahkanlah pintu pintu ku
Bebaskanlah diri ku
Mendapatkan mu

Aku menyerah diri
Kepada mu
Tuhan ku

My God
I distance myself from you
I suffer
I draw close to you
I face hardship

My God
There is only one God

You
There is only one truth
You
There is only one way
To you

Hold my hands
Open my eyes
Soften my heart
Free my mind
Open your doors
Release me
To embrace You

I surrender to you
My God

Not only a poem but also a book was born from this imprisonment. Published in 1999 by Kairos Research Center in Malaysia, the one-hundred-page *Circumcised Heart* remains in demand in the biography section in national bookstores.

Hilmy writes about walking blindfolded to interrogations. Years later, whenever he leaves a room, he still automatically extends his wrists for handcuffs. He writes about losing thirty-five pounds. He writes about watching his wife, May Lee, recede into the distance.

One Christmas when he is in solitary confinement someone down the corridor sings "Silent Night." Hilmy closes his eyes and pictures May Lee and the church festivities. He smells the curry at one friend's open house and tastes the special pastries at another. It hurts too much. He curls up to sleep.

Yet God walks with him through the pain. As a result, after he is released, he hosts a lunch for his two interrogators. "How could I forgive them? Love them and pray for them? Ridiculous. Yet the Lord taught me how."

Earlier, when Hilmy wrote his poem, a prison guard approached him with a request. "Your poem is not bad. You have talent. I wonder . . . could you possibly compose a poem for my mom's birthday?"

"I'm not a poet," Hilmy answered. "I just wrote from my heart. You can do it too. Write something for your mother from your heart."[18]

I DID NOT ASK TO BE GOLD

"God spoke to me personally and deeply during a seminary class," says Patricia Vergara, a Peruvian writer.

> The professor was praying that we would discover the unique purpose He has for each of us . . . for which He had formed us in the womb.
>
> I shivered with emotion. I felt that the Spirit was telling me that I had to give priority to writing, leaving other things aside . . . that my future ministry would be through publications, and that through them I would continue pastoring, exhorting, and edifying.
>
> I thought about the church, and my responsibilities.

Patricia was a pastor's wife. "The faces of the people who needed me and absorbed my time passed through my mind. I cried, because I realized that truly I would have to make adjustments in order to fulfill my call."[19]

During a five-minute recess, Patricia fled to the bathroom to dry her tears. In the corridor the school secretary handed her the printout of an e-mail message.

"How strange!" Patricia murmured. "I never receive E-mail here at the seminary."

It turned out to be a note from the wife of a pastor in Chile. She had read Patricia's book *Yo No Pedi Ser Oro (I Did Not Ask to Be Gold)*. "With words tender and beautiful, she told me how the book had ministered to her," Patricia says. "She asked me to continue writing. And she told me that she always would be praying for me."

Patricia and her husband formed a publishing company called *Verbo Vivo* (Living Word) and she writes books for children, adults and teens. "There is a great empty field in literature for adolescents in Spanish," she says. Two of her books are devotional guides for teens. Each contains one hundred lively devotionals.

The whole family promoted Patricia's first book, which was poetry. When her husband preached evangelistically, the family dramatized the poems with music and dance. Nonbelievers responded, confessing faith in Jesus. Patricia was not surprised. "Art speaks," she says simply.

Bookstores were less enthusiastic. Some refused to take the books on consignment until readers demanded them. As *Verbo Vivo* developed regular advance publicity and employed an agent/distributor, sales increased.

While raising three small children and serving actively in the church, Patricia has continued to sharpen her mind. For many years she has maintained a regular reading schedule and a habit of filing interesting articles for later reference. A graduate of the prestigious San Marcos University, Patricia went on to complete her M.A. at the Facultad Teologia Latinoamericana. Her thesis was on God in modern Peruvian novels.

More than once Patricia has been honored by invitations to take part in the annual poetry reading at San Marcos University. One year she read a poem that responded to the theory of evolution and others that narrated Jesus' encounters with the adulterous woman and with Lazarus. Another year she read a series on conjugal love, as well as poems about the death and resurrection of Jesus.

The audiences were not Christian. Many other poems had erotic themes. "I, too, sang of love," says Patricia, "but I transmitted values that the world had forgotten. It was a privilege to share my Christian worldview by reading simple authentic poems."[20]

Writers like Patricia and Hilmy are treasures. In too many nations translations fill Christian book tables. These do not tell the local stories nor tap into local wisdom. From pastors to peanut vendors, readers deserve more. Imports can turn people into strangers in their own countries. Yet stories are everywhere. All a writer has to do is catch them as they float by.

WHERE IMAGINATION COMES FROM

Where does creativity come from? God formed us in his image, imprinted us with creativity and set us in a world of possibilities.

When God made the world, He could have finished it. But he didn't.

He left it as a raw material—to tease us, to tantalize us, to set us thinking, and experimenting, and risking, and adventuring.

And in this we find our supreme interest in living.

He gave us the challenge of raw materials, not the satisfaction of perfect, finished things.

He left the music unsung, and the dramas unplayed.

He left the poetry undreamed,

In order that men and women might not become bored,

But engaged in stimulating, exciting, creative activities

That keep them thinking, working, experimenting, and experiencing

All the joys and satisfactions of achievement.[21]

First God imagined turquoise and garlic and the long-horned narwhals of the arctic. Then he bestowed imagination on *us*. We were designed to doodle, to draw on the walls of caves and to weld massive sculptures in bronze. To synchronize our violin bows in great orchestras and to hum while we wait for a bus. To dream and to spangle word pictures across the community's consciousness.

Singers in Cambodia and the Amazon, storytellers in Ghana, writers in Malaysia and Peru, and Internet connectors everywhere use a variety of genres to communicate God's good news. There are also graphic artists like Makoto Fujimura. Based in New York, he interweaves the Japanese Nihonga technique with abstract expressionism as he paints about redemption and hope.

Some who sing and story and act and write are communicators more than they are artists. For them art is a tool to be used for witness or discipling. Others aim for "purer" art, seeking to express more than to teach. Nevertheless, what they feel to be true will emerge in their work. Quality art will reveal the artist's priorities, whether the primary elements are chaos or pain or the struggle for justice or human dignity or a mythic story or beauty or sacrificial love.

Many serious artists in Asia, Africa and Latin America find that social commentary is integral to their work. "Could I paint abstract landscapes when poor people are being gunned down in the streets?" they ask. They feel the weight of history resting on their shoulders.

It is possible that artists see a little more deeply than the average person. According to anthropologist Claude Levi-Strauss, the universe is more full of meanings than normal or rational thought can discover. In the Amazonian cultures he studied, he observed that a traditional ceremony, rich in imaginative symbols, could bring together meanings that otherwise would remain ungathered. The singer, the poet, the dramatist, the shaman provided "fireworks" for the community. This emotional purging served as a catharsis for the larger society.[22] Aristotle noted the same function for drama.

In his essay "The Mission of Metaphor in Expressive Culture," James Fernandez suggests that art is composed by people who feel their inchoateness more keenly than the mass, and so are pushed to "leap" to other realms in order to find wholeness. This opens the other realms to those who stayed home, the bulk of society who never dared to take the leap.[23] In the words of C. S. Lewis, "One of the functions of art is to present what the narrow and desperately practical perspectives of life exclude."[24] Imaginative communication is not rocket science. It is something more.

Whether we are primarily communicators or primarily artists, if God's original creation gifts us, and God's transforming salvation energizes us, new life will vibrate inside us. New creations will emerge. Some of this will be art, and glimmers of a worldview will shine through it.

WHEN YOU
GO THROUGH FIRE

Jesus' People in Africa

"My sisters," Joseph stammered. "I kneel here to represent all the men who have raped you. All the men who have beaten you, all the men who have forced you to evil and caused you pain, all the men who have violated your bodies and broken your spirits." Slowly Joseph sank to his knees and flung his body forward, coming to rest with his forehead on the floor. A group of men and women sat in front of him.

Joseph was not a rapist. He was a trauma counselor, part of a team that was helping Rwandans heal their wounds. In her book *After the Locusts*, third-generation Rwandan resident Meg Guillebaud describes how healing has happened.[1]

Beautiful little Rwanda—"the Switzerland of Africa"—has two major peoples, the cattle-herding Tutsi and the agricultural Hutu. They speak the same language and once intermarried freely. But the gap between them widened after European colonial rulers arrived. Under the new governments, identity cards were issued, stating a person's tribe,

Hutu or Tutsi. If your family had more than ten cows, you were Tutsi. So were all your descendents forever afterward.

The colonial rulers—first German, then Belgian—used one group to control the other, and sometimes switched favorites. Divisions deepened. Widespread bloody ethnic savagery erupted in 1912, 1959 and 1973.

In 1993 President Habyarimana signed a peace accord, hoping to increase power-sharing all around. Eight months later he died when his plane was shot down while landing at the national airport. Then all hell broke loose. In an organized, methodical way, armed Hutu hunted Tutsi and killed them in every brutal fashion imaginable. Some of the victims were their neighbors. Babies and children were not spared. Women were ravaged. In a four-year period, it is believed that over three hundred thousand women were raped. In the first one hundred days, eight hundred thousand people were killed. Two million scrambled out of the country by plane, by car and by foot. Many ended up in refugee camps governed by brutal guards and overrun with cholera. Even inside the camps there were reprisal killings, sometimes massacres. Throughout the region murders continued. Hutus targeted Tutsis, and Tutsis retaliated against Hutus. Sometimes the Tutsis struck first.

When the camps themselves were attacked two years later, people fled back home. A degree of peace had been achieved there, so they tried to rebuild their lives. But their wounds were profound, and their anger and pain were intense. A man looked across the street and saw the man who had hacked his wife and children to death. A woman looked up and saw the man who had raped her. In their agony, some people accused those who were innocent, simply because they were from the tribe that had hurt the accuser. Sometimes the accuser wanted the other person's property. These innocent people spent years in jail awaiting trial, while their families tried to cope without them.

Ruth's story. Ruth had been married five years. She had one child and was expecting another when the violence swooped down. Her husband was slaughtered. So were her parents. So was her three-year-old toddler. Ruth herself was herded into a camp, and over the next months raped by so many men that she lost count.[2]

She nearly starved. When she was seven months pregnant, a Congolese Christian volunteer found her and handed her over to the care of foreign aid workers. She had a baby girl.

The aid workers built her a hut. Someone burned it down. They gave her a job looking after orphans. Others muttered, "This Tutsi is like a rat, able to find a life after everything." When major violence erupted and she tried to escape, she fell in a hole, seriously injuring her baby.

Yet in time she married and had another baby.

Then she discovered that she was carrying AIDS.

What next? She thought of her husband. She loved him. Had she infected him? Had she passed AIDS on to him? She thought of her children. Now she must plan ahead for the time when they would be orphans if her husband died too. She thought of her daily trips to market, when she saw some of the men who had raped her.

There are hundreds of thousands of people like Ruth. Meg Guillebaud has recorded many of their stories in her book. How can these survivors cope? How can healthy communities be built in such a wreck? How can individuals get on with their lives when they bear such deep grief and rage? How can Jesus' people worship him and truly love their neighbors?

Nail your grief to the cross. Several Christian groups have begun to work for healing and reconciliation. African Evangelistic Enterprise is one of these. Antoine Rutayisire, a Rwandan, and Rhiannon Lloyd, a psychiatrist from Wales, began to hold AEE healing seminars in all the major cities in the country.[3]

To begin a workshop, Rhiannon would talk about her childhood in Wales. She hated the English. They had restricted her people's rights and ravaged her country, she felt. But one day an English woman apologized to her for the sins of the English, and Rhiannon learned to let go of her hatred.

The workshop then reviewed Rwandan history. What stimulated genocide in Rwanda? They discovered contributing causes. But they didn't stop there. Our human stories don't stand alone. They are played out in the context of God's great story, perplexing as that appears. So the workshop participants talked about who God is and what he is like.

Next, people wrote down on paper the worst things that had happened to them or that they had seen or heard about. Then in groups of three they shared some of their stories. Whenever possible the groups were ethnically mixed. Sharing took at least an hour.

A large wooden cross had been erected in the front of the room. Participants were invited to hold their paper of pain up to Jesus, to tell him about their grief and eventually to give it to him by nailing it to the cross. A hammer and nails stood ready at hand.

The cross was carried outside, and the papers were removed and burned. As the smoke wafted upward, they remembered Isaiah's words that God can bring beauty out of ashes. They prayed for those on either side of them.

Returning to the seminar room, they tried to turn their thoughts to how God had been with them through the pain.

"I can tell about a Catholic orphanage," someone said. "Killers arrived and shouted, 'Point out the Tutsi children!' "

But the nuns refused. "We only have children of God here," they said.

Furious, the killers herded the whole orphanage to a mass grave. The nuns began to sing a hymn of praise. The children picked it up. That did not faze the killers. One by one each person was murdered. The nuns were the first. But the children kept on singing until there was just one treble voice wafting into the sky. Even when only a single child was left, that child was still singing.

As the seminar participants remembered nobility and courage and sacrificial love, and wrote these good memories on a wall chart, spontaneous worship began. It lasted into the night. The final words of the day were from John 1:5: "The light shines in the darkness, and the darkness did not overcome it" (NRSV).

My people's sin. The next morning many participants would relate a new sense of freedom. Everybody would have a chance to share. That is where Joseph found himself kneeling in identification with rapists, and expressing repentance on behalf of all men who have abused women. He hadn't planned it, but he felt compelled to fall to his knees and open his mouth.

Rhiannon Lloyd was right behind him. "My sisters and brothers, I kneel here as a European. So often we have acted like we are more human than you are. As though we deserve more safety, more medicine, more pay. Yet much of our wealth was made possible by cheap slave labor. And to get that wealth we intensified divisions between Rwandans, and sowed the seeds of genocide. I repent on behalf of my people."

To their surprise, a Hutu knelt next, repenting on behalf of the Hutu killers. Then a Tutsi came forward. "In the beginning, we may have been victims, but how quickly we plunged into murder. Even though I did not kill anyone with my own hands, I wished for their deaths in my heart. I repent to you."

Sometimes men have knelt before AIDS orphans to repent for men who brought AIDS into the family.

Taking their people's guilt on themselves sounds like some of the prayers of Moses, Daniel, Nehemiah and Paul. The workshop leaders call it "standing in the gap." Rwandan pastor Meg Guillebaud says, "We must be prepared to stand in the gap wherever we meet people who have been injured because of actions taken by our own people group, government, church or other institution, even if we did not agree with the action taken."[4] This has become the final step in the workshop.

Chantal's story. Through this kind of teaching, Rwandans have experienced deep healing. Chantal had ten brothers and sisters. They lived in peace with their Hutu neighbors. Yet just twenty-four hours after the president's plane was shot down, all the Tutsis in the neighborhood were dead, as well as the Hutus who worked for them. Chantal herself was staying with a relative. In that community Tutsis were rounded up and shot two by two, but several of the girls were saved to become the "wives" of a soldier, and Chantal was one of those. They were kept in a small hut in his compound. The girls somehow got hold of a grenade and prepared to kill him, but he was spared because he was called away one day and never returned.[5]

When things calmed down, Chantal discovered that only one brother and one sister had survived. She tried to make a home for them, but she worried about AIDS and a possible pregnancy, and was consumed by hate. So she conspired to accuse a Hutu neighbor whose house and family had survived intact. Before a judge she swore a false testimony. Ntanturo was imprisoned, and Chantal was happy to see that a Hutu was hurting.

A Christian school, a Christian boyfriend who became her husband and a church changed Chantal's perspective. She began to feel guilty over what she had done. She asked God to forgive her. But what should she do about Ntanturo? If she recanted, she might be imprisoned for giving false testimony.

One day at church she encountered Ntanturo's son. As she opened her mouth to apologize, he told her he had become a Christian and had been praying for her.

Before long Chantal found herself visiting Ntanturo in prison. By now he had spent five years there. Chantal herself was married and had a baby.

Although she had a lot to lose, she knew she had to confess her false testimony. Her church prayed for Chantal as she returned to court.

"Why are you changing your story?" the judge asked.

"Because God has convicted me," she answered.

The judge accepted her testimony and did not imprison her. Then Ntanturo wrote her a magnificent letter in which he offered to become her father, since Chantal's father was dead.

"My beloved daughter," he wrote,

> I have such a deep love for you now that you have spoken the truth. As you wept in court yesterday, I realized the depth of your sorrow for what you have done. I now want to honour you as a member of my family. I want our hearts to be one. I will not be a bad parent to you, and will give you a father's gift when your next child is born. The doors of my family are always open to you whenever you come. My daughter, I want to thank you. If ever you have a problem, don't hesitate to come to me or my family for help. What you did yesterday will never be forgotten. The other prisoners here greet you. Read these Bible verses for your comfort: Numbers 6:24-26; Hebrews 13:18-19; Romans 9:25-29; Psalms 25; 26; 35; 1 Timothy 1:1-18.[6]

When Chantal's next child was born, Ntanturo did give her a "father's gift." Africans treasure multiple generations. If violence or sickness decimates families, they lose not only individual persons; they also lose the network of roles that gives each man and woman a place in the universe and helps them remember who they are. By the grace of God, Chantal and Ntanturu began a new network.

Many ministries rebuild families. Seniors are connected with adult children who adopt them, help them and love them as their own children would have done if they had lived. Orphans are connected with "aunts" and "uncles." One of their key responsibilities is to sponsor the orphans when they marry.

Rape in the Sunday school curriculum. Raped women are a special set of people. In ethnic violence across the globe, mass rape is a tool of aggression. As I write this, great numbers of women—some as old as seventy and some as young as three—are being violated in eastern Congo. Some African men force themselves upon young girls in order to avoid AIDS, or because of a myth that sex with a virgin will cure AIDS.

Solace is the name of a Rwandan ministry that serves raped women like Ruth, who was described earlier in this chapter. Pastors should speak from the pulpit about rape, Solace says. They should help the raped women in their congregations see that they are not responsible for what happened to them. They should pray that these women's negative views of themselves will be taken away. They should bless these women's sexuality, sanctifying it once more. Each church should train a group of women to listen to these hurt women and to love them.

Water is a better metaphor than blood for such women, Solace finds. Jesus offers living water, cleansing and purifying. Jesus also restores what has been stolen. In this regard, John 10:10 is quoted: "The thief comes only to steal and kill and destroy; I have come that they may have life, and have it to the full." Strangely, the thought of Jesus hanging naked on the cross also comforts these women. Often they have been left naked and bleeding by the side of the road, with their legs spread wide open. They have had to crawl until they could find help. It has been very shameful. Seeing Jesus' shame soothes them.

Out of such healing ministries remarkable forgiveness has grown.[7]

NO MORE THIRD CHEEK

Ethnic violence is not the only knife that slices Africa. Muslim-Christian violence bloodies the continent too.

"Run!"

"But mama, did you see? That man is bleeding. I think somebody stabbed . . ."

"Run anyway!" Eyes rolling with fear, a woman sprinted down the road, dust billowing under feet. Her little daughter puffed and panted not far behind.

Nahor groaned. "So it has come to this?" He glanced around quickly. Clamor reverberated in nearby streets. Out in the courtyard he could see his wife winnowing grain, bouncing it up into the air from a flat basket again and again. How lovely she looked in her everyday blue turban and robe. What a source of comfort she represented. Their toddler, the youngest of five, tugged on her clothes.

Yet they must flee. Again! Five years earlier, Nahor's church had been burned to the ground. Now his new church had been torched and reduced to cinders. This time the senior pastor was murdered.

"But it cannot continue, cycle after cycle," Nahor determined. "Burning. Killing. Fleeing. What future is there in that?"

Some Christian friends argued for a violent response. "No more third cheek! The time has come to retaliate. We were patient. We offered the second cheek, just as Jesus advised, and it has been slapped. Now it is time to fight back."

Nahor thought differently. "Our priority is to share the good news of God's love in Jesus with our Muslim neighbors," he reasoned. "We can't do that in a setting of conflict, but only in a setting of peace. So I am going to support dialogue."

"The enemy is whatever stops us from loving." Christians and Muslims had lived in peace in northern Nigeria for generations. As a child, Na-

hor was welcome in his Muslim friends' homes, and they were welcome in his. They ran back and forth, in and out, finding lunch in one place and a snack of bananas in another. Their fathers discussed land and water issues, and their mothers helped each other in childbirth. On religious holidays, they might invite the other families for a meal or send some of the holiday food to their neighbors as a friendly gesture. Nahor longed for the easy give-and-take that he remembered.

But some Nigerian Muslims disagreed. They longed for a society governed by the law of God, as they understood it. Only this kind of society would prosper, they believed. Secular law, which allows all religions equal status, leads toward ethical looseness, they argued. It opens the door to all kinds of immorality in the community. Pornography, adultery, babies without fathers, drugs, robbery and murder increase in modern urban society. While a relaxed approach might have worked in traditional communities, firmer structures are needed today. Sharia, or Muslim law, provides those structures. Under sharia the whole community acknowledges God and is guided toward living by God's rules.

Today several states in northern Nigeria are governed by sharia law. Nahor lived on the borderline. Here the struggle flared up intensely from time to time. As he watched the violence spiral out of control once again, Nahor committed himself to peacebuilding. There were people of good will on both sides. True, the pastor had been murdered. But other church members had been rescued by Muslims who had compassion on them.

Nahor remembered another community where militant Muslims had moved in. When violence erupted throughout the region, moderate Muslims in that town were caught up in the fervor and urged the militants to burn the Christians' homes and stores and churches.

"Why should we do that?" retorted the militants. "Only the Christians were kind to us when we arrived in this community. You didn't welcome us. But they were good neighbors."

Grassroots peacebuilding can succeed in places like this, Nahor affirms. If you start from the top, peace will not last. The Peace Declaration that was developed in Karuna in 2000 did not hold. Violence soon

erased it. Yet while high-level agreements were failing, there were villages where Muslims and Christians knew each other and determined
to stay calm even when outside agitators tried to stir up trouble. And
they did keep the peace. Grassroots community-based dialogue holds
great promise.

In situations of religious conflict some Christians avoid witness because they fear that it will fan the flames. But Nahor believes witness is
intrinsic to worship. Jesus' people testify. They share the good news.
That is the most powerful way that we can love our neighbors. That is
the best thing we can give them. "The enemy is whatever stops Christians from loving and from evangelism," Nahor says. He works for peace
in order to develop a better milieu for witness.

"Oh, I wish I was one of those women!" Nahor expects the church to
grow as a witnessing community in the middle of struggles and persecution. New Life for All is a powerful lay evangelistic movement. Not
long ago they announced a witnessing event in a state governed by sharia law. When the participants converged from several states, arriving in
the backs of open trucks, officials met them.

"You know evangelism is prohibited here. Please come to our office
immediately," the officials said.

The leaders of the event complied. The followers climbed out of the
trucks and began dancing in the plaza, offering free entertainment.
Then they slipped away to visit houses. While the leaders were warned
and fined, people heard the good news that God has come close to us in
the person of Jesus.

Joy and vitality draw people. One day Nahor was riding a bus that
passed a number of Christian women singing on the sidewalk. A Muslim woman was riding near him. "Oh! I wish I was one of those
women!" she said.

Another day a veiled woman came to Nahor's office. "May I speak
with you, Pastor?"

"Certainly. Please be seated," he answered. "How may I serve
you?"

"I want to receive Jesus," she told him.

"Is your husband aware of this?" Nahor asked.

"Yes," she said.

"Bring your husband to see me," Nahor said.

The next day both the wife and the husband were waiting at his office.

"Did your wife tell you something?" Nahor asked.

"Yes," said the husband.

"What was it?"

"She wants to receive Jesus."

With the husband's knowledge, this veiled woman committed her life to Jesus as Lord. Today both wife and husband follow Jesus and witness actively to their Muslim friends.

Twenty-four hours a day. Discipling Muslims is not easy. They need a structure, a community and a sense that God is in touch with their immediate needs. Many African churches provide that. "When a Muslim comes to Christ, we surround him immediately with community. We love him. We are there for him 24 hours a day," Daniel Coulibaly of Mali told me. "How else could he survive all the powers that will beat down on him?"

Witness is alive across Africa. If churches are burned, leaders emerge from the fire. Five thousand two hundred Nigerian missionaries serve in fifty-six countries today under the umbrella association of NEMA, the Nigerian Evangelical Missions Association. This is a network of more than one hundred Nigerian denominational and parachurch organizations.

Nigeria's Deeper Life Christian Ministry works in thirty countries across the continent.

Traders and businesspeople also spread the word. When they move to new places to practice their professions, they are not shy about their faith. As a result, churches are born where they never existed before.

Even a poor country like the Democratic Republic of Congo pulsates with witness. Africa's big transnational languages are English, French and Portuguese, alongside Swahili, Arabic and the thousands of "heart languages" in which mothers croon lullabies, toddlers lisp and lovers whisper. Congo is part of French-speaking Africa. Like the Portuguese-speaking region, the French zone does not have as much Christian infrastructure and materials as the English-speaking area. But Congolese Christians do not let that stop them. "Not hindered by a vision of missions requiring a four-wheel drive vehicle and a salary, they seem to be accomplishing the most for the kingdom, much of it undocumented."[8]

Indeed, undocumented successes shimmer across Africa. Believers do have shortcomings, and we will explore some. Yet African churches—vibrant, creative and often surprisingly mature—sparkle with everyday heroes who practice virtue without fanfare, as we have seen in Rwanda, Nigeria and Congo. Undocumented they may be, but the God who knows every hair on our heads and every single bird in the sky (Mt 10:29-30) certainly knows every unsung hero in Africa.

FAILED STATES

Money matters. Spiritual and community richness make life worth living, but without material sustenance there will be no life at all. Many Africans face that hard truth. Seven of the top ten "failed states" in the world are on the continent of Africa. In these states governments are so weak that they have little practical control over much of their territory. They can't protect citizens against rogue armies that invade from outside or against death squads that roam around inside the country itself. Bullying and corruption squeeze profits. The economy languishes. Electricity is erratic. Transportation is so expensive that students hardly can afford to get to classes. Jobs are scarce. Malaria and tuberculosis and AIDS run rampant. Healthy toddlers die from polluted water. Women die during normal childbirth. Citizens are too malnourished to mobilize their energies optimally. Nevertheless, millions of uprooted people have to keep moving to avoid sweeping violence. The more educated people flee the country and the epidemic of "brain drain" spirals.

The irony is that Africa is rich in resources. Tragically, this is part of the problem. "Africa is cursed—with riches. In an era of rising petroleum prices, African oil is drawing new interest from major companies around the globe," according to John Ghazvinian in *Untapped: The*

Scramble for Africa's Oil.[9] His title reminds the reader of "the scramble for Africa" that took place in 1877, when European countries divided up a map of Africa, allocating the resources in each part to some nation north of the Mediterranean. Centuries earlier, both Arab and European traders had looted Africa's most precious resource—its people—in order to sell them as slaves.

In an ideal world big oil companies' investments should create jobs, which should improve African nations' economies. Wage earners would have money to spend. Stores and businesses would multiply in order to serve the employed workers. That remains the hope, as money pours in. China is investing $12 billion in Congo in exchange for the right to mine copper ore of equal value. This is three times Congo's annual national budget and ten times the aid Western donors have promised annually. The money will build railways, roads and mines.[10] Because Africa has high-quality oil, multinational oil companies will invest $70 billion dollars in oil exploration in Africa by the end of the decade. Surely all this should give African economies a shot in the arm?

Unfortunately, most of this investment will not trickle down. The cash circulates among the foreigners, the elite and the government officials. It is a hard truth that oil money tends to corrupt politicians. If governments depended on taxes, the citizens would have a whip to crack. However, most African governments are not dependent on taxpayers.

Meanwhile, prices rise.

"Between 1970 and 1993, countries without oil saw their economies grow four times faster than those of countries with oil," Ghazvinian notes, adding that oil exports inflate the value of a country's currency, making its other exports uncompetitive. At the same time, workers flock to booming petroleum businesses. That saps other sectors of the economy. "Your country becomes import dependent," he says. "That decimates a country's agriculture and traditional industries."[11]

Angola is a very poor country. Luanda is its capital and also the hub of its oil business. Here luxury high-rise apartments are renting for

$15,000 a month to oil executives. Somebody is making money. But that money is not going for schools, clinics, job training or safe public transportation. Multinational companies argue that that is not their concern. It is the politicians' job to worry about that. "The oil companies will often say that they would like to invest in infrastructure or schools, but they don't have the expertise," Ghazvinian notes. "That's glib. Exxon Mobil is making billions and can hire consultants. They could do more. They don't have to usurp the role of government to do something useful in the countries where they are operating. At the very least, the oil companies might come together and fund some sort of petroleum engineering university so more Africans could work in the industry."

Meanwhile, violence rockets out of the Niger Delta. This is the site of an unusually valuable cache of fuel. Yet the people live in stick huts. Many evenings, little boys will drill holes in pipelines and suck oil out. One hundred thousand barrels a day can disappear through this kind of sabotage. Their families will sell the fuel or pass it on to the rebels who are fighting for a more equitable future. At present, a thousand people are killed in small-scale clashes here every year.

TRAINING GODLY LEADERS

People who think about God, study about God, connect with the writings and teachings of others throughout time and feel a passion to explain this to the rest of us are called theologians. From the first days of the church, Africa has birthed theologians. Shortly after Jesus returned to heaven, Peter preached to Jews from many nations who had gathered in Jerusalem for a festival (Acts 2). Two thousand of those who listened placed their faith in Jesus. Some had come from the Jewish communities that flourished in cities across North Africa. They returned home to plant some of the first churches in Morocco, Algeria, Tunisia, Libya and Egypt.

Not long after that an Ethiopian official encountered the apostle Philip. When Philip explained the good news, the official opened his heart to Jesus. He asked Philip to baptize him. This Ethiopian took the gospel back to East Africa, where a strong church with its own distinctive flavor developed (Acts 8:26-38).

How Africa shaped the Christian mind. Ethiopia, North Africa, Egypt and Sudan (Nubia) all hosted early Christian communities that spread across their lands. Christianity did not come to Africa through Western missionaries. It was the other way around. So many early Christian thinkers lived in Africa that we might say Africa shaped European Christian thought. That is the argument made very persuasively by Thomas Oden in his book *How Africa Shaped the Christian Mind*.[12]

Augustine is known to every theology student, and Augustine was Algerian. Other theologians noted in historical theology courses are Origen, Didymus, Tyconius, Tertullian, Cyprian and Cyril. All of these early Christian thinkers were born and lived in Africa.

Great libraries blossomed in Egypt, Libya, Tunisia and Algeria in the centuries immediately following Jesus' time on earth. Exegetical study of texts was honed. Diaspora Jewish communities were seedbeds of ideas. When members of the communities became Christians, they applied these resources to Christian thought. Early doctrines were polished in Africa in areas like creation, grace, sin, atonement and eschatology.

Preaching, debating and conferring all were cultivated by early African Christians. The two great opponents in the Nicene Creed controversy—Arius and Athanasius—were African.

Spiritual formation through monasticism began in Africa. Antony was a pioneer who went far into the desert to find a place where he would not be distracted. Developing rhythms of prayer, study and work, the monastic community pattern eventually spread as far as Ireland and influenced all of Medieval Europe.

Building with the pieces. Centuries later, Western missionaries came to Africa along with explorers and businessmen. While they were children of their time,

> the missionaries of the colonial era were, on the whole, a remarkable lot. Like Rowland Bingham of the Sudan Interior Mission (SIM, now Serving In Mission), they were a tough-minded breed who often buried their colleagues and kept going. Like George Grenfell of the Baptist Mission Society of Congo, they were tire-

less explorers and enemies of the slave trade. Like Albert Sch-
weitzer of Gabon they were often humanitarians. Like Mary Sles-
sor of the Calabar mission, many were single women who gave
their entire lives to the work. Like P. A. Bennett, acting secretary
of the CMS in Nigeria, they were sometimes incorrigible racists.
But like Archdeacon Dennis, also of the CMS in Nigeria, they
more often opposed racism with equal vigor. Like Father Shana-
han of Nigeria they aggressively founded schools. Most important, like Carl Christian Reindorf of Ghana, they mastered the
vernacular languages of the people and like George Pilkington of
Uganda, they translated the Scriptures and trained indigenous
evangelists. This last factor, vernacular translations and the training of national evangelists, accounts for the remarkable church
growth that took place during the colonial decades.[13]

"What is a missionary's job?" Paul Bohannan was chair of the department of anthropology at Northwestern University when he asked
that question in his book *Africa and Africans*.

What is a missionary's job? It turns out that, besides the purpose
he goes over to achieve—the spread of his religion—he has an
important secondary task. That secondary task is to hold the
pieces of a society together when it smashes, and, ultimately, to
put them back together again in a new pattern. . . . In 1960 (when
Nigeria achieved independence), 96% of the schools in Nigeria
were mission-operated schools. . . . It was the missionaries who
taught Africans to read and write, and thereby supplied government clerks and traders' clerks and ultimately the national leaders.
It was they who did the constructive job. Missionaries are very
often blamed because they destroyed and misunderstood, and so
they did. But so did everybody else. And missionaries are the only
people who *built* below an institutional level.[14]

Today there are hundreds of Bible-training institutes and theological seminaries shaping leaders in Africa. In chapter three we have
traced three of the many themes that African theologians are explor-

ing. Significant publications are emerging like the *Africa Bible Commentary,* completely written by competent Africans. The *Dictionary of African Biography* has collected thousands of grassroots stories, sent them in annual updated CDs to African Bible schools and trained students in those schools to gather such data. The Africa Evangelical Alliance is one of many networks that connect brothers and sisters across the continent.

You're the one I've been waiting for. Beyond formal schools, leaders have been shaped though personal Bible study using guides published by Scripture Union and through university groups related to the International Fellowship of Evangelical Students. InterVarsity is part of the IFES network.

In 2005, IFES opened work in its 150th country, Equatorial Guinea. For a year Nigerian staff worker Gideon Para-Malam had prayed about this wretchedly poor and dismally governed nation. Then he started making daily visits to the Equatorial Guinean embassy. Often he felt like he was butting his head against a wall. There were so many arbitrary conditions that he almost gave up.[15]

Finally a tourist visa came through. The hassles did not end, however. On Gideon's arrival in Equatorial Guinea, the customs woman ransacked the travelers' luggage and demanded money. Two security guards collected Gideon's passport and demanded still more money. Another Christian traveler paid for him. Gideon was repulsed by the experience but also challenged: How much this country needed a spiritually alive student movement! What a difference it could make.

The next day he shared a taxi to the university with a young stranger named Adolfos.

"Are you a professor?" Adolfos asked.

"Yes. I teach students the Bible."

"You're exactly the one I've been waiting for!" Adolfos exclaimed. "I've been looking for someone who could teach me about the Bible."

In the taxi Gideon shared the story of the good news. Adolfos wanted to follow Jesus. He became Gideon's first interpreter.

Next Gideon met with a pastor from another African country, Ghana. This pastor ministered to English-speaking foreigners like himself, but he longed to bless the people of Equatorial Guinea directly. When he learned that IFES was rooted in indigenous leadership, he was eager to be part of it.

Finally, meeting with four students, Gideon told stories about IFES in various countries, with its focus on discipleship, evangelism, missions and leadership development.

"Do you want to spearhead a movement here?" he asked.

"Yes!" they answered enthusiastically.

Any meeting larger than five people required special permission. Usually that permission was denied. Yet when Gideon returned six months later there were fifty students who gathered. Four months later they had sent their first representative to an IFES conference on AIDs in Nigeria. Through such student groups, godly leaders are nurtured.

HEALTH AND WEALTH

Africa is more than suffering and sacrifice. The world's biggest worship auditorium is in Nigeria—Winner's Chapel, with fifty-four thousand seats. So is the world's biggest InterVarsity student Christian movement—forty thousand students. Many Christians are outstanding in civil service, professions, management and education. Their sense of honor, responsibility and motivation are renewed weekly in worship, daily in prayer and Scripture and family fellowship, and through special answers to prayer in times of crisis.

Traditionally, wealth and blessing have been linked in Africa. Political leaders have resources. Otherwise they are not leaders. In stable times in the past, this was not viewed as private, individual wealth. It was to be used for the common good. Leaders accumulated wealth in order to redistribute it.

This is an ideal picture, of course. Unequal power always can be exploited by the unscrupulous. In any case, stable, self-contained societies no longer exist, if they ever did. Slave-trading, colonial governments, modernity, the global ecónomy, national corruption and tribal enmity all have weakened the sense of mutual obligations within communities.

God wants his children rich. Some churches still draw the traditional connection between wealth and blessing. Jesus will make you prosperous, their pastors say. A car, a house, a husband or wife, unbeatable physical health, runaway professional success—all are at your fingertips.

"God has made provision for his children to be wealthy. . . . When I say wealthy, I mean very, very rich," says Pastor Michael Okonkwo from his gold-plated throne on the platform in front of four thousand worshipers.[16]

"Would you like to have a blessing? Come forward and invest in the future," invites Okonkwo's assistant. The equivalent of two hundred dollars would be a good sum to give, he recommends. This is a country where teachers earn about $150 a month. Yet three hundred people scramble forward to make the donation and to receive an anointing of oil on their hands, as observed by reporters Isaac Phiri and Joe Maxwell.

Other pastors oppose this. "Their god is their belly," snorts Joseph Ojo when asked about such pastors. Ojo is national secretary of the Pentecostal Fellowship of Nigeria. "The kingdom of God is built on the cross, not on bread and butter," admonishes pastor David Oginde of Nairobi.

Inevitably some people are harmed by this teaching. Oginde remembers a bewildered student who told him, "I 'planted' my school tuition money in the offering, just like my church advised. But you know what happened? My college kicked me out for not paying the fees. I gave my money to God, but it did not come back. Why not?"[17]

The idea that Jesus will bring prosperity is not unique to Africa. Some of the teaching originated in the United States and has been spread through massive Christian TV networks. Today there are probably "prosperity" churches on every continent but Antarctica.

Yet the "prosperity gospel" teachers are partly right. Christian faith often helps the family budget. People get drunk less. Their lives become more orderly. They become more accountable. Many churches help people in dysfunctional situations—street children, prostitutes, drug addicts—to find more secure footing. Some churches teach business skills. Members may patronize each other's shops and share resources when needed. Non-Christians prefer honest merchants who will not sneak their thumb onto the scale to make unjust profits. The joy of the Lord can put a spring in the step and a sparkle in the eye that will brighten any transaction. Christian faith encourages and inspires and motivates. Renouncing idols and serving Christ blesses individuals and can also bless communities and nations.

Or does he? Does God want us to be rich? Of course. Silks and oil and wine and spices and land and ores and harvests sparkle throughout Scripture as signs of the good life. God intends us to be rich.

But not while God's other children are ragged. We dare not focus on our own prosperity and ignore our neighbor. Long ago the prophet Amos blasted God's people for this imbalance:

> Woe to you who are complacent in Zion. . . .
> You lie on beds inlaid with ivory
>   and lounge on your couches.
> You dine on choice lambs
>   and fattened calves.
> You strum away on your harps like David
>   and improvise on musical instruments.
> You drink wine by the bowlful
>   and use the finest lotions,
>   but you do not grieve over the ruin of [the people next door].
> Therefore you will be among the first to go into exile;
>   your feasting and lounging will end. (Amos 6:1, 4 -7)

A writer of proverbs recommends:

> Give me neither poverty nor riches,
>   but give me only my daily bread.
> Otherwise, I may have too much and disown you,
>   and say, "Who is the LORD?"
> Or I may become poor and steal,
>   and so dishonor the name of my God. (Prov 30:8-9)

Choosing Pygmies Over Multinationals

Pierre lives in Central African Republic, a country so weak that it cannot defend its own borders. Soldiers from Chad, Sudan and Congo invade whenever they feel like it.

Because he was a bright boy, Pierre won a scholarship to study overseas. The grant came from China, a country eager to cultivate ties with Africa's future leaders.

Pierre's first year at university was spent learning the Chinese language. After that, he studied agricultural economics. Although Pierre was not a committed Christian, a relative had tucked a Bible into his suitcase. Alone in China, he read the Bible and came to vital faith in Jesus. Then he began to look around for other Christians.

"You coming tonight?" Peter asked Fula one evening after dinner in the campus dining hall.

"To the worship group? Yes, I'll be there. At 7:00, right?"

Overhearing the exchange, Pierre realized that other African students believed in Jesus too.

"May I join you?" he asked. In that fellowship group Pierre discovered Christian love and learned to grow as a disciple.

Later the Africans found a Chinese house church that welcomed them. Eventually they went out to share their faith in villages. The sight of five large black men striding into a village was sure to draw an audience.

By the time Pierre graduated, he was fluent in Chinese, English, French and his own language. Even though he had his pick of jobs across the globe, he chose to return to his own weak country. Today he runs a discipleship-training center that trains poor pygmies in gardening and marketing of produce, and witnesses to powerful Muslims in the name of Jesus. The only prosperity Pierre is pursuing is long term in the kingdom of God.

If Our Culture Is Going to Survive

At the height of the gory conflict pictured so graphically in *Hotel Rwanda*, Hutu students were killed by Tutsis on campuses in Burundi.

Others fled into the mountains. Tutsi Christian students followed them and brought them food and clothes. Later they brought more, even for strangers whom they did not know. Because of this some of their families rejected them.

When the non-Christian university president heard about this, he made a noteworthy observation. "Our culture is disintegrating," he said. "On our campus there are three types of people: Hutus, Tutsis and Christians. If our culture is to survive, we must follow the example of the Christians."[18]

WAY OF THE CROSS

BLOOD SPURTED IN GREAT GOUTS WHERE QAZI ABDUL KARIM'S RIGHT
ARM SHOULD HAVE BEEN. Jagged flesh quivered from his gaping arm-
hole. Against the wall the bailiff lounged, his sword dripping.[1]

Qazi wobbled.

"Recite the creed: 'There is no God but Allah and Muhammad is his
prophet,'" the judge commanded, unmoved by the gory spectacle.

Through waves of pain, Qazi held on to one truth. Jesus was the
center of his life. He would not swear loyalty anywhere else. He
stayed silent.

A fly buzzed, and the judge roused himself to lecture Qazi, ignoring
the red streams pouring down. "Your arm is gone. You can live with
that. We have one-armed men. But if you persist in this heresy, you will
lose everything. Is that what you want?"

"Jesus is everything," Qazi breathed.

"Off with his left arm," the judge snarled to the bailiff.

Son of an Afghan Muslim judge, Qazi had found a job in a hospital
just across the border in Pakistan. There he became a Christian. When
he had spare time, he witnessed about Jesus all along the frontier. Eventually he was arrested.

Since he would not deny Jesus, a seventy pound chain was placed around his neck and a bridle put in his mouth. He was marched three hundred miles from Kandahar to Kabul and abused all along the way.

It was in Kabul that he lost first his right arm, then his left. When, armless, he still refused to recite the creed, his captors beheaded him.

Twenty-five years later, an Afghan man visited a Christian home in Iran. "I was there in the court that day," he said. "I was a boy of ten or twelve at the time, but I have never been able to forget it. I saw a man tortured and hounded to death for his faith in the streets of Kabul. He was a Christian. The remembrance of the light of the peace on his face remains with me to this day. I can never forget it. Tell me the secret of it."[2] This man committed his life to Jesus and returned to Afghanistan.

Twenty five years after Qazi's death, his life was still speaking.

One of the toughest places. Afghanistan's terrain is forbidding and its history troubled. Opium supports a great deal of the economy. Some of the toughest men in the world stake out their positions here. Huge numbers of widows scrabble to feed their children. Islam is the official religion, and it is a fundamentalist version. Human rights of any kind—religion, press, assembly, gender—don't get much attention. Weapons keep arriving from all directions. Busses are blown up. Journalists are kidnapped.

Can Afghans choose Jesus in the middle of all this? Qazi Abdul Karim and the man who followed him twenty-five years later show that even in crushing circumstances they can.

A thousand years ago there were more people in Asia who called themselves Christian than in all the rest of the world. A good number of those believers lived in Afghanistan. Old Afghan coins bear an inscription "In the name of the Father, Son and Holy Ghost, one God." Ancient rug patterns display crosses. Monuments and cloisters stand as reminders of great mission-training seminaries here.

What happened? The Bible was not translated. Teaching was through Bible stories rather than doctrines, and leaders' understandings remained shallow. Far from the rest of the world church, the clergy became corrupt. Then Genghis Khan arrived. He slaughtered a million people in the Herat valley, which had been a strong Christian center. Shortly after that, Islam moved in.

Still, Bible sellers continued to visit now and then. Some Afghans believed. Eventually foreign Christian doctors and nurses and research scientists worked inside the country, while a praying "circle of love" outside the nation's borders surrounded Afghanistan like a necklace. People in this circle prayed faithfully and talked with Afghans who traveled beyond the boundaries. *Afghanistan: The Forbidden Harvest* by J. Christy Wilson recounts the stories of those working inside as well as those in the outside circle. Some are in Afghanistan now, building up the nation.

Meanwhile, an Afghan diaspora is sprinkled around the world. This includes many gifted people who mourn the tragic state of their homeland and look forward to the time when it will flourish again. Some of these people are meeting Jesus.

The brilliant blind man. In the long line of Afghan believers is a sightless scholar named Zia. In 1964, when he was fourteen, Zia enrolled a school for blind students. Here he met Jesus.[3]

"Do you know that student named Zia?" one teacher asked another. "English isn't enough challenge for him. Now he's tackling German."

"What's his tribal language? Dari? Or Pushtu?"

"He speaks both. Arabic, too. But get this. When he finishes learning German, he plans to tackle Russian."

"Well, that makes sense, since Russia may invade any day."

Zia not only learned to speak those languages but also to read Braille script for all those that had it. He went on to graduate from the University of Kabul with a degree in law, focusing on Islamic law so he could defend Christians. On the side he read Calvin's *Institutes of the Christian Religion*.

Russia invaded, as predicted. Zia's teachers departed, but they left him Isaiah 42:16:

> I will lead the blind by ways they have not known,
>   along unfamiliar paths I will guide them;
> I will turn the darkness into light before them

and make the rough places smooth.
These are the things I will do;
   I will not forsake them.

Zia was appointed director of the school for the blind during the Russian occupation.

"There's just one problem, said the education department representative. "Your administration is fine, your human relations are good, your ability to connect with people from different regions and even different countries is very helpful. But you haven't joined the Party. That's a requirement for someone in your position." The representative voiced this complaint whenever he visited.

If Zia joined the Communist Party, he would have to deny God.

"You aren't even a Muslim. Why make this an issue? It's just professional protocol," the representative would argue.

But Zia would not join the Party. As a result, he was removed from his position and eventually thrown into prison. After some time, he escaped to Pakistan disguised as a blind beggar (which he was).

There Zia dived into translating the Old Testament.

"Great news for you! You've been awarded a scholarship to study Hebrew in the U.S.," a fellow translator told him one day.

For a man with so much intelligence and curiosity, this was a wonderful opportunity. However, Zia turned down the scholarship. "I'm too busy ministering right here," he explained. Yet he did take time to learn Urdu as his seventh language in order to reach out to Pakistanis.

Eventually he was martyred. His wife and children were rescued by a friend.

OTHERS WERE TORTURED AND PUT TO DEATH

Chapter eleven in the book of Hebrews is known as the "faith chapter" because it begins each Bible character's story with the phrase "By faith . . . "

"By faith, Abel . . . By faith, Enoch . . . By faith, Noah . . . By faith, Abraham . . . " Glorious triumphs roll out. Through faith, these biblical characters "conquered kingdoms, administered justice, and gained what was promised; [they] shut the mouths of lions, quenched the fury of the flames, and escaped the edge of the sword; [their] weakness was turned to strength; and [they] became powerful in battle and routed foreign armies. Women received back their dead, raised to life again" (Heb 11:33-35).

Heady stuff. We love it. But suddenly the mood changes.

> Others were tortured. . . . Some faced jeers and flogging, while still others were chained and put in prison. They were stoned; they were sawed in two; they were put to death by the sword. They went about in sheepskins and goatskins, destitute, perse-cuted and mistreated—the world was not worthy of them. They wandered in deserts and mountains, and in caves and holes in the ground. (Heb 11:35-38)

The gospel is not only good news. It threatens established systems and powers. Those systems and powers fight back. This has happened throughout history right up to the present. More Christians have been killed in the twentieth century than in any previous era. In the past few years Pakistani churches have been bombed with the worshipers inside. Indonesian Christian women have been raped by the dozens. Multiple Vietnamese pastors have languished in cruel jails. Korean and Filipino workers have been martyred in Saudi Arabia. Tens of thousands of Christians have been slaughtered for their faith in Sudan. Christian women in India and Turkey have seen their husbands burned to death and their throats slit. In both nations these women have gone on TV to forgive the killers. Though they cried, these women were confident of joy ahead. This sent ripples of shock throughout the societies, impacting many.

Rami Ayyad directed the Palestinian Bible Society's office in Gaza. He was known for his friendliness. Yet on the evening of October 6, 2008, just as he was closing his office, he was abducted. The next day his body was found, brutally murdered.

In the months before Ayyad died, threats had arrived at his office. But he had stayed at his post because he believed the work deserved to be continued.

Elizabeth was a young Christian girl who was kidnapped and forced into prostitution in Southeast Asia. She wrote verses from Psalm 27 on the wall of her prostitute's crib:

The LORD is my light and my salvation—
 whom shall I fear?
The LORD is the stronghold of my life—
 of whom shall I be afraid?
When evil men advance against me
 to devour my flesh,
when my enemies and my foes attack me,
 they will stumble and fall.

Elizabeth looked to God for rescue, and it came. The International Justice Mission discovered and freed her. Today she is a college graduate. Now she quotes from Psalm 34, "I sought the LORD, and he answered me; / he delivered me from all my fears."[4]

If we combed world history stretching from Japan to Uganda, from Siberia to Mexico, we could fill whole libraries with stories of suffering Christians. Some who suffer in our time are delivered, like Elizabeth. Others, like Rami Ayyad, are not. Either way, they follow the "suffering Servant" "who for the joy set before him endured the cross, scorning its shame" (Heb 12:2).

Chhirc Taing was a Cambodian church leader martyred by the Khmer Rouge. The night before he died, he encouraged believers to obey authorities (Rom 13:1), to be gentle as doves yet wise as snakes (Mt 10:16) and to rise up as an "Elisha generation" (2 Kings 2:13). (The prophet Elisha accepted the call to be a leader when his mentor Elijah died.) Then, according to the songwriter Barnabas Mam, "knowing this was the end of his life, Chhirc Taing went out and began witnessing on the streets." Barnabas saw Chhirc Taing arrested and assassinated. "He became my Elijah," Barnabas says.[5]

BRINGING GOOD OUT OF EVIL
Suffering can yield positive results. God can bring good out of evil. In

Bible history Joseph's brothers sold him to be a slave in Egypt. Later, when he had risen to a position of power, he rescued his extended family from famine. If he had not served his time in Egypt, he would not have been able to help. "You intended to harm me, but God intended it for good to accomplish what is now being done, the saving of many lives," he told his brothers (Gen 50:20).

Sometimes when Africans look at black Americans, they wonder, *You are the richest black people on earth. Why have you taken so long to come and help us?*

For their part, African Americans have wondered, *Did your ancestors sell mine into slavery?*

Remembering how Joseph rose out of slavery to bless his people, some African Americans have formed a nonprofit organization and named it the Joseph Assignment, based on Genesis 45:4, 7 (KJV): "I am Joseph your brother. . . . God sent me before you to preserve for you a posterity in the earth, and to save your lives by a great deliverance."[6]

They aim to follow Joseph's example and turn their heritage of suffering into a platform for good.

A wealthy African American church in Chicago began this ministry. With many medical professionals in the church, they formed short-term teams to run regular clinics in Ghana, focusing on five health issues: malaria, TB, typhoid, ringworm and immunizations. In every six-day clinic they treat about fifteen hundred people and provide medicines for others.

They also help in schools, wells and clean water projects, agriculture and economic development, church planting, and pastoral training. Raising funds for these activities keeps the church busy. They gather donations of all sorts of supplies from library books to eyeglasses. The church also supports some African staff.

A little African boy has been adopted by the senior pastor in Chicago. This child was so near death from malaria, and his organs were so enlarged, that the orphanage had not bothered to give him a name. Today he is a bouncy five-year-old. The pastor's wife displays two photos—the first when they got him, and the second as he is now. "This is the face I fell in love with," she says as she holds up the first photo. Then she raises the second. "This is the face that love created."

Culturally, African Americans are quite different from Africans. Yet, inspired by Joseph, this church is strengthening those ties and redemptively bringing good out of evil.

SERVING IN SCARY PLACES

"You saw it yourself. Arms strewn around on the floor. Legs. God help us, you saw Jose Rinaldo's head. They hacked it off, stuffed other body parts in his mouth, and played soccer with it. Now you want to go in there? Who says you'd ever come out?"

"The Lord."

The Colombian governor grimaced, swiped his hand across his mouth, and eyed Oscar Osorio across his desk. Oscar smiled back. He was walking the way of the cross. Sometimes that leads to death. Other times it leads to service in hard places.[7]

Bellavista Prison crammed four thousand men into a space meant for fifteen hundred. Some called it the deadliest prison in the world. *Caciques,* local bosses, ruled every cell block. They determined where men slept, whether they ate, even whether they lived. Although Marxist terrorists were housed separately from right-wing death-squad members, revenge murders ricocheted back and forth. Even if you lived, it was a struggle. Some blocks had no toilets at all, and the stink was gagging.

Art, literature, history, philosophy, style and etiquette have a rich heritage in Colombia. People who appreciate the refinements of civilization have made a mark in this nation. But killing has a long heritage here too. When Colombians fought for freedom from Spain, the policy on both sides was, "Take no prisoners!" If you were captured, you were executed. Vengeance smoldered. In the middle of the twentieth century, atrocities erupted into "La Violencia"; politicians, unions, megabusinesses and the military whacked each other brutally, all grasping for power. Two-hundred-thousand Colombians were annihilated in riots and retaliations. To stay alive, small farmers had to ally with their local *patron,* the big man who held the power.

Though some violent leaders have been captured recently, several strong Marxist rebel movements continue, including FARC and ELN. Civilians have organized regional death squads. Periodically both right and left take the law into their own hands, and murder according to their own codes.

Bellavista Prison is one place where they end up. When Oscar and the governor faced off in 1990, Bellavista was in crisis.

How much to kill a cop? "What choices do our security forces face?" the governor lamented. "'Silver or lead!' Take a bribe or take a bullet. How much is Escobar paying to kill a policeman now?" Pablo Escobar was the drug kingpin, one of the richest men in Latin America.

"$4,000 for a cop. $8,000 for a narcotics cop," Oscar answered. "If you're desperate, it's a way to make a living."

"No wonder the prison guards are on strike!"

So many guards had succumbed to pressure that weapons were smuggled into the prison freely. Two deaths every day was normal inside the walls. Corpses littered corridors until the cleanup crew arrived. Some were hacked two hundred times. Graffiti was etched on walls in human blood. Loud buzzing around a corner announced that flies were feasting. Even outside the prison, guards were not safe. At a bus stop or even at home with their families, death could come calling.

"No more!" they announced in 1990. They walked off the job, locked the gates, and refused to allow anyone inside, not even the governor. "Send in the military!" they demanded as they picketed the prison, distributing handbills to passing motorists, asking for public support for a military takeover.

Enraged, the prisoners went wild. Deaths escalated. Eight, twelve, twenty-four deaths were reported daily in the media. Everyone expected military action. A bloodbath seemed imminent.

But Jesus' followers had not been absent from this hellhole. Local believers, sometimes under the auspices of the Association of Evangelicals in Medellin or the Salvation Army or Prison Fellowship regularly had distributed clothes and hygiene articles to the men. They had rounded up books for the prison library. They had run a prison football league, an eighty-voice prison choir, and classes in literacy, gardening, beekeeping, psychology and Bible.

These stories fill David Miller's holy thriller, *The Lord of Bellavista*. One character is Oscar. As a former criminal and inmate himself, Oscar felt the prisoners' frustrations. He knew the hopelessness. He also knew life could change.

"We can't guarantee your safety," he was advised when he started ministering in the prison. But he walked behind the bars anyway.

Preaching at the latest murder. "Where was the latest murder?" he would ask. "I'll preach on that spot."

"Watch out!" someone called. If Oscar didn't sidestep nimbly, urine drenched him. Prisoners stored up bags of it for the entertainment.

When some prisoners read Bibles, others ripped the pages out. The thin paper was ideal for making cigarettes.

"Look at this, pastor!" The young believers complained as they held up their Bibles, gouged and torn.

Oscar shrugged, ripped out more pages, wrote "Jesus Loves You" with felt tip pen on the pages, and slipped them under cell doors.

Dozens attended worship. Soon hundreds were coming. Lives changed. Then the guards' strike erupted, order collapsed and massacre loomed.

"Come pray with me," Oscar invited believers in the churches in Medellin. A group of older women took up the challenge. They traipsed to a bluff overlooking the prison. For six days they took turns fasting and praying. Then Oscar experienced a vision. That prompted his appointment with the governor.

"Tell me again," the governor said.

A huge hand cradles the prison. "I saw a huge hand reach down and cradle Bellavista in the palm. Then, clear as a bell, a voice said, 'Organize an evangelistic campaign inside Bellavista. Bring singers and preachers and amplifiers. Play the national anthem and ask the prisoners to raise white flags.' "[8]

Absurd. But since there was nothing to lose, the governor granted permission. Oscar then turned his attention to the *caciques* inside the prison. He negotiated. Would they allow safe conduct for evangelists?

Their response filtered back: No one would touch the Christians during the "white flag campaign."

Oscar and his wife sat down at their kitchen table, scissored white paper into thousands of triangles, and pasted the triangles onto plastic straws. For the next two months, preachers and singers from the Covenant Evangelical Free Church and Prison Fellowship would wave white flags and sing and dance and read the Bible and speak about Jesus inside the prison every day.

Right away Oscar handed a white flag to every inmate. Then the national anthem soared over the loudspeakers. Like many national anthems this song speaks of liberty and of suffering. Such suffering helps us "comprehend the words of the One who died on the cross," it continues. Yet from Jesus' pain, and from ours, good things can come, the song concludes.

The men stood in the prison yard as these lyrics they had heard from childhood floated through the air.

When the music drifted away, Oscar asked the inmates to raise their flags and bow their heads. "Lord Jesus, we ask you to forgive us. Forgive us for shedding so much blood. Forgive our kidnappings, our homicides, every one of our crimes," he prayed.

Earlier that day, in preparation for the meeting, the 120 baptized prisoners had walked through all the corridors and prayed at every junction and in every room. Now they prayed silently.

Killings dropped to zero. Oscar anointed with oil the places where people had been murdered, as well as the walls where satanic symbols were scrawled in blood. Holding out a burlap bag, he invited prisoners to come forward and drop their guns and bloodied knives and ice picks into it. Soon his bag was full. Many turned to follow Jesus. Even those who didn't acknowledged, "Something is here. Even though I don't believe in God, what he does is real."[9]

Killings dropped to zero. For the next two years, no deaths occurred. The governor wrote a note of appreciation to Prison Fellowship of Colombia, detailing how anarchy had been transformed to blessing. Even seven years later, when there were riots in every other prison in

Colombia, there were none in Bellavista.

But one day Oscar was threatened. "You're ruining my drug business, preacher," a *cacique* grated. "Nobody buys drugs. They're all reading the Bible. I'm going to stop it." He dragged Oscar into his cell, and put a gun to Oscar's head.

God prompted Oscar to look the *cacique* in the eye and say, "If God gave you permission to harm me, you may. But if God did not give you permission, you cannot lay a finger on me."[10]

The drug boss couldn't move. He trembled, and slipped out of the cell.

Throughout Latin America, many churches and agencies serve prisoners. In Argentina, for example, 10 percent of the nation's prisoners are estimated to be committed evangelical Christians, and in some prisons the number is as high as 50 percent.

In Bellavista, Christian prisoners are nurtured by a prison Bible school that grew out of the Bible Seminary of Colombia. Jeannine Brabon, a bookish professor of Hebrew, was the link. When Colombia became so dangerous that most foreign missionaries were ordered home, Jeannine had stayed. Then she met Oscar, who asked her, "Will you help me train leaders?"

Today there is a two year Bible school for prisoners. There is a sewing business in a women's prison. There is a relationship with the prison transfer office, so that prisoners can complete their Bible school certificate before being transferred, and can be transferred to specific prisons where the team hopes to plant new churches. There are weddings in the prison and restoration of broken families. There are churches outside that welcome prisoners' families. There is a halfway house for men who are released. And there is a mandate and purpose for lifers—a sense of call to be of use to others as channels of the love of God. Prisoners have written to the Prosecutor General to tell him they pray for him. Prisoners also raise money to support ministry in other prisons.

All this happened because volunteers followed the way of the cross, which led them into the prison. The cross does not always mean death. Sometimes it means the hard work of love.[11]

BEST PRACTICES TO LIMIT SUFFERING

Suffering is part of the human condition in a sinful world. Bible professor Robert Wall says:

> If I read the creation account right, God's interaction with creation is typically brokered by the folks God has asked to steward it. And typically those human agents don't do a very good job. "Natural" disasters are made so much more disastrous by institutional malfeasance and human incompetence, sin and foolishness. We have met the enemy and s/he is us.[12]

Incompetence and foolishness are not just traits of evil people. Christians can be ignorant and careless too. Because of this, sometimes we bring suffering on ourselves. Occasionally it is our fault. In Afghanistan, where this chapter began, workers recently learned some hard lessons about this.

Twenty-three Korean short-term missionaries were bouncing through Afghanistan in a bus in 2007 when they were abducted. For forty-two days they were held hostage. Two died. Although the other twenty-one were released, all were traumatized.

To achieve their release, the South Korean government bargained directly with the Taliban terrorists. Suddenly, instead of being seen as a marginalized rogue fringe, the Taliban were raised to the level of significant players, worthy of international negotiation. There is a persistent unconfirmed report that the government also paid a large ransom. Due to the way this incident was handled, missions and philanthropic organizations expect kidnappings to increase in the future.

As part of the agreement, the Taliban required all Korean Christian workers, aid workers, and noncombat troops to leave Afghanistan.[13]

Meanwhile, back in Korea, the sending church's senior pastor apologized to the nation, then resigned from his pastorate. He was one of the most respected pastors in the country. The church, taking comprehensive responsibility for the care of their missionaries, arranged a debriefing team to meet the former hostages as soon as they returned. For ten days they were counseled individually in a safe environment. Then they went through a week of group therapy. The church also reimbursed the government for its costs.

Eventually the pastor was reinstated. Nevertheless, mission work was tarnished throughout the country.

Could this tragedy have been avoided? Following the incident the World Evangelical Alliance developed a set of "best practices" for violent contexts.[14] What do these best practices involve? At a minimum, we should avoid stirring up an angry response.

Unfortunately, during the year preceding the attack in Afghanistan, other Korean groups had sent thousands of short-term missionaries to that country. These short-termers conducted massive rallies in Kabul, threw tracts over courtyard walls and confronted strangers in the marketplaces with their testimonies.

Afghan media protested. So did long-term Christian workers in the country, including Koreans. Eventually the Afghan government deported the eager witnesses. But the damage had been done. The following year, others suffered the backlash.

In general, what are some activities that provoke angry and violent responses? Confrontational preaching. Noncontextualized preaching. Ignoring social structures, so that leaders are insulted. Child evangelism, which causes parents and elders to worry that their children will be drawn away from them. Loud singing. Christian promotions during other religions' sacred seasons. Disrespectful comments about other faiths. Prominent foreigners. An opulent lifestyle in a poor country. Expensive ministry equipment. Using social and economic programs as "bait." Dissension among Christians. Introducing contradictory elements that disrupt long-term ministry programs. Breaking the law of the land by activities such as forging passports. If these are characteristics of our ministry, we may bring punishment on ourselves.

In a "worst case scenario," Crisis Consulting International (www .CriCon.org) is a highly professional service that helps Christians in dire situations like kidnappings. Websites about suffering Christians include Barnabas Fund (www.barnabasfund.com), Christian Freedom International (www.christianfreedom.org), Christian Solidarity Worldwide (www.cswusa.com), Open Doors International (www.od.org), World Evangelical Alliance's Religious Liberty Commission (www.worldevan gelicals.org/commissions/rlc) and Assist News Service (www.assist news.net).

Clearly, we should take steps to keep out of trouble in the first place. "Pure passion is not enough for missions. We need wisdom too," says Korean researcher Steve Moon. He warns against excessive activism and optimism, a compulsion to leave visible results, and neglecting to learn from and share with workers in other organizations. "Churches need to create a corporate learning culture" and a humble, teachable attitude, he advises.[15]

BLOOD AS SEED

"Anyone who does not carry his cross and follow me cannot be my disciple," Jesus said (Lk 14:27). The way of Jesus leads to the way of the cross. God suffered for us, and in a sinful world we too suffer as we live for him. This may range from inconvenience or marginalization to tor- ture and death.

We do not seek suffering. Like the apostle Paul who asserted his Ro- man citizenship in order to avoid unnecessary torture, we claim rights when we can. We look ahead confidently to the awesome kingdom where there will be no more tears.

But right now, while spiritual kingdoms are still in conflict, we stand vulnerably in the arena, looking to the example of the cross.

> If you suffer for doing good and you endure it, this is commend- able before God. To this you were called, because Christ suffered for you, leaving you an example, that you should follow in his steps. . . . When they hurled their insults at him, he did not retali- ate; when he suffered, he made no threats. Instead, he entrusted himself to him who judges justly. He himself bore our sins in his body on the tree, so that we might die to sins and live for righ- teousness; by his wounds you have been healed. (1 Pet 2:20-21, 23-24)

The blood of the martyrs is the seed of the church, it is said. Consider China.

Though some regions are more tolerant than others, persecution continues. Christians' houses have been searched without warrants and their properties have been confiscated, leaving aging mothers and tiny children with no food or shelter or future support. During interrogations, Christians have been stunned with cattle prods, burned with cigarettes and even stabbed.

Some have died in government custody. Prisoners' bodies have displayed deep rope burns on their ankles from being hung up and beaten. Yet relatives have been told, "He died of natural causes." "She fell." "He tried to escape." "It was a sudden illness." One family was told that the prisoner died of a stroke and then committed suicide by poisoning himself.[16]

In spite of persecution China's church has grown to eighty million, one suffering witness at a time. Will a similar story someday be true for Afghans? Afghanistan is a hard place to live under any circumstances. It is an even harder place to live as a Christian. But Qazi Abdul Karim took up his cross. Zia took up his cross. Today other Afghans follow the way of the cross. And that way leads straight to resurrection and the outpouring of the Spirit.

WAY OF LIFE

"How much?"

"$60,000 per person."

"Ouch."

While China's economy grows by nearly 10 percent per year, conditions in some rural areas are tough.

"But there's a way to a better life," a whisper spread in south China. "If you can make it to America, you can earn enough to lift your whole extended family. Then you can come back and live comfortably."

"How would we get there?"

"Ah, there are ways." Gangs of human smugglers—"snakeheads"—spread the bait, and enterprising men and women took it. Though the price was beyond their grasp, they were assured that they would earn it back in the new land.

Little did they know that some of them would become Jesus' people. In this final chapter we explore two contrasting frames for Christian experience, the global and the local. Both perspectives are essential. The smuggled Chinese illustrate the global network that cuts across cultural and national boundaries.

On the docks where ship containers were loaded, the brave would-be migrants slipped silently past longshoremen and slithered into the cavernous boxes. Shortly afterward, the metal rectangles were sealed. Great cranes clutched the units in their claws, lifted them abruptly, and swung them onto ocean liners. With a thudding jar they were released. More metal boxes crashed down on top until the stack rose high. Engines growled and rumbled, and the caged people were underway.

They had packed food and water and blankets, but of course what they could sneak in was minimal. They designated areas for toilets and for seasickness. When the ship rolled, however, the contents sloshed all across the floor.

As the days passed, food and water began to run out. People got sick. Others began to go a little crazy. Then came the deaths. Now the living shared the dark, shuddering, smelly, clanging space with the corpses.

What a shock for the dockyard workers in the West Coast cities who opened the crates. The stink was putrid. Bodies tumbled out. But wait! Did that one move? Yes. And what about that one? On a ship that docked in Seattle in 2000, thirty-four men were found alive.

Most were dispatched to the hospital. When they had recovered enough, they were transferred to the U.S. Immigration and Naturalization Service Detention Center where they would stay until they were deported. (The INS has been merged into the Homeland Security program, which runs the jail now.)

Hundreds of people exist in this bleak, sterile fortress with iron bars on the window. Most have no attorneys, family visits or friends. Many do not speak English. They do not understand the rules or the procedures or their future prospects. Some stay in this bland featureless space for years. Yes, they have food, beds and a clean environment. What they lack is hope. And people who understand and care.

Who cares about them? While these stowaways were vomiting their way across the Pacific, Chinese Christians in Seattle enjoyed *dim sum* together. Asians constitute a big part of the population here. Even a governor of the state of Washington has been Chinese. Some Chinese have lived in this region for over one hundred years. Among them are Christians, both

those who brought their faith from China and those who found Christ in
the United States. Although they belong to various churches, they fellowship across denominational boundaries now and then.

When they heard of the plight of the "container Chinese," their
hearts were moved.

"Who cares about them?" they said to each other. "The U.S. is angry
with them. China is angry."

"The smugglers are angry! And their families are angry, because
somehow they must come up with the money to pay the smugglers that
exorbitant fee!"

"Do they have lawyers?"

"No chance."

"Do they have anybody who cares?" The Chinese outside the walls
looked at each other, and felt an obligation. Who would care for these
forgotten men if they did not? They began to importune the INS to let
them hold Sunday worship services in the Detention Center.

It was risky to rattle that cage. The INS had a reputation for being
tough, and some of the petitioners were not U.S. citizens. Yet they persisted. In time their perseverance bore fruit.

Twenty-five detainees came to the services. They walked in with
stony faces. But "the love of Christ through individual volunteers
opened the Chinese up," according to Cal Uomoto, one of the coordi-
nators. Twelve Chinese churches provided eighty volunteers. As the
prisoners experienced love and care, their hopelessness melted. Tears
rolled down their cheeks. They came to Jesus. Sixteen of the thirty-four
men were baptized a few months after the ministry began. Others were
baptized later.

They became powerful in prayer. They started composing worship
songs and eventually burned their own CD. When the jail got too full,
some of the Christians were transferred to other detention centers across
the state. They went as missionaries, and soon there were prisoners in
those jails asking for baptism.

Happiest scum of the earth. When the INS saw the benefits, they
took an unprecedented step. "Would you be interested in minister-

ing beyond the Chinese to more of the prison population?" they
asked the volunteers.

This was not the plan. World Relief sponsored the ministry, but the
work was done by volunteers. They were stretched thin already. But
they said yes.

Around 2002 I was part of a gathering of ethnic ministers. A Hispanic pastor had reported on his activity. Following him, Jonathan
Soepardjo spoke about the detention-center work. "Something new is
happening, and we don't know quite what to do about it." Jonathan
added. He leaned toward the Hispanic pastor. "The Chinese are not the
major population in the jail. It's the Mexicans."

The Hispanic pastor nodded. Latin Americans constitute the biggest minority population in this state, though many lack legal residence documents.

"And Mexicans are coming to our Chinese services," Jonathan continued. "They can't understand us. We can't understand them. But they
sense that God is present, and they are so desperate that they come, hoping that somehow a crumb of his grace will fall from the table to them."
He smiled at the Hispanic pastor. "Brother, come over and help us!"

He did. Today there are six services, three on Saturday and three on
Sunday. The jail has been enlarged to nearly one thousand beds. There
are detainees from seventy countries. Many petition to come to the
Christian services—Chinese, Mexicans and also Arabs, Afghans,
Sikhs—maybe even al-Qaida!

The ministry force continues to be volunteers. Prisoners who believe
and show transformation of life are baptized and receive a certificate
admitting them to the rite of communion. In December 2008 sixty
were awaiting baptism. Despite huge language hurdles, the lay volunteers attempt to teach discipleship.

There is even a Fijian choir that formed when the pastor and elders
of a Fijian church were arrested for irregular paperwork! Their wives
formed a choir in the women's section of the jail.

Here in prison people who have been considered the scum of the
earth are finding new life in Christ. When they are deported, they go

home carrying the good news. "Now I know why I came to the U.S.—so I could be detained and deported to take the gospel to my people," one says.

"The happiest days of my life have been here in the detention center," says an Egyptian professional who met Christ.

Sometimes the volunteers help people avoid deportation. A Cambodian boy came to the United States as a small child with his family. He grew up speaking English, married and had four children. But one day he got angry and was arrested for domestic violence. Because he was not a citizen, he was to be deported.

His attorney lost the case against deportation and lost the appeal. There was only one chance in a million that he would be able to stay. Volunteers mobilized. They helped him write to the governor, asking for a pardon. They helped his children's school friends write letters of support. On the day of his final hearing, half the room was full of his supporters. The pardon came through.

Taking God from jail to the world. What happens to those who are deported? When the first "container Chinese" were sent back to China, volunteers scrounged to find clean jeans and tennis shoes for every deportee to wear home. They wrote letters to the prisoners' families. They contacted house churches. A couple of the volunteers themselves traveled to Fujian, the region from which most of the detainees had come. They spoke personally to local pastors, guaranteeing the authenticity of the testimonies of those who returned. They pled for mercy for these men and women who had failed and had suffered. To this day, volunteers Jonathan and Sherry Soepardjo travel to China every year to visit newly returned deportees and their families and churches.

Eight Sri Lankans came to the United States to make their fortune in the fish-processing business in Alaska. Each paid a middleman $8,000 for a work visa. They borrowed the money from loan sharks, intending to repay it with the wages that they would earn.

But the arrangement was a scam. The Sri Lankans were jailed and deported. In the jail, however, they became Christians. When they returned to Sri Lanka, they started a church. They are worshiping there today.

In the sixty Russian and Ukrainian churches in the Seattle area, some members keep track of believers who are to be deported. They alert the churches back home. A church in Russia or Ukraine then sends a delegation to the airport to meet the returning deportee and welcome him into the family of Christ. So far this has happened nine times. A seamless web has been woven as ethnic churches have kept the lines of communication open.

"The Holy Spirit goes ahead of us," says Cal Uomoto, "and God's witnesses move from the jail to the ends of the earth."

NETWORK GLOBALLY BUT FOCUS LOCALLY

Today all kinds of people are scattered across our country. There are refugees who have had no choice but to flee bad situations. There are immigrant families who have uprooted themselves deliberately in hope of a better future. International students. Merchant seamen. Massive migrations of laborers, as well as complex international business networks. There is even diversity in our jails. Taken all together, these are called "global flows."

But most of the important experiences of life are local. When we try to get our minds around vast movements of peoples, we talk in abstractions. At the global level we swim in virtual realities—sports scores, the stock market, packaged music and news flashes in which great tragedies are juxtaposed with beer ads. If we stay at that level, however, we will miss out on the real rhythms of nature and society. Seed time and harvest. Friendship, courtship, marriage, parenting, aging and dying. Creation, use, maintenance and repair.

There are rhythms to living in God's world. These are expressed locally. Knowing these helps us know ourselves, our potentialities and our limits, and the resources and sequences that weave the fabric for happy choices. Raising a child, for example, is not virtual. Being fired from a job is not a media experience. Having a baby is not a packaged game. Coping with cancer is not abstract.

The particular matters, including particular cultures. When Chinese Americans reached out to Chinese in jail, they crossed cultural and national boundaries with the love of Christ. As the prisoners return to China, those transnational ties will continue. But they will not dissolve all differences. People need their own cultures. In spite of variations within them and variations over time, cultures matter. Being a world citizen is too vague to provide motivation and meaning. It makes the common person feel insignificant. On the other hand, if you are a member of a distinct culture or local group, you have celebrations which give zest, values which give a cognitive framework, action patterns which give direction to your days, and associational ties which root you in a human context. You have a place in time in the universe, a base for the conviction that you are part of the community of life flowing from the past and pulsing on into the future. You have a story. You have words and phrases in your language that give coherence to your thoughts.

Global fellowship is glorious, but it rests on local fellowships. Weak national churches do not make a strong world church, any more than weak families make a strong neighborhood. Links need something to link. So while the global dimension is vital, so is the local. On one hand, we must network as broadly as we can. On the other hand, we must love the local as deeply as we can. The worldwide church is built from a thousand thousand communities of grace, one story at a time.

JESUS' PEOPLE IN BURMA

To illustrate the local we will explore one more body of believers, the Christians of Burma. When I taught in that nation a few years ago, I met a two-year-old named John. I can still see him standing secure between his mother's knees, swaying back and forth and piping out John 3:16, first in Burmese, then in English and then in Chin, his father's language. Next came John 15:5: "Jesus said, 'I am the vine; you are the branches. . . . [A]part from me, you can do nothing." Then more verses tumbled out.

Leaning forward to hear him, John's grandparents beamed. They were highly placed Buddhists who had opposed their daughter's marriage to a Christian. But now as they listened to John recite, they glowed with pride.

Six years earlier John's mother had had questions about life. These led her to Jesus. Now she and her husband are part of a hundred-member church with many new believers. The church was not planned. Christians simply shared their own stories and responded to others' questions as they encountered them in the workplace and the neighborhood. A motley set of inquirers blossomed into a congregation. Already the church has given birth to a Bible school with a two-year course of study and thirty part-time students.

Meanwhile, up in the hills of Burma, ethnic groups like the Chin, Karen, Kachin and Lisu treasure century-old denominations with hundreds of congregations, multiple Bible schools, and several missionary movements. While the outside world knows little about Burmese believers, they are taking responsibility for their own faith development generation by generation.

Also known as Myanmar, this country is one of the poorest and most oppressed nations in the world. It is also one of the most thoroughly Buddhist. The massive Shwe Dagon Pagoda dazzles the eye. Spires shimmer with gold. Poor people buy and apply the gold leaf by leaf in order to earn merit. The tyrants in power use Buddhism to buttress their right to rule. The opposition party of the long-imprisoned Aung San Suu Kyi interprets Buddhism to argue for an alternative. In the middle of this sad confusion, Buddhists continue coming to Jesus.

How to kill a tiger. What did John's mother believe before she encountered Jesus?

To explain Buddhism as he described his own conversion, my friend Chaiyun Ukosakul painted a graphic word picture for me. "When you get angry, a tiger grows in your heart. But when you are enlightened, the tiger dies."

How do you kill the tiger? You must get to the place where your desires do not dominate you. Desire must be destroyed, according to the Buddha. If you live morally and donate to monks and build up merit and meditate on spiritual subjects, eventually an insight will pull it all together and raise you to a higher plane of existence. You will be transported into a sphere of tranquility. The tiger in your heart will die, although this may take many reincarnations.

In the process you will learn not to cling to things. You will hold everything in an open hand since it is all passing away anyway. You will not make judgments on other people, since truth is relative. You will realize that a person who clings to absolutes is a slave to the desire for clear answers.

People themselves are not valuable, according to Buddhism. Although each of us feels that we are the center of a world, actually each person is just a temporary psychophysical event. Like a candle flame or a drop of water, we are here today, gone tomorrow. And that is good, because we want to break free from the treadmill of existence.

Once there was a blind man named Bartimaeus, according to a story by the famous Thai writer Kukrit Pramoj. Every day Bartimaeus shuffled to the outdoor market and sat down in his customary spot. Vendors greeted him and dropped a little food in his bowl. Birds sang. Children laughed. A woman named Ruth, who had been burned badly in a fire, befriended him, and they fell in love.

Then Bartimaeus heard that Jesus was coming through town and that he could heal blind eyes.

"Have mercy on me, and heal my eyes!" Bartimaeus called out.

Jesus did.

When his eyes were opened, Bartimaeus's tranquil routine was shattered. Suddenly he saw the sewage and the flies. He saw the vendors' faces lined with weariness and bitterness. He saw the children dressed in rags, their skin pocked with sores. He saw the gross burn scar that oozed where Ruth's face should have been, and he could not stand to look at her.

Later he saw Jesus crucified. Then he fell to his knees and cried, "Oh God, give me back my blindness!"

This is a Buddhist response to the gospel, according to its author. Like a muddy pond, life is pretty ugly. We cannot do much about the pond. We can only shoot up like water lilies and lie clean and untouched on top.[1]

Grassroots leadership. Does that view of life satisfy? If there were no God, it might provide a degree of serenity. But we are created for more than serenity. We are made for love. Buddhists crave this like everyone else. Students in one Burmese Bible school have planted many churches with simple expressions of God's love.

"I know I'm not going to be reborn as a dog. How about you? Do you know what will happen after you die?" they ask the common people. This catches attention because people long for assurance of salvation.

Or the students ask, "Who cares for you? We come from good homes to sleep and eat with you just as you are. Who else does that?"

In a country where there is hardly any decent health care, where most of the population is neglected at basic levels, these questions tug at people's hearts.

Besides Bible schools, there are a couple of graduate level seminaries with Ph.D. professors, small but significant libraries, classes in Greek and Hebrew, and a commitment to excellence. I walked five flights up a dark, narrow cement stairway to visit one of these schools. It was housed in nine adjacent rented rooms. Flipping through theses based on local research, I envisioned how it would bless Burma in the years ahead.

Burmese also send out missionaries. Poverty and politics pose problems for these mission movements. Yet some of their difficulties are unique. For example, several years ago the 3/300 Movement trained and commissioned three hundred young Kachin to be missionaries for three years in Tibet, China, India and unreached peoples in Burma. The trainers faced an unusual challenge. Thirty of the missionary volunteers were drug addicts.

How did this happen? In the Golden Triangle region opium poppies flourish. Addiction is common. Church members' children had become ensnared. These desperate parents sent their young adult children to the mission training school, hoping for some improvement in their lives.

Amazingly, the school did not turn them away. It accepted the challenge. Its first order of business was to detoxify the potential missionaries! Most of them went on to live for Jesus and to serve as part of the three hundred.[2]

Faithful ordinary families make such ministry possible. In some tribal communities they measure out a cupful of uncooked rice every day and set it aside. Once a week the church truck passes through the neighborhoods, the households' rice donations are collected, and eventually the rice is sold to support missions

While little John buzzed through one verse after another, his tummy bouncing in and out between his mother's knees in sync with his phrases, she stroked his shoulders and smiled radiantly. There is a new generation rising in Burma, and it includes children raised as Jesus' disciples. In two ethnic groups some Christians run their own preschools. From age three to age six, preschoolers are taught three alphabets: English, Burmese and their own language. They also learn Bible and Christian doctrine. The parents know that when their children enter public school, they will be bathed in Buddhism. They want them well grounded before they start.

Almost a dozen years ago a wealthy Burmese woman abducted several young girls in her community. She sold most of them as maids but donated one to a temple. Although this girl had been born into Christian family, her head was shaved and she grew up as a Buddhist nun.

One Burmese ministry donates thousands of gift boxes to monks and nuns at Christmas. Along with candy and toiletries, each box contains a New Testament and a Jesus video. When this nun opened her box, she rediscovered the gospel she had heard as a child. In the monastery she became a true follower of Jesus. Shortly after that, her family found her. They had been searching for her all these years. Now she is back with them.

Ten of the eleven biggest churches on the globe are in the Buddhist country of Korea. Elsewhere in the Buddhist world, there are four hundred churches in Mongolia and four thousand in Thailand. But nowhere does Jesus enliven Buddhists and enable them to experience his presence more than in the tragic, upside-down circumstances of Burma.

THE EVERLASTING KINGDOM

While the apostle John was incarcerated on the prison isle of Patmos, he must have meditated on the book of Daniel. One day he had a vision.

Like Daniel, he saw a king on a throne. Like Daniel, John also saw a hero enter, approach the throne and receive worship on all sides.

The throne represents the ruler of the universe. The creator who began it all. The sustainer who holds it together. The conqueror of all powers, the lawgiver, the reconciler, the culminator who will bring everything to fulfillment at the end of time. A metaphor for such power is the lion (Rev 5:5).

But the hero who enters is not a lion. He is a lamb. As the story progresses, it turns out that only a lamb is strong enough to open the book of the secrets of the universe.

Two kinds of praise resound in this vision. The king is praised for *creative* power and for the *unity* that holds all things in existence together.

> You are worthy, our Lord and God,
>   to receive glory and honor and power,
> for you created all things
>   and by your will they . . . have their being. (Rev 4:11)

The lamb is praised for *transforming* power and for the *diversity* that he causes to flourish:

> You are worthy . . .
>   because . . . with your blood
> you purchased men for God
>   from every tribe and language and people and nation.
>   (Rev 5:9)

There are models for us in this vision. Jesus' people are called to be strong, like lions. As stewards of the king, we are to take care of this earth, to create order and justice and beauty. To build. Where much has been given, much is expected.

Jesus' people also are called to be lambs. To serve vulnerably, sharing in suffering until resurrection power is let loose.

And we are called to rejoice in the *created order* of God's world, the *transforming* new beginnings made possible by his grace, the *unity* of global fellowship and the *diversity* of local fellowships.

The Cuban American theologian Justo González has compared a vision from the book of Daniel—Nebuchadnezzar's vision—with the apostle John's. He says,

> There is a vision according to which all peoples and nations and tribes and languages must bow before the beast and worship it. That is the vision of Nebuchadnezzar. . . . If we live by that vision, we shall be content with a world order in which . . . peoples and cultures have no other purpose in life but to enrich those [at the top]. According to that vision, the nations and peoples and tribes should remain subjected, for that is their place in the scheme of things. . . .
>
> But that is not the vision of John of Patmos. According to his vision, out of those many nations and tribes and peoples and languages, God will build a kingdom in which all have royal and priestly honor. According to that vision, a great multitude, from all different nations and cultures will jointly sing, "Holy, Holy, Holy, Lord God Almighty!" According to that vision, our music and our worship must be multicultural, not simply because our society is multicultural, but because the future from which God is calling us is multicultural. . . . Not just so that those from other cultures may feel at home among us but also so that we may feel at home in God's future. . . . Because, like John of Patmos, our eyes have seen the glory of the coming of the Lord; because we know and we believe that on that great waking-up morning when the stars begin to fall, when we gather at the river where angel feet have trod, we shall all, from all nations and tribes and peoples and languages, we shall all sing without ceasing, "Holy, Holy, Holy! All the saints adore thee, casting down our golden crowns before the glassy sea, cherubim and seraphim; Japanese and Swahili; American and European; Cherokee and Ukrainian; falling down before thee, who wert, and art, and evermore shall be!" Amen![3]

When I taught a Christian writers' workshop in Burma, I was given a piece of art to hang on the wall. Made of semiprecious stones—local gems—it displayed the ancient palace at Mandalay. From the time of Ann and Adoniram Judson down to the present, being a Christian in Burma has been hard. Yet when I unwrapped this representation of their old capital, all the faces were wreathed in smiles. What joy they took in their heritage.

Like the Chinese prisoners in the American INS jail, these Burmese brothers and sisters live in a particular culture and speak a particular language. They also network globally. (After all, they invited me.) Yet neither the local nor the global is the context that defines them. Like the prophet Daniel so long ago, like the apostle John on his prison island, both the Burmese and the Chinese and we ourselves have one more home—the kingdom of everlasting dominion that will never be destroyed.

NOTES

Introduction

[1]Melba Maggay, unpublished letter, December 2005.

[2]Isabelo Magalit, "I Have a Dream," in *The Message, Men, and Mission* (Manila: InterVarsity Christian Fellowship of the Philippines, 1971), pp. 5-8.

[3]Ruth Callanta, "Transforming Strategy: Toward Filling the Hungry with Good Things," in *The Church and Poverty in Asia*, ed. Lee Wanak (Manila: OMF Literature and Asian Theological Seminary, 2008), p. 155.

[4]Ibid., p. 151.

Chapter 1: These Are My People

[1]David Bebbington, quoted in J. I. Packer, "Reflection and Response," *Crux* 43, no. 1 (2007): 7.

[2]Packer, "Reflection and Response," p. 10.

[3]Philip Jenkins, *The Next Christendom: The Coming of Global Christianity* (Oxford: Oxford University Press, 2002), pp. 1, 2, 3.

[4]Ibid., p. 18.

[5]Eugene Peterson, *Reversed Thunder: The Revelation of John and the Praying Imagination* (San Francisco: Harper & Row, 1988), pp. 51, 55.

[6]Alfred Lord Tennyson, "In Memoriam A.H.H.," in *Masters of British Literature* (Boston: Houghton Mifflin, 1958), p. 535. Tennyson lived from 1809 to 1892.

[7]Paul Hinder quoted at the laying of the foundation stone in John Terrett, "Christian Church Rises in Arabia," *Aljazeeranet*, March 25, 2007 <http://english.aljazeera.net>.

[8]This event was described by Lindsay Brown in *Shining like Stars: The Power of the Gospel in the World's Universities* (Nottingham, U.K.: Inter-Varsity Press, 2006), p. 178.

[9]God expects us to use our minds. In Philippians 1:9-10, Paul urges us to grow in knowledge so as to discern what is excellent. In 1 Corinthians 14:15 he says, "I will pray with my spirit, but I will also pray with my mind." And he says,

"In regard to evil be infants, but in your thinking be adults" (v. 20). Ten times in Romans and Corinthians the question "Don't you know?" appears. Colossians 1:28 indicates that Christian leaders should aim to present every person mature in Christ, with all wisdom. Similarly in the Old Testament God expects his people to cultivate their minds (Is 1:18; Dan 10:12; 1 Kings 3:11-12).

[10]Abraham Duran, "The Beauty of Jesus as an Evangelistic Factor," in *From the Straight Path to the Narrow Way*, ed. David Greenlee (Waynesboro, Ga.: Authentic, 2005), pp. 265-74.

Chapter 2: The Elephant in the Room

[1]Paul Hattaway, *China's Book of Martyrs* (Carlisle: U.K., Piquant, 2007), p. 577.

[2]Stephen C. Smith, *Ending Global Poverty: A Guide to What Works* (New York: Palgrave Macmillan, 2005), p. 5.

[3]"Sons of Heaven," *Economist,* October 4, 2008, p. 47.

[4]Ibid.

[5]"The Spring of Life," part one of *The Cross: Jesus in China* video, Petaluma, Calif.: China Soul, 2003.

[6]Hattaway, *China's Book of Martyrs*, p. 587.

[7]"The Spring of Life."

[8]Paul Hattaway, *Back to Jerusalem* (Waynesboro, Ga.: Gabriel Resources, 2003), p. 26.

[9]Tim Stafford, "A Captivating Vision," *Christianity Today* 48, no. 4 (2004): 85.

[10]Hattaway, *Back to Jerusalem,* p. 58.

[11]This view is supported by works such as Chan Kei Thong, *Faith of Our Fathers: God in Ancient China* (Shanghai: China Publishing Group, Orient Publishing Center, 2006); and Ethel Nelson and Richard Broadberry, *Genesis and the Mystery Confucius Couldn't Solve* (St. Louis: Concordia Publishing, 1994).

[12]How Chuang Chua, "Revelation in Chinese Characters: Divine or Divined?" *Contextualization and Syncretism,* ed. Gailyn Van Rheenen (Pasadena, Calif.: William Carey Library, 2006), pp. 229-42.

[13]David Bentley-Taylor, *The Weathercock's Reward: Christian Progress in Muslim Java* (London: Lutterworth, 1967), p. 132.

[14]Ibid., pp. 134-35.

[15]Hattaway, *China's Book of Martyrs*, p. 557.

[16]Ibid.

[17]Ibid.

Chapter 3: Word

[1]Anne Judson, quoted in John Waters, *Storming the Golden Kingdom: A Biography of Adoniram Judson* (Kent, U.K.: STL Publishers, 1989), p. 42.

[2]Adoniram Judson, quoted in Waters, *Storming the Golden Kingdom*, pp. 131-32.

[3]Anne Judson, quoted in Waters, *Storming the Golden Kingdom*, p. 50.

[4]Eugene Peterson, *Eat This Book: A Conversation in the Art of Spiritual Reading* (Grand Rapids: Eerdmans, 2006), p. 102.

[5]Joel Carpenter, "Back to the Bible," review of *The New Faces of Christianity: Believing the Bible in the Global South*, by Philip Jenkins, *Books & Culture* 13, no. 3 (2007): 23.

[6]Kwame Bediako, "Scripture as the Interpreter of Culture and Tradition," in *Africa Bible Commentary*, ed. Tokunboh Adeyemo (Grand Rapids: Zondervan, 2006), p. 3.

[7]Robert Schreiter, *Faces of Jesus in Africa* (Maryknoll, N.Y.: Orbis, 1991), pp. vii-viii.

[8]Yusufu Turaki, "The Role of the Ancestors," in *Africa Bible Commentary*, p. 480.

[9]Ibid.

[10]Bediako, "Scripture as the Interpreter," p. 4.

[11]Anne Nasimiyu-Wasike, "Christology and an African Woman's Experience," in *Faces of Jesus in Africa,* ed. Robert Schreiter (Maryknoll, N.Y.: Orbis, 1991), pp. 76-77.

[12]Lindsay Brown in *Shining Like Stars: The Power of the Gospel in the World's Universities* (Nottingham, U.K.: Inter-Varsity Press, 2006), p. 162.

[13]Ibid., p. 163.

[14]Ibid., p. 114.

[15]Ibid., p. 119.

[16]Franz Kafka, quoted in George Steiner, *Language and Silence* (New York: Atheneum, 1970), p. 67.

[17]Peterson, *Eat This Book,* pp. 1-2.

[18]Justo Gonzáles, *Mañana: Christian Theology from a Hispanic Perspective* (Nashville: Abingdon, 1990), p. 86.

[19]"Living Word for a Dying World," conference sponsored by the Forum of Bible Agencies, Dalfsen, Holland, April 20-25, 1994.

Chapter 4: Pulsating Passion

[1]Lindsay Brown in *Shining Like Stars: The Power of the Gospel in the World's*

Universities (Nottingham, U.K.: Inter-Varsity Press, 2006), p. 53.

[2]John Maust, *Peace and Hope in the Corner of the Dead* (Miami: Latin American Mission, 1987).

[3]Ibid., p. 178.

[4]Ibid., p. 170.

[5]Tetsunao Yamamori and Donald Miller, *Global Pentecostalism: The New Face of Christian Social Engagement* (Berkeley: University of California Press, 2007).

[6]Juan Pérez Alfonso quoted in Michael J. Watts, "Oil as Money: The Devil's Excrement and the Spectacle of Black Gold," in *Reading Economic Geography,* ed. Trevor J. Barnes, Jamie Peck, Eric Sheppard and Adam Tickell (Hoboken, N.J.: Wiley-Blackwell Publishing, 2003), p. 205

[7]Yamamori and Miller, *Global Pentecostalism,* p. 56.

[8]Ibid., p. 57.

[9]Ibid., p. 87.

[10]*Evangelicos* is a term for Protestants in Latin America. It connotes their emphasis on reading and preaching the Bible, the evangel.

[11]Felipe Vásquez Palacios, "Democratic Activity and Religious Practices of Evangelicals in Mexico," in *Evangelical Christianity and Democracy in Latin America,* ed. Paul Freston (Oxford: Oxford University Press, 2008), pp. 56-57.

[12]Ibid.

[13]Timothy Steigenga and David Smilde, "Wrapped in the Holy Shawl: The Strange Case of Conservative Christians and Gender Equality in Latin America," in *Latin American Religion in Motion,* ed. Christopher Smith and Joshua Prokopy (New York: Routledge, 1999), p. 180.

[14]John Burdick, *Looking for God in Brazil: The Progressive Catholic Church in Urban Brazil's Religious Arena* (Berkeley: University of California Press, 1993), p. 112.

[15]Brown, *Shining Like Stars,* p. 118.

[16]Pablo Deiros, "Where Is the Latin American Church Going? What Dangers Do We Face?" to be published in a collection of essays by faculty members of PRODOLA (Programa Doctoral en Teologia, also known as LADP, Latin American Doctoral Program), ed. Nancy Thomas (2009).

[17]Orlando Costas, "Mission and the Liberation of Man," in *The Church and Its Mission: A Shattering Critique from the Third World* (Wheaton, Ill.: Tyndale House, 1974), pp. 219-64.

[18]Yamamori and Miller, *Global Pentecostalism,* p. 214.

[19]Brown, *Shining Like Stars*, p. 59.

[20]Ibid., p. 60.

[21]Ibid., p. 61.

[22]Ibid., p. 63.

[23]Bruce Olson, with James Lund, *Bruchko and the Motilone Miracle* (Lake Mary, Fla.: Charisma House, 2006), and David Miller, "An Interview with Bruce Olson," *Evangelical Missions Quarterly* 44, no. 4 (2008): 472-79.

[24]Olson, *Bruchko and the Motilone Miracle*, p. 147.

[25]Ibid., p. 158.

[26]Miller, "An Interview with Bruce Olson," p. 477.

[27]Brazilians, who speak Portuguese rather than Spanish, prefer the inclusive term *Iberoamericans* when referring to both groups, but for simplicity we are using the term *Latin Americans* for both.

[28]Barbara Burns, "Brazilian Antioch Community, Spirituality, and Mission," in *Global Missiology for the 21st Century: The Iguassu Dialogue,* ed. William Taylor (Grand Rapids: Baker Academic, 2000), p. 516.

[29]Ibid., p. 517.

[30]Antonia van der Meer, "The Scriptures, the Church, and Humanity: Who Should Do Mission and Why?" in *Global Missiology for the 21st Century: The Iguassu Dialogue,* ed. William Taylor (Grand Rapids: Baker Academic, 2000), p. 155.

[31]M. Daniel Carroll R., *Christians at the Border* (Grand Rapids: Baker Academic, 2008), p. 61.

[32]Van der Meer, "The Scriptures, the Church, and Humanity," pp. 159, 150.

Chapter 5: Spirit

[1]Fyodor Dostoevsky, *The Brothers Karamazov* (New York: Heritage Press, 1949), p. 279.

[2]Gerard Manley Hopkins, "God's Grandeur," *Hopkins Poems and Prose* (New York: Alfred Knopf, 1995), p. 14. Hopkins lived from 1844 to 1899.

[3]Ibid.

[4]Sara Glerum, "Weekly Travel Essay," *Seattle Times*, March 30, 2008, p. K2.

[5]Elizabeth Gilbert, *Eat, Pray, Love* (New York: Penguin, 2006), p. 130.

[6]Kim Comer, comp., *Wisdom of the Sadhu: Teaching of Sundar Singh* (Farmington, Penn.: Plough, 2000), p. 29.

[7]Ibid., p. 30.

[8]Ibid., p. 43.

[9]Ibid., pp. 25, 40.

[10]Ibid., p. 40.

[11]Tetsunao Yamamori and Donald Miller, *Global Pentecostalism* (Berkeley: University of California Press, 2007).

[12]Vishal Mangalwadi, *Truth and Social Reform* (New Delhi: Nivedit Good Books, 1986), pp. 46-47.

[13]Ibid., p. 47.

[14]J. I. Packer, *Systematic Theology Overview: Theology Course Lecture Notes* (Vancouver: Regent College Publishing, 2001).

[15]Paul Hattaway, *China's Book of Martyrs* (Carlisle, U.K.: Piquant, 2007), pp. 597-98.

[16]Dean Gilliland, "How 'Christian' Are African Independent Churches?" *Missiology* 14, no. 3 (1986): 259-272.

[17]International Orality Network/Lausanne Committee for World Evangelization, *Making Disciples of Oral Learners* (Bangalore, India: Lausanne Committee, 2005), p. 47.

[18]Packer, *Systematic Theology*, sec. 24.

[19]Minnie Abrams, *The Baptism of the Holy Ghost and Fire,* 2nd ed. (Kedgaon, India: Mukti Mission Press, 1906), p. 67.

[20]Macartney, quoted in V. Raymond Edman, *They Found the Secret: Twenty Transformed Lives* (Grand Rapids: Zondervan, 1960), p. 20.

[21]Ibid.

[22]Eugene Peterson, *The Jesus Way* (Grand Rapids: Eerdmans, 2007), p. 132.

Chapter 6: Axis of Hope

[1]Iranian is a broader category than Persian because Iranians include all citizens of Iran, including Kurds, Jews and tribal peoples.

[2]"The Moment of Truth," *Economist*, July 25, 2008, pp 29-32.

[3]Ibid., p. 32.

[4]Krikor Makarian, "Today's Iranian Revolution: How the Mullahs Are Leading the Nation to Jesus," *Mission Frontiers* 30, no. 5 (2008): 6-13.

[5]Ibid.

[6]William McElwee Miller, *Tales of Persia* (Phillipsburg, N.J.: Presbyterian & Reformed, 2005), p. 25.

[7]William McElwee Miller, *My Persian Pilgrimage* (Pasadena, Calif.: William Carey Library, 1989), p. 22.

[8]Miller, *Tales of Persia*, pp. 28-35.

[9]Miller, *My Persian Pilgrimage*, pp. 253-54.

[10]Miller, *Tales of Persia,* p. 120.

[11]Sarah Belle Sherwood, trip report, Wheaton Ill.: Billy Graham Center Archives, 1899.

[12]Letter from Miss Dean, *Women's Work for Women* 10, no. 6 (June 1880), p. 209.

[13]Letter from Miss Poage, *Women's Work for Women* 10, no. 3 (March 1880), p. 100.

[14]A good discussion of Jesus as Word, Spirit and Messiah in the Qur'an is found in Warren Larson, "Jesus in Islam and Christianity: Discussing the Similarities and the Differences," *Missiology* 36, no. 3 (2008): 327-37.

[15]For further discussion see Miriam Adeney, "Rajah Sulayman Was No Water Buffalo: Gospel, Anthropology, and Islam," in *No Other Gods Before Me? Evangelicals and the Challenge of World Religions,* ed. John Stackhouse (Grand Rapids: Baker Academic, 2001), esp. pp. 79-83.

[16]The more complete story is recorded in Miriam Adeney, *Daughters of Islam: Building Bridges with Muslim Women* (Downers Grove, Ill.: InterVarsity Press, 2002), chap. 11.

[17]H. B. Deqani-Tafti, *The Hard Awakening* (New York: Seabury, 1981), pp. 113-14.

Chapter 7: Catastrophe

[1]Stephen C. Smith, *Ending Global Poverty* (New York: Palgrave Macmillan, 2005), pp. 132-34.

[2]Brian Fikkert, "What Do You Think?" *Mandate E-Newsletter* 2 (2008) <http://chalmers.org/staging/mandate/august_2008/from_the_director.php>.

[3]David Bussau and Russel Mask, *Christian Microenterprise Development* (Waynesboro, Ga.: Paternoster/Regnum, 2003), p. 77.

[4]Augustine, quoted in Carolinne White, *The Confessions of St. Augustine* (London: Frances Lincoln, 2001), p. 14.

[5]Smith, *Ending Global Poverty,* p. 148.

[6]Muhammad Yunus, "The MicroLoan," *Seattle Post-Intelligencer,* September 29, 1996, pp. E1-3.

[7]Bussau and Mask, *Christian Microenterprise Development,* passim.

[8]Ibid., p. 24.

[9]Ban Ki Moon, "Quenching a Global Thirst," *International Herald Tribune,* March 21, 2008, p. 8.

[10]Afif Tannous, *Extension Work Among the Arab Fellahin*, quoted in Earl Bell, *Social Foundations of Human Behavior* (New York: Harper & Row, 1961), pp. 492-93.

[11]Ajith Fernando, *What Should We Be Doing Now?* unpublished paper, 2005.

Chapter 8: Mystic Servants

[1]J. Herbert Kane, *A Global View of Christian Mission* (Grand Rapids: Baker, 1975), p. 107.

[2]H. L. Richard, *Following Jesus in the Hindu Context* (Pasadena, Calif.: William Carey Library, 1998).

[3]Ibid., p. 94.

[4]Ibid., p. 77.

[5]Ibid., p. 69.

[6]Ibid., p. 62.

[7]Rochunga Pudaite, "The Shadow of the Untouchable," in *The Quest for Freedom and Dignity: Caste, Conversion, and the Cultural Revolution*, ed. Vishal Mangalwadi (Willernie, Minn: South Asian Resources, 2001), p. 160.

[8]Joseph D'Souza, *Dalit Freedom* (Centennial, Colo.: Dalit Freedom Network, 2004), p. 38.

[9]Mangalwadi, ed., *Quest for Freedom and Dignity*, pp. 11-20.

[10]Joseph D'Souza, *On the Side of the Angels* (Colorado Springs: Authentic Publishing, 2007), p. 86.

[11]For example, Donald McGavran describes a church split when low-caste members created their own church "because they felt: (1) that they were not taken seriously but were despised and humiliated; (2) they were underrepresented in diocesan councils and boards; (3) the pastoral care provided by the Church of South India failed to look after them; and (4) at the social level, nothing was being done for them" (*Ethnic Realities and the Church: Lessons from India* [Pasadena, Calif.: William Carey Library, 1979], p. 252).

[12]J. Waskom Pickett, *Christ's Way to India's Heart* (Lucknow, India: Lucknow Publishing, 1938), pp. 29-30.

[13]Stephen Neill, *Builders of the Indian Church* (London: Livingstone Press, 1934), pp. 131-32.

[14]Sam George, "Director's Desk" <www.parivarinternational.org>.

[15]See J. Waskom Pickett, *Christian Mass Movements in India* (New York: Abingdon, 1933); and Frederick Stock and Margaret Stock, *People Movements in the Punjab* (Pasadena, Calif.: William Carey Library, 1975).

[16]Krishnasamy Rajendran, *Which Way Forward Indian Missions: A Critique of Twenty-Five Years 1972-1997* (Bangalore, India: SAIACS Press, 1998). When K. Rajendran did his research, Operation Mobilization paid for missionary children's schooling through college. Friends Missionary Prayer Band paid for boarding school or for part of the school fees if the children stayed with their parents. FMPB provided a loan for college costs, which the graduate repaid when he or she got a job. Smaller missions might not provide for any of these needs, however. Some Indian missionaries are "half-trained, half-paid, and half-starved." By contrast, Rajendran continues, "For comparison we may look at the *Waqfh* Board of the Muslims and the Hindu Temple trusts. They do their homework in caring for their priests. Each State in India has schemes to care for them," including death benefits, medical benefits, scholarships for children, benefits for the marriage of each child, and pensions (p. 120).

[17]Ibid., p. 179.

[18]Ibid., p. 193.

[19]Roger Hedlund, "Christianity in India," *International Church Growth Quarterly,* April-June 1986, p. 154.

[20]Donald McGavran adds: "To recapitulate some part of our thinking, it is highly desirable for such Indian missionaries to divest themselves of the trappings of Western missions. It is not necessary for missionaries to be college graduates or to live in seeming affluence. It is not necessary for them to have cars and hospitals. It is necessary that they be full of zeal, know their Bible from cover to cover, and be sent out by the Holy Spirit to the work to which He has called them (Acts 13:2-4). It is essential for Indian missionaries to be thoroughly trained in cross-cultural evangelism" (*Ethnic Realities and the Church*, p. 238).

[21]Phil Parshall, *New Paths in Muslim Evangelism* (Grand Rapids: Baker, 1980), pp. 47-48.

[22]E. Stanley Jones, *Christ of the Indian Road* (London: Hodder & Stoughton, 1925), pp. 158-64.

Chapter 9: Song

[1]Barnabas Mam as told to Bruce Hutchinson, "Communicating the Gospel Through Story and Song in Cambodia," in *Communicating Christ Through Story and Song: Orality in Buddhist Contexts*, ed. Paul DeNeui (Pasadena, Calif.: William Carey, 2008), pp. 203-36.

[2]Ibid., p. 205.

[3]Eugene Nida, *God's Word in Man's Language* (New York: Harper & Row, 1952), p. 83.

[4]International Orality Network and Lausanne Committee for World Evangelization, *Making Disciples of Oral Learners* (Bangalore, India: International Orality Network, 2005), pp. 43-44.

[5]Ibid., pp. 44-46.

[6]Ibid., pp. 48-49.

[7]Jan Vansina, *Oral Tradition as History* (Madison, Wis.: University of Wisconsin Press, 1985), p. 16.

[8]Bruce Olson, *Bruchko* (Lake Mary, Fla.: Charisma House, 1995), p. 145.

[9]Paul Jewett, "America's First Black Christians and Their Songs," *Bulletin of Systematic Theology III* (Pasadena, Calif.: Fuller Theological Seminary, 1983), p. 14.

[10]Clifford Geertz, "Religion as a Cultural System," *The Interpretation of Culture* (New York: Basic Books, 1973), p. 100.

[11]Jewett, "America's First Black Christians," p. 12.

[12]Jeremy Begbie, "Music in God's World," *Books & Culture*, September-October 2007), pp. 30-31; and Jeremy Begbie, *Theology, Music, and Time* (Cambridge: Cambridge University Press, 2000).

[13]Delbert Rice, "Developing an Indigenous Hymnody," *Practical Anthropology* 18 (1971): 97-133.

[14]Clive Thompson, "Clive Thompson Explains Why We Can Count on Geeks to Rescue the Earth," *Wired* 15, no. 9 (2007).

[15]From an interview with David Hackett, Director of the Internet Evangelism Network <dhackett@visionsynergy.net>.

[16]Andrew Walls, quoted in Joyce Chaplain, *Adventure with a Pen* (Kumasi, Ghana: Africa Christian Press, 1966), p. 15.

[17]Hilmy Nor, *Circumcised Heart* (Kuala Lumpur: Kairos Research Center, 1999), p. 9.

[18]First published in *Interlit* 41, no. 2 (2004): 23.

[19]Patricia Adrienzen de Vergara, "¿Qué Haré Con Lo Que Me Has Dado?" in *La Aventura de Escribir: Testimonios de 14 Escritores Cristianos*, ed. Adriana Powell (Lima, Peru: Ediciones Puma, 2003), p. 22.

[20]First published in *Interlit* 41, no. 4 (2004): 23.

[21]A. A. Stockdale, "God Left the Challenge in the Earth," *His* 25 (1964): 20.

[22]Claude Levi-Strauss, *Structural Anthropology* (New York: Basic Books, 1963), p. 182.

[23]James Fernandez, "The Mission of Metaphor in Expressive Culture," *Current Anthropology* 15 (1974): 119-45.

[24]C. S. Lewis, *Of Other Worlds: Essays and Stories* (New York: Harcourt, 1966), p. 10.

Chapter 10: When You Go Through Fire

[1]Marguerite Guillebaud, *After the Locusts* (Oxford: Monarch Books, 2005).

[2]Ibid., p. 122.

[3]Ibid., pp. 81-84.

[4]Ibid., p. 100.

[5]Ibid., p. 104.

[6]Ibid., p. 108.

[7]Ibid., pp. 15, 159, 194.

[8]Sue Devries, "African Mission Boards and Societies," *Evangelical Dictionary of Mission*, ed. A Scott Moreau (Grand Rapids: Baker, 2000), p. 44.

[9]John Ghazvinian, *Untapped: The Scramble for Africa's Oil*, reviewed in " 'The Resource Curse': Why Africa's Oil Riches Don't Trickle Down to Africans," October 31, 2007 <http://knowledge.wharton.upenn.edu/article.cfm?articleid=1830>.

[10]"A Ravenous Dragon: Special Report on China's Quest for Resources," *Economist*, March 15, 2008, p. 3.

[11]Ghazvinian, quoted in "Resource Curse," p. 3.

[12]Thomas Oden, *How Africa Shaped the Christian Mind* (Downers Grove, Ill.: InterVarsity Press, 2008).

[13]Mark Shaw, "Africa," *Evangelical Dictionary of Mission,* ed. A Scott Moreau (Grand Rapids: Baker, 2000), p. 41.

[14]Paul Bohannan, *Africa and Africans* (Garden City, N.Y.: Natural History Press, 1964), p. 23.

[15]Lindsay Brown, *Shining like Stars* (Nottingham, U.K.: Inter-Varsity Press, 2006), pp. 190-92.

[16]Michael Okonkwo, quoted in Isaac Phiri and Joe Maxwell, "Gospel Riches," *Christianity Today*, July 2007, p. 23.

[17]Phiri and Maxwell, "Gospel Riches," p. 28. All quotes in this section are from Phiri and Maxwell's "Gospel Riches."

[18]Brown, *Shining like Stars*, p. 134.

Chapter 11: Way of the Cross

[1]J. Christy Wilson, *Afghanistan: The Forbidden Harvest* (Elgin, Ill.: David C.

Cook, 1981), p. 121.

[2]Ibid., p. 122.

[3]"The Amazing Life of Zia: Afghanistan's Apostle Paul," Atascadero Calif. International Outreach, 1990.

[4]Sharon Cohn Wu, "RSVPrayer: Answering God's Invitation," *Prism* 15, no. 6 (November–December, 2008): 23.

[5]Barnabas Mam as told to Bruce Hutchison, "Communicating the Gospel Through Story and Song in Cambodia," in *Communicating Christ Through Story and Song: Orality in Buddhist Contexts*, ed. Paul DeNeui (Pasadena, Calif.: William Carey, 2008), p. 207.

[6]Judith St. Clair Hull, "African American Strategies and Motivations in Short Term Missions," paper read at the Evangelical Missiological Society Annual Meeting, Minneapolis, 2007.

[7]David Miller, *The Lord of Bellavista* (London: Triangle, 1999), p. 69.

[8]Ibid.

[9]Ibid., p. 73.

[10]Ibid., p. 75.

[11]Regrettably, Oscar Osario was removed from this ministry in 1998 for mismanagement of funds. This does not negate the blessings that occurred, nor the continuing team ministry. Oscar continues to work with prisoners in another setting.

[12]Robert Wall, private communication with School of Theology faculty, Seattle Pacific University, February 7, 2008, used by permission.

[13]David Tai Woong Lee, "The Case of Korean Hostage Incident," *Connections* 7, no. 1 (2008): 17.

[14]See numerous articles in *Connections* 7, no. 1 (2008).

[15]Steven S. C. Moon, "Seven Lessons Learned from the Hostage Case of Koreans in Afghanistan," ibid., p.18.

[16]Paul Hattaway, *China's Book of Martyrs* (Carlisle, U.K.: Piquant, 2007), p. 584.

Chapter 12: Way of Life

[1]Kukrit Panoj, "The Hell Which Heaven Forgot," *Practical Anthropology*, May-June 1966.

[2]Grace Hla Young, *Prayer Arrows and Love Bullets* (Yangon, Myanmar: Chit Myat Noe Press, 2002).

[3]Justo González, *For the Healing of the Nations* (Maryknoll, N.Y.: Orbis, 1999), pp. 111-12.

Image Credit Information